the cook's
garden

McArthur & Company
Toronto

Canadian Gardening

the cook's garden

100 Favourite Recipes and Expert Growing Advice
from Canadian Gardening Magazine

Edited by LIZ PRIMEAU　　　Foreword by ALDONA SATTERTHWAITE

First published in 2003 by
McArthur & Company
322 King St. West, Suite 402
Toronto, Ontario
M4V 1J2

Editor: Liz Primeau
Design: Carol Moskot Design + Direction
Cover Photo: Roger Yip

National Library of Canada Cataloguing in Publication

the cook's garden: 100 recipes and expert growing advice
from the editors of Canadian gardening magazine /
edited by Liz Primeau; foreword by Aldona Satterthwaite.

Includes bibliographical references and index.
ISBN 1-55278-347-2

1. Cookery (Vegetables). 2. Cookery (Fruit).
3. Gardening—Canad—Miscellanea.
I. Primeau, Liz II. Title. III. Title: Canadian gardening.

TX715.6.C6695 2003   641.6'5   C2003-900110-5

The publisher would like to acknowledge the financial
support of the Government of Canada through the Book
Publishing Industry Development Program (BPIDP) and the
Canada Council for our publishing activities. The publisher
further wishes to acknowledge the financial support of the
Ontario Arts Council and the Government of Ontario through
the Ontario Media Development Corporation's Ontario Book
Initiative for our publishing program.

Printed in Canada by Transcontinental Printing Inc.

10 9 8 7 6 5 4 3 2 1

This book is dedicated to hardy gardeners
everywhere who cope with early frosts
in fall, late frosts in spring, drought, blight
and humidity to grow and cook some of the
best food on Earth.

contents

SPRING

SUMMER

WINTER

FALL

foreword

Since its founding, *Canadian Gardening* magazine has had just three editors—Liz Primeau, Beckie Fox and me—and we're passionate gardeners and good cooks all. Is this a coincidence? Hardly. Like gardening, cooking is a creative and sensual pursuit, so the two are natural complements. Done in tandem, they provide wonderful nourishment for the body as well as the soul.

It's supremely satisfying to plant seeds or seedlings, watch over them as they grow, then harvest your bounty to prepare and serve at the table. There are other benefits as well. Home-grown produce can be enjoyed fresh picked and pesticide free. (And even if you're short on space, take heart. You'll be amazed at what you can achieve in pots and containers on a sunny balcony.)

These information-filled growing stories and simple-to-follow recipes are some of the best we've ever published in the magazine; many of the original articles were edited by Christina Selby and art directed by Bonnie Summerfeldt. But a book is a thing apart, and this one is a finely seasoned stew of only the very best ingredients from those stories, judiciously chosen by editor Liz Primeau and freshly designed by Carol Moskot.

Too many cooks? Not in this case. Happy growing and bon appétit.

Aldona Satterthwaite

Aldona Satterthwaite
Editor, *Canadian Gardening*

introduction

One of my earliest memories is working in the garden with my mother, tending her small vegetable garden. Although most of her wonderful garden was flowers, the vegetable patch was my favourite. Maybe it was because when we tended it we had a chance to chat with our backyard neighbours, who we didn't see as often as our side neighbors. Or it may have been because I knew that the fruits of our labours would be cooked for supper in one of Mom's special recipes. But although my favourite foods didn't include vegetables, I knew that when they came from our garden they would taste wonderful, so the struggle my parents usually went through to get me to eat my vegetables was not nearly as intense.

Today, my husband, Gavan, and I have taken over the tradition of the fruit and vegetable patch. And just as Mom now passes along her Dutch garden secrets to my family, *Canadian Gardening* magazine, with the support of McArthur & Company, is passing along to you the best of our food-growing techniques and recipes. Like gardening tips, recipes are meant to be shared, and it's our hope that the combination of our favourite growing articles and the great recipes that appeared with them will inspire you in both in the garden and the kitchen. I trust that after browsing through this book your most difficult choice will be whether to keep it with your cook books or your gardening books. Either way, I wish you happy growing, cooking and eating!

Jacqueline Howe
Publisher, *Canadian Gardening*; President Avid Media Inc.

spring

We wait for spring. Eventually, as the song says, it creeps over our windowsills, blasting the blues and opening up the gardening season—and life itself. For spring is life in all its bounding glory. It brings new growth, renewed energy and sunshine. Plants embrace spring and grow as they will never grow again. Most vegetables are annuals, and they put all their energies into one year's growth, producing food for our tables and seed for new plants next year. Perennial vegetables, such as asparagus, which opens our section on spring on the next page, also embrace spring with new shoots that pop their heads through warming soil, or bright green leaves unfurling to greet the season. Gardeners love spring for the same reason plants do as well as for the promise of fresh salad greens, peas to be sampled as they're picked, and tart-sweet rhubarb for pies and crisps. Gardeners, raise your trowels to the new season!

Even in a small garden you can grow the tender spears of spring

asparagus

recipes

asparagus, scallop
& shrimp soup

spring risotto

asparagus &
mushroom strata

The season for asparagus (*Asparagus officinalis*), one of the first vegetables harvested in spring, is tantalizingly short. All too soon, the sweet, melt-in-your-mouth spears have vanished. Yet unlike other vegetables, they miraculously reappear next spring.

Knowing that asparagus is a true perennial is the key to growing it: commercial growers usually count on 15 to 20 years of harvest; many home gardeners keep theirs going 40 years or more. That means you have to be especially picky about where you plant it: seldom would you put it in the middle of the vegetable patch. Its deep root system would be a major obstacle when you till the soil in spring. If you grow only a few plants—and two or three are probably sufficient for a family—it's best to grow asparagus at the edge of the vegetable patch, or in a perennial border. The long, branching green stems and delicate, cut-leaf foliage form a tall (to 150 centimetres), attractive plant that adds height and volume at the back of the border.

If you want dozens of plants, prepare a special bed just for them—or let them share one with that other perennial vegetable, rhubarb. The bed can be any size or shape you want, as long as there's ample room for plants. BY LARRY HODGSON

GARDENER'S TIPS
- Freshly picked asparagus is high in fibre and contains beta-carotene, vitamin C and the mineral selenium. Winter asparagus is less nutritious—by the time it's arrived in Canada from the south it's lost two-thirds of its vitamin content.
- Asparagus stimulates the urinary system. Some people notice their urine has a slight green tint and a strong odour after they've eaten it.
- Year-old plants are preferable to those two years old or older, and usually less expensive.

growing

Soil should be close to neutral (pH 6.5 to 7.5); do a soil test and correct the pH if necessary. Asparagus prefers soil dug at least 40 centimetres deep and turned over. Remove rocks or debris; then work in plenty of compost or well-decomposed manure. Good drainage is crucial: create raised beds if your garden is in a low spot or the soil is clay. Plant in full sun or light shade. Asparagus will shade out other plants, so plant it to the north of its neighbours.

You can grow asparagus from seed or plant young plants, called crowns. Seed is comparatively inexpensive and has a high germination rate. The downside is you'll have to wait until the third spring to harvest. Soak the hard seeds in warm water for 48 hours, then sow four centimetres deep in early spring, indoors or out. Germination is slow and sporadic (anywhere from 10 to 24 days), but usually every seed sprouts. By fall, the seedlings will be large enough to move to their permanent spot. Let them grow a full year in their new home, and start with a light harvesting in year three. Normal harvests begin in year four.

Even though they are more expensive, most gardeners plant crowns, available in garden centres and by mail order, usually in spring. Price is offset by quality—only a few are required and harvesting can begin the following year. Dig individual planting holes or, if planting an asparagus bed, a trench. Plant with the tip of the crown set about 15 centimetres below the ground, then cover with three to five centimetres of soil, gradually filling in the hole or trench as the shoots become taller. Space plants 30 to 45 centimetres apart, with the same distance between rows.

Because of its open growth habit, asparagus's worst enemy is weeds. Since plants are easily damaged by hoeing, hand weeding is best. To control weeds, mulch plants to a depth of eight to 10 centimetres. Compost or rotted manure makes an excellent mulch and provides additional minerals; asparagus is a heavy feeder. If your mulch is less nutritious, fertilize plants three times a year—spring (before harvest), midsummer and early fall—with a slow-release organic fertilizer with a high first number, which means it's richer in nitrogen than in phosphorus and potassium. Asparagus, although drought-tolerant, is more productive when kept slightly moist; provide some irrigation in hot, dry weather.

For extra-early spears, rake off the mulch at snow melt so the ground warms up more rapidly. Once the sprouts are up, keep the harvest weed-free by pushing the mulch back into place, adding more as needed to maintain an eight- to 10-centimetre layer.

Through the winter, insulate plants from the damaging freeze/thaw cycle with a 15-centimetre layer of light, airy mulch such as straw; or cover plants or rows with landscape fabric. Where there's abundant snow cover, no extra protection is needed.

harvesting

Harvestable shoots begin appearing in mid-spring and continue until early summer. The first year of harvest, take only a few spears so the plant can build up strength. The following years, harvest all spears over 1.5 centimetres in diameter, leaving the others to grow. In most years, you'll have a four- to eight-week harvest period. Cut the plants down to the ground in late fall or early spring for more accessible spears and tidier plants.

Harvest asparagus by cutting or snapping it off. To cut, hold the spear with one hand and cut it about two centimetres below the ground with a sharp knife; you'll probably have to snap off the fibrous base before serving. To snap, simply bend the spear until it breaks. It will separate naturally just where the edible part begins.

Asparagus is best eaten fresh but can be stored for a few weeks in the refrigerator. Plunge the base of newly harvested spears into three to five centimetres of cold water, drain and store upright, wrapped in plastic, in the coldest part of your fridge. You can also store them unwrapped, upright in a few centimetres of water in the fridge. Blanch and freeze the surplus.

diseases and pests

Although asparagus is generally problem-free, here's what to do if trouble strikes:

Asparagus rust This rarely occurs in modern varieties. You'll know it if you see it: stems are covered with rust-coloured pustules. Destroy infected plants.

Crown rot Plants rot away at the base. It can occur if you're growing asparagus in poorly drained or excessively acidic soil. The best long-term solutions are to plant in raised beds and correct the pH level every few years.

Asparagus beetles Dispatch the striped or spotted bugs or aphids with a few sprays of insecticidal soap, repeating every three days as needed.

green or white

Europeans have customarily grown white asparagus, maintaining it's tastier and more tender than the green. The plants are the same, but the spears of white asparagus are blanched, or kept from light while growing. This is done by either mounding up soil over the plants in the spring or covering the plants with an opaque cloche, called an asparagus jar. Mounds and jars are removed after harvesting. Asparagus plants will die if permanently deprived of light. Today's asparagus is much less fibrous than older cultivars, and white asparagus isn't seen often in North America. It's easy to blanch asparagus in a home garden by mounding the emerging stalks with soil and keeping them covered till harvest time.

varieties

Female plants are short-lived and less productive than males; they also tend to produce unwanted seedlings and become weedy. Most hybrid seed lines produce far more male plants, but open-pollinated types are closer to 50/50. Even purchased crowns aren't guaranteed to be male. The only way to tell them apart is to wait until summer: if berries form, you've got a female plant. Dig them out in favour of the male plants.

Mail-order sources for both seeds and plants usually give you the best choice. Older, open-pollinated varieties such as 'Mary Washington' and 'Martha Washington' are still available, but are not productive or disease-resistant enough to compete with the more modern types. 'Viking' (also sold as 'Viking KB-3'), developed at Vineland Station in Ontario, is probably the best asparagus overall for cold-climate growing; it's hardy to Zone 4. An open-pollinated cultivar, it produces quite a number of female plants, so expect to do a lot of culling. You might want to try the newer, extra-hardy 'Guelph Millennium'. It has yet to be widely tested but so far has proved hardy to Zone 3 and quite disease-resistant.

The California hybrids ('Jersey Giant', 'Jersey Knight', 'Jersey King') and a few other hybrid strains, such as 'Supermale', are highly productive and nearly all male but are hardy to Zone 5 only.

Finally, novelty varieties such as 'Purple Passion' and 'Purple Jumbo', both disease-resistant and hardy to Zone 5 (4, with mulch), have attractive deep purple rather than green spears, which unfortunately turn green when cooked.

extending the season

In addition to the traditional spring crop, it's possible to have a summer crop if you have a lot of plants. Choose one or two of the most vigorous plants and harvest none of their spears in the spring. In early July, cut the whole plant back to the ground—it will begin producing dozens of thick spears. As with the spring crop, harvest until the new spears are too thin for the table. You can keep a healthy plant on this summer schedule for a decade or more, but if it begins to weaken, switch it back to a spring harvest format.

When cooking asparagus, choose spears of uniform thickness. Thin ones—which you often get at the end of a crop—are good in soups. More substantial dishes such as risottos or pasta can accommodate thicker spears, but they should be cut into short lengths to fit a fork.

asparagus, scallop & shrimp soup

SERVES 6

Although asparagus soup is often thought of as rich and creamy, this light-as-air version is even better suited to this harbinger of spring. A touch of red, in the form of very finely diced red bell pepper, is a colourful addition.

1	lb. (450 g) thin asparagus spears, cut into 1/2-in. (1-cm) lengths
1	tbsp. (15 mL) butter
3	green onions, trimmed, thinly sliced
1/2	cup (125 mL) dry white wine
6	cups (1.5 L) homemade or high-quality chicken stock
1/2	tsp. (2 mL) salt
1/4	tsp. (1 mL) white pepper
1/2	lb. (225 g) medium-sized shrimp, deveined, peeled, halved lengthwise
1/2	lb. (225 g) scallops, halved
6	4-in. (10-cm) lengths of fresh coriander

1 In a medium-sized saucepan, bring 2 cups of lightly salted water to a boil. Add asparagus and cook just until tender-crisp, about 3 minutes. (Alternatively, you could steam the asparagus.) Drain and refresh under cold water; drain and set aside.

2 Rinse saucepan, then melt butter over medium heat. Add green onions and sauté gently–do not brown–until softened, about 3 minutes. Add wine and bring to a gentle boil. Add stock, salt and pepper, and return to a boil. Reduce heat to low, cover loosely and simmer for about 4 minutes. Rinse shrimp and scallops with cold running water and add, along with asparagus, to hot broth. Simmer very gently (not at a boil) until shrimp turn pink and begin to curl, about 3 minutes. Garnish with coriander and serve immediately.

spring risotto

SERVES 4 TO 6

Risotto makes a lovely luncheon or supper dish. Vary the vegetables according to what's available. Leftover risotto can be stored in the fridge for a couple of days, then shaped into small patties and sautéed in a little butter or oil until golden brown.

6   asparagus spears, trimmed,
     cut into 1-in. (2.5-cm) lengths
1   cup (250 mL) tiny peas
     (fresh or frozen)
6   cups (1.5 L) homemade or
     canned chicken stock
1/4   cup (60 mL) extra virgin olive oil
2   tbsp. (30 mL) butter
1   onion, finely chopped
2   cloves garlic, minced
2   cups (500 mL) arborio or other
     short-grained rice
1/2   cup (125 mL) dry white wine
1   small yellow or green zucchini,
     trimmed, diced
1   cup (250 mL) grated
     Parmigiano-Reggiano cheese
2   tbsp. (30 mL) fresh basil, chopped
2   tbsp. (30 mL) flat-leaf parsley,
     chopped
Salt and freshly ground pepper, to taste

1 In a large pot of lightly salted boiling water, cook asparagus and peas (if fresh; frozen peas are added at the end) for 2 minutes or until tender-crisp. Drain and refresh under cold running water; drain and set aside.

2 In a large saucepan, bring chicken stock to a boil. Reduce heat, keeping the stock at a slow simmer.

3 In a heavy-bottomed saucepan, heat olive oil and butter over medium-high heat. Add onion and cook for 2 minutes or until translucent. Stir in garlic and rice; cook for 2 minutes or until grains are well coated with butter and oil. Pour in wine; stir for 1 minute or until wine is absorbed.

4 Using a ladle, add simmering stock 1/2 cup (125 mL) at a time, stirring rice constantly to keep from sticking to saucepan; do not add more stock until last addition is absorbed. If stock is absorbing too quickly, reduce heat to maintain a slow, steady simmer. Repeat process, ladling in stock and stirring, for 15 minutes. As the end of the cooking time nears, reduce amount of added stock to 1/4 cup (60 mL) at a time. (You may not need all the stock.)

5 Stir in asparagus and zucchini—and peas, if frozen. Continue to cook, adding more stock as necessary, until rice is tender but with a firm heart and overall creaminess; the risotto should not be soupy or runny. One minute before completion, stir in cheese, basil and parsley. Season with salt and pepper and serve immediately.

asparagus & mushroom strata

SERVES 6

The new-found popularity of these savoury bread puddings is doubtless due to their delicious versatility. They work well as a breakfast, brunch, lunch or light supper dish and can be prepared the night before and baked the next day. For slightly heartier fare, add cooked sausage or ham to the filling.

3   tbsp. (45 mL) butter
8   slices dry bread (use good bakery
     bread, not too thinly sliced)
1   cup (250 mL) grated Gruyère
     or Swiss cheese
2   cups (500 mL) asparagus, in 1-in.
     (2.5-cm) pieces, steamed until tender
1/2   cup (125 mL) mushrooms,
     thinly sliced
1/2   cup (125 mL) chives, finely chopped
6   eggs
2   cups (500 mL) milk
Salt and freshly ground pepper, to taste

1 Lightly grease an 8-inch square (2-L) glass or ceramic baking dish with a small amount of butter. Use the remaining butter to spread on one side of each slice of bread. Place one layer of bread in baking dish, buttered side up. Sprinkle with half the cheese. Scatter half each of asparagus, mushrooms and chives over the cheese. Add remaining slices of bread and repeat layering.

2 In a mixing bowl, whisk together eggs, milk and seasoning. Pour mixture over bread layers, pushing the top layer down into the mixture, if necessary, to ensure all slices are coated. Cover with plastic wrap and refrigerate for at least 6 hours or overnight.

3 Remove from refrigerator about 45 minutes before baking. Preheat oven to 375°F (190°C). Remove plastic wrap and place strata in upper part of oven for 30 to 35 minutes, until it has puffed up and turned brown, and a tester inserted in the centre comes out clean.

4 Remove from oven and let stand for about 15 minutes before serving.

Raw or cooked briefly, peas can't be beat

peas

recipes

pea & carrot curry

maltese scampi
with peas

fresh pea soup

fettuccine with smoked
salmon & peas

chicken & snow peas
in black bean sauce

Peas are a popular choice for home gardeners because nothing surpasses the flavour of fresh ones: frozen ones are so-so, canned ones are egregious, and dried peas are a different animal altogether. And peas aren't difficult to grow, although some requirements must be met. Peas must mature during cool weather—spring or fall—yet they need full sun. They also require moderately rich, deeply worked, well-drained soil with a pH of 6.0 to 6.8. Avoid nitrogen—it encourages more vines than pods. Phosphorus and potassium are what's important for pod production; some growers recommend applying 5-10-10 fertilizer several days before planting. Another option is to work healthy amounts of bonemeal and wood ashes into the soil, but to temper wood ashes' tendency to raise soil pH, you may need to add pine needles or peat moss.

Peas also need something to climb, and supports should be considered before planting. Elaborate trellising isn't necessary—wire works well, as do branches from tree prunings. To use wire, stretch two or three lengths about eight centimetres apart between posts. Plant peas as soon as the ground can be worked, usually about six weeks before the last expected spring frost or six weeks before the first fall frost. In some parts of Canada, this may mean as early as March. A caveat: if the soil is too wet the seed will rot or refuse to germinate. BY LAURA LANGSTON

GARDENER'S TIPS
▪ A cup of fresh peas contains about nine grams of protein, 5.4 grams of fibre and 122 calories. Snow peas have less protein and fewer calories, but are high in vitamins.
▪ Pick peas every day during the harvest period, and pick carefully, using small scissors or fingernails to pinch off pods.
▪ Kids will love an edible hideaway of 'Sugan Snap' or 'Sugar Daddy' peas. Lash bamboo poles in a teepee shape and cover with plastic netting to support the growing plants.

pea varieties

- 'Knight', an early variety, has a high percentage of large double pods, 60 centimetres tall. Strong resistance to powdery mildew, wilt and enation virus. Matures in 56 days.
- 'Green Arrow' has large yields of peas in each pod and many double pods. Freezes well, too. Resistant to mildew and wilt. About 70 centimetres. 70 days.
- 'Alaska' is hardy and early, with a lower sugar content than most peas. Also dries well. Ideal for hot summers. Grows to 90 to 120 centimetres. 55 to 60 days.
- 'Little Marvel' is prolific, with an excellent sweet flavour. Peas also freeze well. About 50 centimetres. 65 days.
- 'Alderman' (or 'Tall Telephone') has huge, plump pods. Excellent flavour, but not resistant to enation virus. About 100 centimetres. 70 days.

Peas can be left to sprawl on the ground, but they produce better and remain healthier if supported on a trellis. They also add a vertical design element to the vegetable garden. Purple-podded peas like the one on the opposite page are decorative as well as an important food crop.

fixing the nitrogen in your soil

Growing peas in nitrogen-rich soil—sometimes the result of excessive amounts of manure or compost—is one of the biggest mistakes home gardeners make. The results are lush vines with few pods. To get a sense of the amount of nitrogen in your soil, look at your nasturtiums. Nasturtiums grown in soil low in nitrogen produce lots of large flowers. Rich soil that's high in nitrogen means more leaf growth. Peas require nitrogen, but they take most of it from the air by utilizing soil bacteria. The catch is that peas are planted in cool weather, when soil bacteria are inactive, and bacteria tend to leach out of the soil during early spring rains. To avoid the potential problems of this situation, many gardeners coat pea seeds with a powdered legume inoculant before planting to help the plants gain access to the nitrogen in the soil. Introducing the nitrogen-rich bacteria means quicker growth and healthier plants, without altering the nitrogen levels of the soil. Inoculants are inexpensive, easily available (be sure to buy one meant for peas), easy to use and completely harmless. Just moisten the pea seeds, dust with the inoculant and plant.

planting

Sow seeds about 2.5 centimetres deep and five or eight centimetres apart; gently water in the seeds if rain isn't forecast. They need cool weather to germinate, ideally 20°C, in which they'll sprout in about a week. However, seeds will germinate at temperatures as low as 5°C, but it may take a month. As soon as they germinate, mulch the tiny plants with grass clippings around the base to help retain moisture.

Young pea plants are extremely hardy—they tolerate frost and even a light dusting of snow. At the vining stage, plants can survive -7°C, and -2°C while flowering. On the other hand, if temperatures go above 27°C while the peas are blooming, the flowers won't properly pollinate, which reduces or eliminates yield.

Though plants need moisture and don't like to dry out, they hate saturated soil. They need about 2.5 centimetres of water a week—slightly more at flowering time.

Peas are very sensitive to wind-borne dust and sand—shelter them from strong prevailing winds. A row of sunflowers planted on the windward side of fall-grown peas protects them.

care and maintenance

Weed peas with a light touch. If their shallow, fibrous roots are disturbed, leaves and pods may quickly drop. But do weed the area around plants: weeds reduce yields, and weeds are far more vigorous than the plants, especially in early spring.

Because the leaves and shoots of peas are so succulent and tender, slugs, earwigs and aphids love them. To avoid slug and earwig damage, keep plants off the ground and cover them at night until they're about 15 centimetres tall. Spray regularly with insecticidal soap.

Powdery mildew—greyish patches on the leaves and occasionally the pods—is sometimes a problem. Avoid overhead watering and use a soaker hose or drip irrigation instead. If overhead watering is the only option, water in the morning to give the plants a chance to dry before night; growing a mildew-resistant variety also helps.

West Coast gardeners sometimes encounter enation virus, a wilt that stops the plant from flowering and results in warty, misshapen pods and the eventual death of the plant itself. Aphids spread the disease. Choose resistant varieties and plant early to avoid flowering in hot weather. Less prevalent are common wilt (wilted, dried-up leaves) and mosaic (mottled, curled, yellow leaves that fall off), viruses that can generally be avoided through early planting, crop rotation and good garden sanitation.

harvesting and saving seeds

Like fresh corn, picked peas lose their sweet flavour quickly. Even a two-hour wait between picking and eating can make a big difference. If you must pick peas ahead, put them in the fridge unshelled; shelling encourages them to convert sugar into starch.

The young shoots and blossoms of peas are edible and taste much like the peas themselves. They're pretty in salads and as garnishes on soups and dips. However, never confuse the leaves and blossoms of garden peas, snap peas and snow peas with the leaves and blossoms of sweet peas, which are poisonous.

Pea varieties are non-hybrids, or open-pollinated, which means seeds saved from this year's crop will produce a nearly identical crop next year. However, if you grow more than one variety, plant them at least 30 metres apart to avoid cross-pollination by insects. To save seeds for next year's crop, let the pods dry on the vine until the seeds rattle inside, but don't wait too long—pods may crack and scatter the seeds on the ground. If it rains while the pods are drying, pull the vines

and stack them in a dry, airy spot until peas are dry. Seed peas remain viable for three years if stored in an airtight container in a cool place.

pea types

There are four types of peas: garden peas, edible pod peas, snap peas and dry peas. Within each type are bush or pole varieties. Petit pois isn't a separate type, but sweet, intensely flavored peas that are small when mature.

Garden peas The terms *garden pea* and *English pea* refer to the traditional shelling varieties that yield edible seeds, or peas. Depending on the variety, plants range from rambling 120- to 150-centimetre vines to petite dwarf varieties that measure less than 60 centimetres.

The highest yields are from varieties that bear two pods at each flowering stem. Once peas mature, it's important to harvest every day to encourage continued pod production, although the season is short—about four to six weeks.

Enthusiastic harvesting might result in uprooting the whole plant. To pick pods, hold the plant stem in one hand and pull pods off with the other. Harvest when the pods are plump, lustrous and bright green, and seams are smooth. If the pod is wrinkled, it's old and the peas inside will be bland and pasty rather than sweet and fresh. Start checking for pods about three weeks after vines flowering.

Edible-pod peas The terms *Chinese pea, snow pea* and *sugar pea* are used inter-changeably to describe edible-pod varieties. They're also sometimes called *pois mangetout* by the French, which means "eat all."

Some varieties produce large, flat pods and must be grown on fences at least 120 centimetres tall. Others are dwarf vines that grow only 40 to 60 centimetres. Most gardeners harvest just as the peas begin to swell. Pick often; if pods are left to mature, the vines stop producing.

■ 'Oregon Sugar Pod II' is a heavy producer on 90-centimetre vines. It's mild-flavoured and frequently sets double pods. Highly disease- and enation-resistant. 80 days.

■ 'Oregon Giant' is the first high-sugar content snow pea. It has extra large, flat pods on 75-centimetre vines. Resistant to powdery mildew, common wilt and enation virus. 60 to 80 days.

■ 'Dwarf Grey Sugar' is an early dwarf variety that grows to 75 centimetres and tolerates both heat and cold. 65 days.

Snap peas Sometimes called sugar snap, it was introduced in 1980. Thick, crisp, edible pods with sweet, fat peas. Usually eaten whole. Can be shelled.

■ 'Sugar Snap', the original, is sweet and crunchy. Grows to 180 centimetres. Little disease resistance, so grow early. 70 to 80 days.

■ 'Sugar Daddy' is stringless. Vines reach 60 to 90 centimetres. Enation-resistant. 65 to 70 days.

■ 'Sugar Ann' is a dwarf, early version with plump pods on 45- to 60-centimetre vines. 65 to 70 days.

Dry peas Best suited for drying on the vine and used in soups, dry peas can also be eaten fresh. Harvest when the pods are hard and the peas rattle.

■ 'Blue Pod Capucijners', an heirloom pea from Holland. Two-tone purple blossoms, dark purple pods, greyish peas, sweet fresh or dry. 80 to 90 days.

■ 'Raisin Capucijners' Green pods, with wrinkled brown peas like raisins. 80 to 90 days.

pea & carrot curry

MAKES 2 1/2 CUPS (625 mL)

Eating your peas and carrots takes on new meaning with this fast, colourful curry.

1/4	cup (50 mL) vegetable oil or clarified butter
1	large onion, chopped
1	tbsp. (15 mL) finely chopped fresh ginger
1/2	tsp. (2.5 mL) salt, or to taste
1/4	tsp. (1 mL) black pepper
1	tsp. (5 mL) cumin seed
1/2	tsp. (2.5 mL) crushed dry red chilies
1/4	tsp. (1 mL) turmeric
1	tbsp. (15 mL) tomato paste
2	tbsp. (30 mL) water
2	medium carrots, peeled and thinly sliced
1/2	lb. (225 g) peas, fresh or frozen
1	cup (250 mL) water

1 In large pan or wok, heat oil or clarified butter over medium-low heat and sauté onion and ginger until brown, about 3 or 4 minutes, until the mixture is soft, aromatic and lightly browned. Add salt, black pepper, cumin seeds, red chilies and turmeric. Stir well. Add tomato paste and water. Stir and cook 1 minute.

2 Add peas, carrots and water. Cover and cook until peas and carrots are tender. (If using frozen peas, don't add until carrots are half cooked.) When the water is completely absorbed, continue cooking and stirring until you see oil separating out (forming around the edge of the pan).

maltese scampi with peas

SERVES 6

A beautifully coloured dish inspired by a recipe in *The Victory Garden Cookbook*, by Marian Morash. Serve on a bed of rice and garnish with lemon wedges.

	Shrimp Marinade (recipe follows)
1 1/2-2	lbs. (675 g-1 kg) large raw shrimp or 5-6 shrimp per person
1/4	lb. (115 g) smoked sausage (kielbasa or chorizo)
1-1 1/2	lb. (500-675 g) snap peas
1/2	lb. (250 g) baby sea scallops
1	lb. (500 g) mussels
3	tbsp. (45 mL) butter
	Salt and pepper

	Shrimp marinade	
1/3	cup (75 mL) olive oil	
1/3	cup (75 mL) vegetable oil	
1/3	cup (75 mL) fresh lemon juice	
2	tbsp. (30 mL) tomato paste	
1/4	cup (50 mL) chopped fresh parsley	
1	tbsp. (15 mL) fresh oregano	
1	tsp. (5 mL) fresh basil	
1/2	tsp. (2 mL) salt	
3	cloves garlic, minced	
1/2	tsp. (2 mL) hot pepper sauce	

1 Whisk marinade ingredients together; set aside. Peel and devein shrimp; add to marinade. Marinate at least 4 hours or overnight.

2 Prick sausage with a fork; cover with water, bring to a boil and blanch 5 minutes to release fat. Cool, slice diagonally in 1/4-inch (6-mm) pieces and set aside. Blanch peas in water 1 minute, let cool and set aside. Remove side muscle from scallops. Wash and scrub mussels, remove beards.

3 Remove shrimp from marinade, heat butter and 3 tbsp. (45 mL) of marinade in large pan. Sauté shrimp over high heat until pink on one side, about 3 minutes, shaking pan occasionally. Turn shrimp; add scallops, sausage and mussels. Sauté 2 or 3 minutes, or until scallops are opaque and mussels open. Add peas during last minute of cooking. Add salt and pepper to taste.

fresh pea soup

SERVES 6 TO 8

Chilled pea soup, adapted from *Tastes of the Pacific Northwest*, by Fred Brack and Tina Bell, is an excellent lunch with a chunk of hearty bread, or a lovely first course for a spring dinner.

1	cup (250 mL) finely diced onion
2	tbsp. (30 mL) unsalted butter
	Small bunch of fresh arugula
1	large cucumber, peeled, seeded and chopped
3	cups (750 mL) fresh peas
3	cups (750 mL) chicken or vegetable stock
	Salt and white pepper
1	tbsp. (15 mL) finely chopped fresh mint
1 1/2	cups (375 mL) heavy cream
	Cucumber-mint chutney (recipe follows)

1 In a large saucepan, sauté onion in butter over medium-low heat until soft but not brown, about 5 minutes. Add arugula and cucumber and cook about 2 minutes, until arugula wilts.
2 Add peas, stock, and salt and pepper to taste. Bring to a boil, turn heat to low and simmer, partially covered, until peas are tender, about 10 minutes.
3 Strain soup, reserving liquid. Purée solids, with a little liquid, in a blender. Combine purée with reserved liquid.
4 Stir in cream and mint. Cover and chill thoroughly.

Cucumber-mint chutney

1	cucumber, peeled, seeded and finely chopped
1	cup (250 mL) loosely packed fresh mint leaves, finely chopped
2	tsp. (10 mL) minced fresh cilantro
1/2	cup (125 mL) unflavoured yogurt
1/2	cup (125 mL) sour cream
	Pinch of salt

Lime juice to taste
Dash of red pepper flakes (optional)

Combine ingredients and chill thoroughly. Bring to room temperature before serving.

fettuccine with smoked salmon & peas

SERVES 4 TO 6

For a slightly thinner, lighter sauce, use evaporated skimmed milk instead of cream.

2	cups (500 mL) shelled fresh peas
4	tbsp. (50 mL) water
4	tbsp. (50 mL) butter
1	shallot, minced
1	clove garlic, minced
1/4	cup (50 mL) minced Italian parsley
4-6	oz. (120-180 g) smoked salmon, cut in bite-sized pieces
	Salt and pepper
2	eggs
1/2-1	cup (125-250 mL) heavy cream
1/2	cup (125 mL) freshly grated Parmesan cheese
1	lb. (500 g) fettuccine
1	tsp. (5 mL) minced fresh dill

1 Simmer peas in water with 2 tbsp. (30 mL) of the butter until just tender, about 5 minutes. Over medium heat, sauté shallot, garlic and parsley in remaining 2 tbsp. of butter until soft but not brown. Add smoked salmon and drained peas and sauté gently 2 more minutes, being careful not to break up the salmon pieces too much.
2 Add salt and pepper to taste; set aside.
3 In a large bowl, beat eggs with 1/2 cup (125 mL) cream and Parmesan cheese. Cook fettuccine according to package directions. Drain and toss in bowl with egg/cream mixture; add salmon and peas and toss again. Add

more cream if a thinner consistency is desired. Garnish with fresh dill.

chicken & snow peas in black bean sauce

SERVES 3 OR 4

Most bottled Asian sauces are extremely concentrated and need to be diluted more than North American sauces.

2	tbsp. (30 mL) vegetable oil
6	scallions, cut into 1-in. (2.5-cm) pieces
1	large red pepper, cored and cut into strips
3/4	lb. (340 g) snow peas, stemmed and stringed
1	tsp. (5 mL) minced ginger root
1	lb. (500 g) boneless, skinless chicken breasts, cut into 2-in. (5-cm) pieces
2 1/2-3	tbsp. (35-45 mL) prepared black bean sauce (not fermented beans) dissolved in approx. 3/4 cup (150 mL) water
2	pinches granulated sugar
2	tsp. (10 mL) cornstarch
2	tbsp. (30 mL) cold water

1 Heat wok and add 1 tbsp. (15 mL) oil. Sauté scallions, pepper, snow peas and ginger 2 or 3 minutes, or until vegetables are tender-crisp but still brightly coloured. Remove to a plate. Add remaining oil to wok. Stir-fry chicken until firm and no longer pink inside, 3 or 4 minutes. Return vegetables to wok. Add black bean mixture and sugar; toss to coat. Combine cornstarch and water. When liquid in wok begins to bubble, quickly stir in cornstarch/water mixture. Stir continually until liquid becomes clear and thickens slightly, about 30 seconds. Remove from heat and serve over noodles or rice.

Explore the amazing variety of an unsung vegetable

radishes

recipes

radish, green bean
& potato salad

radish & cream cheese
tea sandwiches

smoked trout with
radishes & watercress

Radishes are about as close as gardeners get to instant gratification. When sown in warm soil, the seeds germinate in two days, and the peppery little roots of the earliest varieties are ready to eat in 21 days. Their skins may be red, white, purple, lavender, black or bi-coloured, with white, red or bright pink flesh. They vary from marble-sized summer radishes to oriental types that can reach 45 centimetres in length.

The radish (*Raphanus sativus*) originated in western Asia, just east of the Mediterranean, and the earliest cultivated variety was probably *R. sativus* var. *niger,* a large, black-skinned winter radish. The ancient Greeks held radishes in high regard—their offerings to the god Apollo included turnips made of lead, beets of silver and radishes of gold. Radishes were appreciated by the Romans as well: they cultivated a large, black-skinned variety that grew to weights of 45 kilograms. By 500 BC the large winter radish (*R. sativus* var. *longipinnatus*) had reached the Far East, and it's been regarded as an important vegetable ever since.

European settlers brought radishes to North America, and many varieties were grown in colonial gardens. A typical Dutch breakfast in mid-18th century New York consisted of tea with brown sugar, and bread and butter with radishes. Thinly sliced radishes on buttered bread are still popular in Europe. BY HEATHER APPLE

GARDENER'S TIPS
- Although black-skinned winter varieties are high in calcium, radishes are low on nutrition. They offer a little vitamin B, potassium and sulphur, which accounts for the hot, sharp taste.
- Chew radishes well—they're hard to digest. A cup contains only 20 calories.
- Radish leaves are edible, particularly the mild and tender leaves of the first spring crop. Also good in soups, stews or stir-fries.
- Grated daikon complements a salad of Chinese cabbage, green onions and sweet red pepper.

Radishes aren't just the red and white nippy addition to a salad. They grow in many sizes, shapes and tastes for cooking and pickling. Left: a green-fleshed radish. Right: 'Round Black Spanish' and 'Easter Egg' which comes in assorted colours.

growing

The key to growing crisp, tasty radishes is to meet all their needs so they grow as quickly as possible. Radishes grown in unfavourable conditions may be hot and pithy.

They can be grown throughout the season, but cool weather gives the best quality. Sow the first crop in spring as soon as the soil can be worked. Because most small radishes mature in three to four weeks, they can be harvested before warm-weather crops such as beans, tomatoes or squash are planted. Some black and oriental radishes produce well when planted in July or August for winter use; for specific growing instructions see sections below.

Plant seeds in full sun in well-drained, loosened soil enriched with compost. Don't use high-nitrogen fertilizers. Make one-centimetre deep furrows, 10 centimetres apart, and sow the seeds about 2.5 centimetres apart and five millimetres deep. Keep soil moist but not soggy, and weed regularly. For a steady supply, make small plantings at one-week intervals throughout the growing season.

harvesting

A radish's quality deteriorates if it's left in the ground too long. Pull them up as soon as they mature—they'll stay crisp for several weeks in the refrigerator.

On the other hand, plants left in the ground form edible flowers and seed pods. If harvested young, the pods are crisp and edible, and can be added to salads, cooked in stir-fries or pickled. The seed can be harvested for another radish crop, or for growing radish sprouts—they also have a peppery taste. Allow plant stems and pods to dry and turn light brown on the plant, then harvest and finish drying in a warm spot. Separate the seeds from the pods and debris; store in a jar in a cool, dark place.

diseases and pests

Home gardeners rarely have problems with diseases if sound guidelines are followed. Radishes are members of the cabbage family and are bothered by the same pests—don't plant them where broccoli or cabbages grew the previous season. Control weeds such as shepherd's purse and wild mustard, and clean up plant debris in the fall.

Flea beetles These shiny black pests chew tiny holes in the leaves and can quickly destroy seedlings. As a preventive measure, place a floating row cover over seeds immediately after planting, and keep seedlings moist. Try growing varieties that have strong, large leaves and produce vigorous seedlings, such as 'Early Scarlet Globe'.

Cabbage root maggots These pale, seven-millimetre long maggots tunnel through the roots of the radish. Protect plants with a floating row cover, and reduce damage by harvesting radishes as soon as they mature.

small salad radishes

'Cherry Belle' An early, mild-flavoured favourite variety with white flesh and bright red skin; stays firm and crisp. Matures in 22 to 24 days.

'Comet' Recommended for late spring and midsummer planting, it has white flesh, bright red skin, and stays firm and crisp. 25 to 28 days.

'Early Scarlet Globe' A quick-growing variety, suited for spring or fall planting, with crisp white flesh, bright red skin and a bold flavour. 24 days.

The exotic looking variety at left has rose and white flesh and bright green skin. On the opening page, a bouquet of two varieties that are a far cry form the usual red radish: 'Valentine', with white skin, and 'China Rose', with pink skin.

'Sparkler' An attractive, flavourful, round radish, red with a large white tip. 25 days.

'D'Avignon' The best non-hybrid French breakfast-type radish. Its cylindrical, bright red roots have white tips. 21 days.

'French Breakfast' The delicately flavoured, scarlet cylindrical roots are white-tipped; it grows well throughout the season. 25 to 30 days.

'Icicle' (includes 'White Icicle'/'Icicle Short Top'/'Long White Icicle') Crisp and mild, these varieties have white skin and flesh and grow to 15 centimetres. 30 to 35 days.

'Easter Egg' Comes in assorted colours—red, purple, lavender or white. Each has white flesh and stays crisp and mild as it gets larger. 28 to 32 days.

'Snow Belle Tender' Mild and crisp, with a round root, white skin and flesh. 28 to 35 days.

'Purple Plum' From the 'Easter Egg' collection, it has deep purple skin and stays deliciously crisp. 28 days.

black radishes

These heirloom radishes store well and are grown mainly for eating over the winter. Sow seeds in July and August, five centimetres apart; thin to 15 centimetres. Keep soil moist but not soggy.

'Round Black Spanish' Rough, black skin covers white, tender flesh with a bit of bite; they can be eaten when the size of a quarter, but for winter storage leave them in the ground to come to their full diameter—eight to 10 centimetres. Store just above freezing in sand, leaves, sawdust or perforated bags, in a humid environment. In mild areas of British Columbia they're winter hardy. 55 to 60 days.

oriental radishes

On average, oriental radishes mature in 50 to 60 days. Different varieties are adapted to sowing at different times—spring, summer or fall—and they won't produce good roots if sown at the wrong time. Grow in full sun in well-drained soil worked deeply and enriched with compost. Harvest carefully with a pitch-fork as soon as they reach full size. Varieties sown in summer should be dug up in the fall. To store, remove leaves and place in sand, leaves, sawdust or perforated bags in a humid environment, just above freezing. Use in stir-fries, soups and stews, pickled, sliced or shredded in salads, or grated as a condiment.

'April Cross' A Japanese fall radish. Sow seed 60 days before the onset of cool weather. Thin seedlings to 15 centimetres apart. The white-fleshed, white-skinned roots grow to 45 centimetres long.

'Spring Song' Sow in spring. It produces long, smooth white roots and is strongly resistant to bolting. 60 days.

'Miyashige' Good for pickling, it has long, cylindrical white roots with a pale green band near the top. Sow in July and early August; stores well. 50 days.

'Daikon' A long Japanese radish with crisp, white flesh and a mildly hot flavour. Sow in early summer and harvest in August or September. 65 days.

specialty radishes

These unusual radishes are fun to grow and eat.

■ 'China Rose' Grows 12 to 15 centimetres long, with rose skin and mild white flesh; stores well. Plant in June or July for fall and winter use—it will bolt if planted when night temperatures go below 9°C. 60 days.

■ 'Shunkyo Semi-long' A hot but sweet-tasting radish from North China with cylindrical roots 10 to 12 centimetres long, deep pink skin and crisp, white flesh. Use the pink stems in salads or stir-fried with the roots; stems can also be pickled. Slow to bolt, 'Shunkyo' can be sown throughout the season. 32 days.

■ 'Valentine' A round, green-and-white-skinned radish that has red flesh at maturity. Sow throughout the summer and use in salads. Matures in 25 days.

■ 'Munich Bier' The long white roots of this variety are sliced and served with draft beer in Munich. Sow in midsummer for a fall crop. Matures in 60 days.

■ 'Misato Rose' A sweet-flavoured fall radish that grows five to 10 centimetres in diameter. Good cooked or in salads, its white-skinned roots have green shoulders and bright pink flesh. Sow in late summer to early fall. Matures in 55 to 65 days.

Radishes should be picked as soon as they mature. They get tough and strong if left in the ground too long, but keep well in the fridge several weeks. Radish sprouts are peppery and tasty in a salad. Above: 'Minowase Spring Cross', an oriental type whose long, cylindrical roots keep well.

radish, green bean & potato salad

SERVES 4

A colourful salad with a delightful contrast of tastes, shapes and textures. Serve with oven-fried chicken or grilled fish. Make sure potatoes are all about the same size.

1 1/2 lb. (750 g)	new potatoes, scrubbed clean and left whole
3/4 lb. (375 g)	thin green beans, stem ends trimmed
6	slices bacon
1/4 cup (60 mL)	plain yogurt
3 tbsp. (45 mL)	extra virgin olive oil
2 tbsp. (30 mL)	white wine vinegar
3 tbsp. (45 mL)	chopped, fresh dill
1	small bunch of radishes, washed, trimmed and sliced thinly

1 In a large pot of boiling water, cook potatoes for 10 to 15 minutes or until tender. Remove with a slotted spoon and reserve. Plunge green beans into the same cooking water and cook until just tender, about 4 to 5 minutes. Drain, rinse under cold water and drain again. Slice beans on the diagonal into 2.5-centimetre pieces. Set aside.
2 Cook bacon until crisp. When cool enough to handle, crumble into pieces. In a large mixing bowl, combine the yogurt, olive oil, vinegar and 2 tablespoons (30 mL) of the fresh dill, and whisk together. Add potatoes, green beans, bacon and radishes; mix well. Scatter remaining tablespoon (15 mL) of dill over the top and serve.

Radishes are overlooked as a vegetable. Even young seed pods harvested right after the plants have flowered are crisp and edible, and can be used in salads, cooked in stir-fries or pickled.

radish & cream cheese tea sandwiches

SERVES 6

The filling is also good for wraps. Or use it as a topping for tiny steamed and halved new potatoes, or as a stuffing for fresh celery.

1	cup (250 mL) minced red radishes
1	tsp. (5 mL) poppy seeds
1	cup (250 mL) soft, spreadable deli-style cream cheese
1	tsp. (5 mL) salt
	Freshly ground black pepper
8	slices dark rye bread, lightly buttered and crust trimmed
1/2	English cucumber, very thinly sliced

1 In a mixing bowl, combine the radishes, poppy seeds, cream cheese, salt and freshly ground black pepper to taste. Blend well. Let stand for a few minutes.
2 Lay out slices of bread on a dry surface. Spread radish filling, about 5 millimetres thick, on 4 of the bread slices. Top with slices of cucumber and the remaining bread slices.
3 Cut into triangles and serve immediately.

smoked trout with radishes & watercress

SERVES 6

A lovely light supper or lunch recipe that lends itself to many variations. Use smoked salmon or good-quality canned tuna (packed in olive oil) in place of the trout. Vary the greens by substituting frisée for the watercress.

1/3	cup (75 mL) fresh lemon juice
2	tsp. (10 mL) Dijon mustard
2	tbsp. (30 mL) light mayonnaise
1/2	cup (125 mL) extra virgin olive oil
2	tbsp. (30 mL) chopped, fresh chives
	Salt and freshly ground pepper
1	lb. (500 g) smoked trout fillets
4	green onions, trimmed and chopped
1/4	cup (60 mL) chopped, fresh parsley
2	cups (500 mL) red radishes, thinly sliced
1	cup (250 mL) white radishes, thinly sliced
2	to 3 bunches watercress, washed, stems trimmed

1 Prepare the dressing by combining the lemon juice, mustard, mayonnaise, olive oil, chives, and salt and pepper to taste in a small mixing bowl. Whisk together until well blended. Set to one side.
2 Pull trout fillets apart into rough chunks and place in a medium-sized bowl along with the chopped green onions and half of the parsley. Toss trout with half of the dressing.
3 In another mixing bowl, combine the radishes and watercress with remaining parsley and dressing. Arrange radishes and watercress on a large oval serving platter. Top with trout mixture. Serve with warm crusty bread and a good Sauvignon blanc.

Rosy stalks that deliver tart taste and a store of warm memories

rhubarb

recipes

rhubarb & ginger cordial

persian lamb with rhubarb

rhubarb custart tart

Each spring, my grandmother's rhubarb patch erupted beside the wire fence at her Ontario farm. It was huge—brawny even. My brother and I delighted in breaking off stalks, dipping the ends in salt or sugar pirated from the kitchen, then shivering as our taste buds exploded. That patch was a marvel. It also had some help.

The rhubarb grew about a tail's length from a cow pasture, which perhaps explains why it produced the greenest, hardiest plants in Murray Hills. Rhubarb pies sprang forth from Grandma's wood stove with juices bubbling to the surface like sweet lava (through fork marks that resembled birds' feet), and rhubarb sauce often kick-started the day with a zesty hit to the back of the throat. My knees still wobble at the thought.

That was more than 35 years ago. Today my wife, Catherine, and I grow rhubarb in British Columbia and in summer our patch is almost as impressive as my grandmother's used to be. Of course I miss her way with pies and sauces, her Findlay wood stove— and those Herefords on the other side of the fence. But a bag of manure mixed with compost seems to stand in rather nicely. And you don't have to clean out the barn. Bring on spring! BY MARK FORSYTHE

GARDENER'S TIPS
- Rhubarb leaves can be composted but should never be eaten—they contain high amounts of oxalic acid.
- The flower stalks are striking additions to vegetable plots or perennial beds. But for tender rhubarb, remove flower stalks as they appear.
- Rhubarb stalks are ready harvest just before the crinkles on the leaves disappear and they're beginning to look like elephants' ears.
- Rhubarb grows best where the average temperatures fall below -6° C in winter and below 25° C in summer.

Rhubarb plants unfurl in spring from a bulbous, shiny red crown and leaves unfold magically into giant ribbed shields on tart-sweet stalks. Don't harvest the first year; allow plants to develop a good root system before taking stalks for pies or crisps.

with 2.5 centimetres—no more—of soil. Water well; mulch with a mixture of compost and straw, hay or shredded leaves to a depth of 15 centimetres, leaving a space in the centre so the crown is uncovered.

Keep the soil moist but not soggy. Feed in midsummer with a layer of compost around the crowns, or a granular organic fertilizer. If your soil is poor, feed every two or three weeks with compost tea (made by soaking a bag of compost in a pail of water overnight).

Remove flower stalks as they appear. In fall, remove dead leaves, fluff up the mulch and lay 2.5 centimetres of new mulch over the crown; use 15 to 20 centimetres in extremely cold climates.

In spring, draw back the mulch, dig in compost or well-rotted manure and granular organic fertilizer, and replace the mulch, avoiding the crown.

growing

Rhubarb is propagated from crowns, or segments, of the parent plant, available at nurseries in spring. Choose crowns that are firm, free of rot and have one or more round, reddish buds. (Three to five plants provide ample fresh and frozen rhubarb for a family of four.) Spring planting is best across the country, except for coastal British Columbia, where fall planting is fine.

Plant in full sun in fertile, well-drained, slightly acidic soil. Take rhubarb's mature size into account when deciding where to place it—plants can grow more than 90 centimetres tall with a spread of 120 to 150 centimetres. Dig a hole 45 to 60 centimetres deep and 60 centimetres in diameter. Add 15 centimetres of compost or well-rotted manure and fill with a mixture of soil and compost, leaving a depression for the crown. Set the crown in the hole, and cover the buds

harvesting

Don't harvest stalks the first year—plants need to devote their energy to developing a good root system. During the second year, harvest only a few stalks during the first two weeks of the season. In subsequent years, harvesting can continue for eight to 10 weeks.

Choose stalks that are at least 30 centimetres long. Grasp the stalk in your hand, slide your thumb down the inner groove as far as it will go, then twist the stalk while pulling up. Take fewer than half the stalks per plant in each picking.

After five to 10 years—earlier if the plant starts producing small, tough stalks instead of large, juicy ones—the crown needs dividing. Divide in early spring before the shoots emerge. Dig up the crown and cut off large side roots. Using a spade, divide the crown into pieces, making sure each piece has roots and at least two buds. Replant as you would a new crown.

The leaves of culinary rhubarb have appeal in the vegetable patch, but several varieties of ornamental rhubarb have been bred simply for their looks. Many have dramatic, coloured foliage, and some have showy flowers meant to draw the eye.

ornamental rhubarb

Rhubarb comes from a family of about 50 close relatives, and some are attractive enough to be ornamental additions to the perennial garden. Their large leaves and small cream, white or red flowers on large stalks can be conversation starters beside a pond or in dappled shade. Grow in enriched, moist but not soggy, soil. Reports differ widely on edibility, so don't experiment.

The most widely grown ornamental is *Rheum palmatum*, 180 to 240 centimetres tall with a 120- to 180-centimetre spread. It has large, round, palmately lobed toothed leaves with tall, branched stalks and tiny pink or reddish flowers. Hardy to Zone 5; with good protection it survives in Zone 4. *R. palmatum* var. *tanguticum*, 150 centimetres tall, has less deeply cut purple-tinged foliage and white, pink or red flowers. 'Atrosanguineum' is a wonderful cultivar whose young, dark purple-red leaves mature to green on top and purple-red on the underside. Flowers are red. 'Bowles Crimson' is similar. 'Ace of Hearts', 120 centimetres, has heart-shaped leaves veined red on the underside. Flowers are white to pink.

pests and disease

When grown in well-drained, fertile soil, rhubarb is usually a healthy, trouble-free crop, but here are a few problems to watch for.

Rhubarb curlico A centimetre-long brown or black weevil usually covered with rust-orange pollen. Adults puncture the stalks and lay their eggs inside. Handpicking should contol the bug; as a last resort, use insecticidal soap. The adults hibernate in weeds and larvae feed on wild dock and related species, so keep the rhubarb patch well weeded.

Crown rot A disease that rots the crown and main roots of the plant. The leaves yellow and wilt, and the stalks collapse. There's no cure, so dig up and destroy infected plants. Plant new crowns in another location. To reduce the risk of crown rot, avoid shady areas and soggy, poorly drained soil. Clean the rhubarb patch thoroughly in fall.

Verticillium wilt Leaves yellow and wilt. The yellowing often occurs first and may be mistaken for a nutritional deficiency. Remove and destroy infected plants. To prevent the disease, don't plant rhubarb where susceptible plants have been grown, such as peppers, tomatoes, eggplants, potatoes, strawberries, raspberries, apricots, cherries, peaches, plums, almonds, roses, okra, mint and sage.

Anthracnose Watery spots appear on the leaf stalks and grow bigger as the disease progresses. Leaves eventually wilt and die. As soon as the first spots appear, apply a natural sulfur-based spray and repeat every seven to 10 days. If this doesn't control the disease after a month, destroy infected plants. To prevent, practise good garden hygiene and clean up garden throroughly in fall—the disease is spread by animals, gardeners and contaminated tools, as well as wind and rain.

rhubarb & ginger cordial

SERVES ABOUT 4 CUPS (1L)

Cordials are old-fashioned liquid refreshments from bygone days. Serve as an aperitif before dinner, or with sparkling water over ice. Keeps for up to a week in the refrigerator.

2	lb. (1 kg) rhubarb, trimmed and chopped
3/4	cup (175 mL) granulated sugar
4	cups (1 L) water
2	in. (5-cm) piece gingerroot, bruised and chopped
3	whole cloves
	Fresh mint leaves

1 In a large stainless-steel saucepan set over medium-high heat, combine rhubarb with sugar, water, cloves and ginger. Gently bring to a boil, then reduce to a simmer until rhubarb is soft, about 5 minutes.

2 Strain through a sieve and serve, warm or chilled. Garnish with fresh mint.

persian lamb with rhubarb

SERVES 4

Lamb and rhubarb have a natural affinity for each other, especially in this Middle Eastern dish. If using shoulder of lamb, increase cooking time by about 30 minutes, or until lamb is tender. Serve over steamed rice.

2	lb. (1 kg) boneless lamb (shoulder or leg)
2	tbsp. (25 mL) unsalted butter
2	tbsp. (25 mL) olive oil
2	white onions, sliced thinly
1	tsp. (5 mL) ground coriander
1	tsp. (5 mL) ground cumin
1/2	cup (125 mL) chopped fresh parsley
1/4	cup (50 mL) chopped fresh mint
2	lb. (1 kg) rhubarb, trimmed and chopped
	Salt and freshly ground black pepper

1 Cut lamb into 2-in. (5-cm) chunks. In a Dutch oven or heavy-lidded saucepan or skillet, combine the butter with the olive oil and sauté onions until golden—not brown—over medium-high heat. Using a slotted spoon, transfer cooked onions to a plate, increase heat to high and brown lamb in batches.

2 When all the lamb has been browned, return it to the pan along with the onions, and add coriander and cumin. Stir to combine well, and add just enough water to cover. Bring to a gentle boil, reduce heat to a simmer, cover and cook gently for about an hour, stirring occasionally.

3 Add parsley and mint, stir to combine well and cook for another half hour, loosely covered, stirring occasionally.

4 About 10 minutes before serving, stir in rhubarb and cook just until softened. Season with salt and pepper to taste.

forced rhubarb

The recipes here use forced rhubarb, and it's important to know the difference between forced rhubarb and rhubarb grown in the garden. Rhubarb available out of season at the grocery store is forced. It requires about half the cooking time of fresh, home-grown rhubarb, and it has a relatively gentle flavour, with less bite. Increase the cooking time for home-grown rhubarb, and adjust the sugar to your taste. Frozen rhubarb may be used in place of fresh. If it's a commercially frozen product, treat it as forced rhubarb.

rhubarb custard tart

SERVES 6 TO 8

A marriage made in culinary heaven—
creamy custard studded with tangy bits of
rhubarb set in shortcrust pastry. Vary the
recipe by combining equal amounts of
fresh strawberries and rhubarb. Serve
barely warm.

	Pastry for a single-crust 9-inch (23-centimetre) pie
4	stalks rhubarb, trimmed and cut into 1⁄2-inch (one-centimetre) pieces
2⁄3	cup (150 mL) granulated sugar
1	tsp. (5 mL) ground nutmeg
1⁄2	tsp. (2 mL) salt
1	tsp. (5 mL) all-purpose flour
3	eggs, beaten
2 1⁄2	cups (625 mL) milk

1 Preheat oven to 350°F (180°C). Line a
pie plate with pastry. Distribute the
rhubarb evenly over the pastry, and set
to one side.

2 In a mixing bowl, combine the
sugar, nutmeg, salt and flour. Add the
beaten eggs, and use a whisk to blend
thoroughly with the dry ingredients.
Set aside. Pour milk into a heavy
saucepan and set over medium-high
heat; remove from heat just before it
boils. Gradually whisk the hot milk
into the contents of the mixing bowl.
When well combined, pour over the
rhubarb in the pie shell.

3 Bake for about 45 minutes, or until a
tester comes out clean. Allow the pie to
cool before serving.

Zesty greens, reds and purples add taste and texture to spring salads

salad GREENS

recipes

greens & cheese strudel

grilled portobello
on greens

arugula & mâche
salad with chèvre toasts

Remember when salads consisted of an anaemic wedge of iceberg lettuce with a few radish and tomato slices smothered in thick, orange dressing? Not any more.

A wonderful assortment of feathery, frilly, curled and serrated plants, often referred to as "greens"—even though some are beautiful shades of red, purple and burgundy—can be grown to create salads with any number of taste, colour and texture combinations.

Greens generally need well-drained, fertile soil and full sun. Amaranth thrives in high temperatures, but many greens grow best in cooler temperatures of spring and fall; they tend to wilt or bolt to seed in high temperatures. Summer heat can also make greens taste bitter or very spicy; sample them before adding to your salad. Arugula, watercress and mâche benefit from light or dappled shade at the height of summer.

Before planting, work generous amounts of compost or composted manure into the soil and keep soil moist but not soggy throughout the growing period. Mulch with hay, straw or leaves. Some greens can be sown more than once per season. Check days to maturity and hardiness in your zone. BY HEATHER APPLE

GARDENER'S TIPS
- Like plain lettuces, fancy greens are high in fibre and low in calories, but they deliver more food value.
- Mustard greens are high in calcium and vitamins A and C, and have substantial amounts of iron, phosphorus and B vitamins.
- Mâche is high in iron, and was a staple in medieval monastery gardens.
- In ancient Greece, cresses were considered brain food, and a cure for both insanity and drunkenness.

amaranth

The tender, young leaves and shoots of amaranth (*Amaranthus tricolor*) taste like spinach with a hint of horseradish, but they become bitter with age, so harvest young.

Plant when the soil reaches 20°C, sowing seed six millimetres deep, 12 to 15 seeds per 2.5 centimetres. As the leaves begin to touch, thin to 15 centimetres apart.

Once plants have a good supply of leaves (at about 50 days), pick individual ones for salad and nip off the end buds to encourage branching.

coveted cultivars

AMARANTH
- 'Joseph's Coat'—variegated red, green and gold leaves

MÂCHE
- 'Vit'—mildew-resistant
- 'Coquille de Louviers'—drought-tolerant
- 'Verte d'Etampes'—drought-tolerant

MUSTARD
- 'Osaka Purple'
- 'Giant Red'
- 'Southern Giant Curled'—frilly, bright green leaves
- 'Kyoto Mizuna'

ORNAMENTAL CABBAGE AND KALE
- 'Tokyo Mixed' and 'Osaka Mixed'—leaves are pink, red or white in the centre; outer leaves are green
- 'White Peacock'—long, serrated leaves, creamy white in the centre
- 'Red Peacock'—long, serrated leaves, rose-pink in the centre
- 'Nagoya Mixed' kale—white, rose or red inner leaves, green outer leaves

arugula

The nutty flavour of arugula—also called rocket or roquette—adds piquancy to salads. The dark green, lobed leaves of common arugula (*Eruca sativa*) form a loose, open bunch that can reach 15 to 25 centimetres across before the plant bolts. Wild arugula (*E. selvatica* syn. *Diplotaxis tenuifolia*) is about half the size, with smaller, more deeply lobed leaves. It has a stronger flavour and is slower to bolt.

Sow in spring as soon as the ground can be worked, planting seeds six millimetres deep, 2.5 centimetres apart in rows 15 to 20 centimetres apart. When leaves of seedlings touch, thin to 10 centimetres.

Arugula is ready to pick 28 to 35 days after sowing for common arugula, 49 to 56 days for wild. Cut off individual leaves for a cut-and-come-again crop, cut off the entire plant just below the root attachment or pull up the plant.

cress

Cress adds a peppery taste to salads; it can also be used in sandwiches and as a garnish. Watercress (*Nasturtium officinale*), the most familiar type, is a perennial that grows wild in streams. Upland cress (*Barbarea verna*), a hardy biennial, tastes similar but is easier to grow.

Watercress can be seeded outside in a rich, neutral soil (pH 7) kept constantly moist. Sow seeds three millimetres deep and thin to 10 centimetres apart when leaves start to touch. Harvest by snipping off the top eight to 10 centimetres of the plant until small, white flowers appear in early summer. Plants mature in 60 days; stems placed in a glass of water in the refrigerator will stay fresh for up to a week.

Upland cress grows best in rich, moist soil and tolerates some shade. Sow six millimetres deep in rows 25 centimetres apart, thinning to 15 centimetres apart when leaves start to touch. In most of Canada, you can mulch plants before the snow falls and enjoy spring greens. Matures in 50 days, but outer leaves can be harvested as soon as the plant produces a rosette of leaves. As the plant ages, harvest milder-tasting leaves from the centre.

Greens are worth planting in the garden for more than their food value. They also have highly ornamental qualities, like the amaranth at right. And a mixture of several greens, such as arugula, mustard greens and cress planted with ornamental kale, is a great annual bed for a shady area.

mâche

Also called lamb's lettuce or corn salad (*Valerianella locusta*), mâche produces a low-growing rosette of tender, mild-flavoured leaves. The leaves lose their succulent sweetness in the heat of the summer but don't become bitter. Mâche is hardy throughout the fall in most of Canada and in the winter and early spring on the coast of British Columbia.

Sow seeds as soon as soil can be worked in spring; germination takes two to three weeks. Plant six millimetres deep, 2.5 centimetres apart in rows 30 centimetres apart, or broadcast seed in a bed. Gradually thin plants to 10 centimetres apart when leaves start to touch.

The succulent, mild leaves of spring mâche can be used alone or to balance the assertive taste of greens such as mustard, arugula and cress. Pick outer leaves or the entire rosette; wash thoroughly and remove any yellow leaves.

mustard

Leaf mustard (*Brassica juncea*) is large-leafed and pungent, and includes colourful varieties—most mature in 45 days. Milder and slower to bolt, mizuna mustard (*B. rapa* var. *japonica*), widely grown in Japan, has deeply cut, feathery leaves.

Plant seeds six millimetres deep, 2.5 centimetres apart, thinning first to five, then to 10 centimetres—20 to 30 if growing for cooked greens—when leaves start to touch. Once plants are 10 to 15 centimetres tall, pick individual leaves or cut the entire plant two centimetres or more above the crown; it will regrow and can be harvested four or five more times.

orach

Orach (*Atriplex hortensis*) plants eventually reach 1.5 to two metres. When the soil warms up, sow seeds six millimetres deep, 2.5 centimetres apart. Germination takes about 10 days. As plants grow, keep thinning until they're 45 centimetres apart.

Orach matures in 42 days. Cut off young leaves and pinch off growing tips and flower stalks to produce branching and delay going to seed.

ornamental cabbage and kale

Ornamental cabbage (*Brassica oleracea* var. *capitata*) and kale (*B. oleracea* var. *acephala*) last into December in many parts of Canada and survive the winter on the coast of British Columbia. Start three months before the first fall frost—seeds germinate at about 20°C. Plants need full sun and rich, well-drained soil with a neutral pH. If sowing directly into the garden, sow seeds six millimetres deep, five centimetres apart. Thin to 30 to 45 centimetres when leaves start to touch. Every four weeks dig in some compost around the plants. Tender young leaves can be harvested a few at a time once the plant has good growth, but cabbage and kale taste better after a frost.

Leaf lettuces in many varieties, such as the 'Osaka Purple', and mizuna mustard leaves, in the bed at right, make a wonderful cut-and-come-again crop. Pick a few leaves from each plant just before a meal; the small new leaves will be ready for next week's salad, and the plant will produce more for a future meal. Swish leaves in a few changes of water to wash off soil and then soak 10 minutes or so to refresh them.

greens &
cheese strudel

SERVES 8

Include hearty greens such as cabbage or kale with leafy ones like amaranth, chard and spinach. Steam them lightly for easier handling. Add leftover cooked vegetables if you have them, or a few thinly sliced mushrooms. If you substitute a different cheese, be sure it's full flavoured.

4   cups (1 L) roughly chopped,
     lightly cooked assorted greens
1⁄4 cup (60 mL) fresh dill, chopped
1⁄4 cup (60 mL) fresh parsley, chopped
1⁄4 cup (60 mL) toasted pine nuts
1   cup (250 mL) shredded
     Gruyère cheese
1⁄2 cup (125 mL) plain yogurt
1   egg, lightly beaten
1⁄2 cup (125 mL) fine breadcrumbs
     Salt and freshly ground pepper,
     to taste
10   sheets phyllo pastry, thawed
1⁄3 cup (75 mL) melted butter

1 Preheat oven to 400°F (200°C). Line a baking tray with parchment paper (or use vegetable cooking spray). In a large mixing bowl, combine greens, dill, parsley, pine nuts, cheese, yogurt and egg; mix together well. Add some of the breadcrumbs if mixture seems too wet.
2 Season with salt and pepper.
3 Unroll the thawed phyllo pastry and place one sheet on a clean, damp tea towel. (Cover remaining phyllo sheets with another damp tea towel.) Brush with melted butter and add a sprinkling of remaining breadcrumbs. Repeat procedure with remaining phyllo sheets; reserve 1 tablespoon of butter.
4 Evenly distribute one tenth of the greens filling over each phyllo sheet along the edge closest to you. Use the tea towel to roll the dough into a strudel shape (like a long tube). Neatly fold each end and tuck beneath the roll. Transfer to prepared baking tray, seam side down. Brush with remaining melted butter and bake for 10 minutes. Reduce heat to 325°F (165°C) and continue baking until lightly browned, another 20 minutes. Let sit for 5 minutes before slicing and serving.

grilled portobello
on greens

SERVES 4

If you don't want to fire up the grill, use a heavy pan to sear the portobellos. Reserve the stems for stir-fries or omelettes.

For vinaigrette
2   tbsp. (30 mL) balsamic vinegar
1   tbsp. (15 mL) fresh oregano, chopped
1   clove garlic, minced
1⁄2 tsp. (2 mL) sugar
1⁄3 cup (75 mL) extra virgin olive oil
     Salt and freshly ground pepper, to taste

For mushrooms and greens
2   lb. (1 kg) portobello mushrooms,
     stems removed (about 6)
3   tbsp. (45 mL) extra virgin olive oil
1⁄2 tsp. (2 mL) coarse salt
6   cups (1.5 L) mixed salad greens
3   oz. (85 g) Parmigiano-Reggiano
     cheese, shaved

1 In a small bowl, combine vinegar, oregano, garlic and sugar. Whisk together until well blended. Add 1/3 cup oil in a steady stream, whisking until well combined. Season with salt and pepper. Set aside.
2 In a bowl, toss portobello caps with 3 tablespoons of oil and salt. Place on hot grill; close lid and grill for 15 minutes, turning frequently, or until edges are a little crispy and mushrooms are tender. (If cooking in a pan, sauté over medium-high heat for 10 to 12 minutes, adding a little more oil if necessary.)
3 Line 4 plates with greens. Slice mushrooms fairly thickly; arrange on greens. Drizzle with vinaigrette; top with cheese. Serve immediately.

Garnish a salad with the small white flowers and delicate green buds of mature arugula—they're delicately spicy. And don't toss out mature arugula plants: Eaten in quantity, the leaves may be too strong and bitter, but they can be snipped and used as an herb in a stew, or as a garnish.

arugula & mâche salad with chèvre toasts

SERVES 6

Arugula has a pleasant bitterness and mâche a nutty, complementary tang.

For dressing

3	tbsp. (45 mL) balsamic vinegar
1/2	cup (125 mL) extra virgin olive oil
1	tsp. (5 mL) salt

Freshly ground pepper, to taste

1/2	tsp. (2 mL) sugar

For salad

4	cups (1 L) each arugula and mâche
6	oz. (170 g) mild chèvre (goat's cheese)
2	tbsp. (25 mL) extra virgin olive oil
1	skinny baguette, sliced diagonally into 18 pieces, 1/4 inch (6 mm) thick
6-8	dried figs, sliced
1/2	cup (125 mL) lightly toasted hazelnuts, coarsely chopped

1 In a large bowl, whisk together vinegar and 1/2 cup of oil. Whisk in salt, pepper and sugar; adjust seasoning.
2 Wash, trim and thoroughly dry greens. Toss together in another large bowl until well combined. In a small bowl, using the back of a fork, soften cheese with 1 tablespoon of olive oil until it's of spreading consistency.
3 Preheat oven to 425°F (220°C). Brush both sides of baguette slices with remaining olive oil. Place on a baking sheet and toast for 5 minutes. Turn over and bake for another 5 minutes or until just golden. Remove from oven and let cool slightly.
4 Slowly drizzle dressing over greens (you may not need all of it) and toss lightly. Arrange greens on salad plates.
5 Evenly scatter nuts and figs on top. Spread softened cheese on warm toasts. Garnish each salad with three chèvre toasts. Serve immediately.

Let's give Popeye's favourite food a fair shake

spinach

recipes

spinach &
chickpea curry

spinach salad

spinach-chicken
dumplings

spinach-cheese tart

For a vitamin-rich green that makes an unbeatable salad and a versatile cooked vegetable, spinach gets a bum rap. But long before Popeye, who enjoyed spinach right out of the can—the most unpalatable way imaginable—some adults appreciated its charms. Ibn-al-Awam, who wrote a book about agriculture in the 12th century in Spain, declared spinach to be "a prince of vegetables." Catherine de' Medici of Florence, who became the wife of Henry II of France and the Renaissance doyenne of fine French and Italian cuisine, was so enamoured of its taste and texture that to this day *à la florentine* means a dish prepared with spinach.

There's something more to know about spinach: not all of it is genuine. New Zealand or Malabar spinach aren't the real thing (*Spinacia oleracea*) but a substitute: *Tetragonia tetragonioides* in New Zealand, and *Basella* spp. in Malabar varieties. There are others, such as orach (*Atriplex hortensis*), also called mountain spinach, and perpetual spinach (*Beta vulgaris*), similar to but milder than Swiss chard. All are as delicious and vitamin-rich as true spinach, and sometimes perform better: many continue to produce edible leaves throughout summer's heat, while true spinach makes a mad rush to go to seed by putting all its energy into the production of a flower stalk. BY HEATHER APPLE

GARDENER'S TIPS
- Spinach is rich in vitamins A and C, iron, potassium, thiamine and riboflavin. It can also be high in oxalic acid and shouldn't be eaten in large quantities.
- Spinach contains three times the protein of lettuce, but it's high in sodium—about 126 milligrams per cup.
- Overcooking spinach is a culinary crime. Cook the leaves in the water that clings to them after washing, and then for just a few minutes.
- Spinach combines well with many flavours, including curry, ginger and citrus.

planting

Spinach (*Spinacia oleracea*) is a cool-weather annual that thrives in early spring and in the fall. Heat and long days that run to 14 to 15 hours cause the plants to bolt, or suddenly send up a single stalk that goes to seed. It likes a fertile, well-drained soil with a good supply of nitrogen and a soil pH of about 6.5. Most vegetables prefer this level, but spinach is unforgiving: if the soil is too acid the plants won't grow; too alkaline and they may develop a manganese deficiency. To be sure your soil has the right balance, test it with a soil-testing kit (available at garden centres) or call your provincial ministry of agriculture to find out where a soil sample can be sent for testing. The pH can be balanced by working lime or wood ashes into too-acid soil or coffee grounds into soil that's too alkaline.

Seed your first crop four to six weeks before the expected last spring frost in your area. The plants are hardy and can stand a little frost. Prepare the bed by digging in generous amounts of compost or well-rotted manure. Choose bolt-resistant varieties such as 'Melody', 'Longstanding Bloomsdale', 'Indian Summer', 'Vienna', 'Tyee', 'Olympia' or 'Italian Summer'. Sow successive crops every two weeks until temperatures rise above 18°C to 21°C and days begin to lengthen.

Plant seeds about 2.5 centimetres apart and one centimetre deep, in rows 30 centimetres apart. In heavy clay soils cover the seeds with sifted compost to prevent the soil surface from crusting. Keep the seedbed moist. When the leaves of the young seedlings begin to touch, thin the plants to eight centimetres, and later to 15 centimetres. Use thinnings in salads.

growing

Keep plants well watered—hot, dry soil encourages bolting. A five- to eight-centimetre mulch of grass clippings or shredded leaves, or a 10- to 15-centimetre layer of hay or straw, preserves moisture and keeps roots cool, thus extending the growing season. When plants are half-grown, feed with compost or manure tea (made by soaking a burlap bag of compost or well-rotted manure overnight in a pail of water). Slow growth and pale leaves indicate the plants need feeding. In poor soils feed every two weeks. Weed carefully by hand, or just scratch the surface with the hoe to avoid damaging feeder roots.

Harvest six to eight weeks after planting. (The cooler the weather, the slower growth will be.) Don't pick until there are at least six large leaves on the plant; harvest outer leaves first, leaving the inner ones to grow on. After this stage, up to half the leaves can be harvested at a time.

Once spinach has gone to seed, pull out the plants and replant the bed with a heat-loving crop such as beans or late-cabbage seedlings. It's not worth trying to grow spinach in the long hot days of summer. Plant a new crop in late summer, four to six weeks before the expected frost date in your area. If the soil is still warm, water the seed bed, plant the seeds and cover with a thin board to keep soil cool. A few days after seeding, check daily for germination; then remove board. Thin plants to 15 to 20 centimetres apart for maximum light.

pests and diseases

Spinach is usually trouble-free. Do a thorough fall clean-up and rotate crops. To discourage moulds, don't water in the late afternoon or evening and maximize air circulation by thinning seedlings and keeping the beds weeded. Plant disease-resistant varieties.

Downy mildew Leaves have yellow spots and fuzzy purple growths on the undersides. Purplish lesions become covered with a downy white fungus. Remove and destroy infected plants.

Spinach blight Leaves turn yellow and curl, plants are stunted. There is no cure, so remove and destroy infected plants. Aphids spread blight, so keep them under control.

Fusarium wilt is generally carried in the soil. Plants turn yellow and lower leaves lose their firmness and wilt. Brown discoloration appears in the veins. Destroy.

Leafminer Plants have irregular, light tan tunnels or blotches on the leaves. Peel to reveal insect waste or the maggot itself.

By the time you notice the damage it's too late. Destroy infected leaves. If serious, cover beds with row covers.

Flea beetle Infested seedlings are pock-marked with little holes and hundreds of tiny black beetles appear. Spray plants with pyrethrum every three to four days.

Aphids Leaves curl and pucker and become stunted; check the undersides for pest. Spray plants vigorously with water every other morning for three sprays. For heavy infestations spray with insecticidal soap under the leaves. Repeat every three days.

the masqueraders

Several green, leafy vegetables taste similar to true spinach. They're well worth growing because they provide greens in hot weather, when regular spinach fails.

New Zealand spinach Its slightly crinkled leaves are a bit firmer than spinach. Plant seeds when soil is warm or start early indoors. Soak seeds overnight to speed germination. Thin seedlings to 30 centimetres. Plants survive drought and poor soil, but water and compost greatly improve the crop. Harvest eight weeks after sowing, pinching eight to 10 centimetres off the tips. Older leaves become tough and strong. Picked regularly, plants yield generously until frost.

Malabar spinach In India and the Far East, it's cultivated as an ornamental and a vegetable in green (*Basella alba*) and red (*B. rubra*) varieties. Slow growing; start indoors eight weeks before the last frost. Soak seeds overnight, harden off seedlings for about a week before planting out. Space 30 centimetres apart and add compost to the planting hole. Plants reaching 90 to 120 centimetres can be left to sprawl on the ground, but to keep dirt-free, support with a trellis. Keep soil slightly moist and feed periodically with compost or manure tea. Wait until the plant has many leaves before harvesting lightly; later, take young leaves.

Mountain spinach Also called orach (*Atriplex hortensis*), it grows in yellow, green and a highly ornamental red, to 180 centimetres. Start seeds indoors or outside in late spring. Thin seedlings to 20 to 30 centimetres. Orach is drought-resistant, but keep watered for a better crop. To harvest, break off young leaves and stalks at the tip of the plant. Side branches grow. Nip off flower buds. Sow every two weeks for young leaves.

Perpetual spinach (*Beta vulgaris*) rarely bolts to seed in hot weather. In mid-spring sow seeds, later thinning to 25 to 30 centimetres. Or start early indoors. Keep well fed and watered and harvest leaves before they're too large.

Strawberry spinach or blite (*Chenopodium capitatum*) can be trained on a trellis or grown as a potted plant. Strawberry-like fruits taste like Swiss chard. Start seeds indoors six weeks before frost. When soil is warm, harden off seedlings and plant outside. Pick throughout summer; water and feed well. After fruiting, the leaves yellow and plants become unattractive. Start successive sowings through the summer, to replace old plants.

Good King Henry (*Chenopodium bonus-henricus*) was once grown for medicinal purposes. Eat leaves cooked or raw; shoots and flowers are good steamed. Plant in sun and rich, well-drained soil. Sow seeds in late spring or start seeds early indoors. Thin to 25 to 30 centimetres, fertilize and water well. Plants are perennials and return for years; they also self sow. Don't pick leaves the first year. After foliage dies in fall, cut it off and mulch bed. Cover emerging shoots in spring with hot caps for an early crop. During summer leaves become bitter, but in late summer new leaves appear and supply tender new leaves even after a frost.

winter spinach

With a little effort, you can have spinach well past the first frost. Sow seeds in a cold frame four or five weeks before the first expected fall frost; plant cold-hardy varieties such as 'Cold Resistant Savoy' or 'Longstanding Bloomsdale'. To enable plants to achieve maximum growth, thin seedlings so the leaves of adjacent plants are just touching. Leave the glass cover off the cold frame until the frost arrives, then cover at night and remove during the day. Once the days become consistently cold, leave the glass on, propping it up during sunny days and closing it at night.

An alternative is to use a row cover: buy or construct a plastic tunnel supported by metal hoops over the spinach once the weather is consistently cold. Make slits in the plastic and leave the ends open to provide ventilation on sunny days. Water as the plants need it.

You can also get a jump on the season by over-wintering spinach. Again, choose cold-resistant varieties. Sow three to four weeks before the first frost. When seriously cold weather settles in, mulch the plants with straw or shredded leaves to protect them against severe winter temperatures and the alternate freezing and thawing of late winter and early spring. Once spring has arrived, draw back the winter protection and enjoy the emerging greens.

spinach & chickpea curry

SERVES 3 OR 4

Curry paste is superior to most curry powders—the taste is more complex—but you can use either. Substitute cooked, diced potatoes for chickpeas.

2	lb. (1 kg) spinach
1⁄4	cup (50 mL) butter
2	tbsp. (30 mL) grated gingerroot
2	tbsp. (30 mL) curry paste or powder
2	cups (500 mL) drained, canned chickpeas
2	tbsp. (30 mL) lemon juice
	Salt and freshly ground pepper
2	tbsp. (30 mL) chopped fresh cilantro

1 Wash and cook spinach—see Spinach-Cheese Tart for method—but don't chop.
2 Heat butter in skillet over medium heat. Add ginger and curry; sauté 1 minute. Add spinach and chickpeas and stir until mixture is hot and has absorbed the spices. Season with lemon juice, salt and pepper; sprinkle cilantro over.

spinach salad

SERVES 4 TO 6

The oilless dressing has a garlic punch.

2	cloves garlic, chopped
3⁄4	cup (175 mL) low-fat sour cream
1⁄4	cup (50 mL) buttermilk
2	tbsp. (30 mL) lemon juice
2	tbsp. (30 mL) chopped fresh dill
	Salt and pepper to taste
6	cups (1.5 L) spinach, washed
4	oz. (100 g) mushrooms, sliced
1⁄2	red onion, thinly sliced
2	Belgian endive, sliced

1 Combine garlic, sour cream, buttermilk, lemon juice, dill, and salt and pepper.
2 Add spinach to salad bowl and toss with mushrooms, red onion and Belgian endive.
3 If salad dressing is too thick, thin slightly with warm water. Toss salad with enough dressing to moisten. Store remaining dressing in refrigerator for up to a week.

spinach-chicken dumplings

MAKES ABOUT 50

These dumplings are a terrific nibbly—make up to a day ahead and reheat in a microwave. Or freeze, uncooked, and cook from frozen.

1	12 to 16 oz. (340 to 450 g) spinach, trimmed, blanched, squeezed dry and chopped
4	green onions, white and light green part, chopped
1	lb. (450 g) ground chicken
2	tbsp. (30 mL) chopped gingerroot
3	tbsp. (45 mL) soy sauce
1⁄4	tsp. (1 mL) Chinese chili paste, or to taste
1⁄4	tsp. (1 mL) granulated sugar
1	tsp. (5 mL) sesame oil
	Salt and pepper to taste
50	wonton wrappers
	Vegetable oil
	Water

Spinach is a great foil for strong, spicy flavours such as curry and ginger.
It goes well with lemon, too, or any citrus fruit. But never overcook it.
For a quick supper side dish, sauté finely chopped onion and garlic with a
teaspoon of ground cumin. Add cooked spinach and a few tablespoons of
yogurt; stir and garnish with lemon quarters for squeezing.

Dip:

2   tbsp. (30 mL) soy sauce
2   tbsp. (30 mL) rice vinegar
1   tsp. (5 mL) grated gingerroot
1   green onion, shredded

1 Combine spinach, green onions, ground chicken, ginger, soy sauce, chili paste, sugar, sesame oil, and salt and pepper in food processor; purée until almost smooth.

2 Brush edges of wonton wrapper with water. Place a heaping teaspoon (5 mL) of filling in centre of each wrapper. Fold corners up to meet in centre and press together to seal. Press bottoms flat, and set aside.

3 Heat 2 tbsp. (30 mL) vegetable oil in non-stick skillet over medium heat. Add dumplings and fry until bottoms are golden, about 1 or 2 minutes. Pour in 1/2 cup (125 mL) water, bring to boil, cover pan and steam dumplings until firm to touch, about 3 or 4 minutes. Uncover and continue to cook until water has evaporated. Repeat in batches, if necessary, until all dumplings are cooked.

4 Combine dip ingredients. Place dumplings on platter and serve with dip.

spinach-cheese tart

SERVES 6

Use fewer cheeses, if desired, or substitute the ones you like best.

2   lb. (1 kg) spinach, stems removed
2   tbsp. (30 mL) butter
2   leeks, white and light green
     part only, sliced
2   cloves garlic, chopped
     Salt and freshly ground pepper
3   eggs
4   oz. (100 g) grated cheddar cheese
4   oz. (100 g) crumbled blue cheese
1/2 cup (125 mL) ricotta cheese
1/4 cup (50 mL) grated Parmesan
1   partially baked 9-in. (23-cm) pie shell

1 Wash spinach well in warm water; shake out leaves. Place in a large pot with just the water left on the leaves after washing, and cook, covered, on medium heat for 5 to 7 minutes, or until spinach is limp. Drain, refresh under cold water and squeeze out moisture. Chop coarsely and set aside.

2 Preheat oven to 375°F (190°C).

3 In skillet, melt butter over medium heat. Add leeks and garlic, and sauté until leeks are limp, about 2 minutes. Add spinach and stir until ingredients are combined. Season with salt and pepper, and transfer mixture to bowl.

4 In separate bowl, beat together eggs and cheeses. Combine with spinach mixture. Pour in pie shell and bake for 30 minutes or until mixture is set. Serve warm or cold.

Plant dayneutrals — they yield bowls of berries all summer long

strawberries

In Canada, summer truly arrives when the strawberry season begins. Festivals honouring the fruit are celebrated across the country, people flock to pick-your-own farms to fill baskets with juicy red berries, and there's an abundance of strawberries and cream, strawberry shortcake, strawberry pie...the list goes on.

The Romans were the first on record to cultivate strawberry plants, but earlier civilizations ate the tiny wild ones that still grow in many parts of the world. Today's garden strawberry (*Fragaria* X *ananassa*) is a hybrid of two New World species: the Chilean strawberry (*F. chiloensis*) crossed with an American species (*F. virginiana*).

Over the years, numerous varieties have been developed. The first produced a single large crop of berries in June, followed by many runners with new plants at the tips. Then came ever-bearing strawberries, with a crop in spring and another in fall. They have fewer runners (plants with runners require more maintenance) and the bonus of a second harvest—but the fruit is smaller and less flavourful. The most recent are dayneutral strawberries, first available to home gardeners in the late '70s and early '80s, which produce fruit continuously from June until fall frost. They're called dayneutrals because, unlike the other types, they don't depend on day length to begin flowering. BY HEATHER APPLE

the dayneutrals

Like ever-bearing varieties, dayneutrals have few runners, but plants yield more fruit with better flavour than ever-bearers. They usually produce more berries than June-bearing plants in their first and second years, and because they bear all summer they're an advantage in areas where late spring frosts destroy early flowers, and reduce the season's crop. But there are a couple of downsides: plants are smaller and less bushy than June-bearers and, with the exception of 'Tristar', the fruit is not as large or quite as flavourful as the old-fashioned strawberry. And because they bear all summer, disease and bugs can be a problem. Botrytis fruit rot and tarnished plant bugs can become entrenched in spring and increase as summer progresses.

planting and growing

Buy certified disease-free plants from a reputable local nursery—local because it sells varieties suited to your area—and plant early in the spring when deciduous trees start to leaf out.

Choose a sunny location with rich, loose, well-drained soil (pH 5.5 to 6.5) and good air circulation, but sheltered from the wind. Avoid low-lying areas where frost can damage flowers.

To prepare the bed for planting, remove all weeds, including underground stems and roots—this is essential for a healthy, productive patch. (Get rid of perennial weeds such as quack or twitch grass, bindweed and thistles the previous season.) Make the beds 30 centimetres wide with paths between them. Except in dry, sandy soil, dayneutrals grow well in raised beds. Mix five to eight centimetres of compost or composted manure into the soil, and lightly sprinkle a balanced fertilizer over the surface and scuffle it into the ground.

Before planting, soak the roots in water for one or two hours, no more. (Plants can be stored for a couple of days in the refrigerator if roots are kept damp but not soaked.) Keep roots damp and cool while planting. Trim off dead leaves, broken roots, flowers and flower buds.

Dig holes 13 to 18 centimetres wide and as deep as the roots are long, 15 centimetres apart in two staggered rows. As you place the plant in the hole, point the roots down and fan them out in all directions, then fill in the hole. Plants do poorly or even die if the crown—the solid area between the roots and the buds and leaves—is not properly positioned. Make sure the roots and the crown's midpoint are covered with soil, and the top part of the crown, where the buds are located, is just above soil level. Press soil firmly around the roots and water well, then check the crowns. If necessary, reposition them by either covering the roots with more soil or gently easing the plant out of the ground a bit to expose the buds.

Immediately after planting, mulch with five to eight centimetres of straw, leaf mould or old hay, nestling the mulch close to the plants. Mulching retains moisture, keeps the soil cool, controls weeds and keeps the berries off the ground. Dayneutrals stop producing flowers and fruit if the temperature reaches 29°C to 32°C.

For the first six weeks after planting, remove all the flowers, and for the first year, cut off runners that form. If you don't do this you'll have small plants with few berries.

Keep plants well weeded for good production and to help prevent disease. Cultivate shallowly to avoid damaging the plants' roots. Because dayneutrals produce fruit continuously, they must be watered and fertilized regularly—less than 2.5 centimetres of water a week results in small, dry berries. Check under the mulch frequently and water whenever the soil's surface is dry, making sure the water soaks deeply into the soil; it may take some time for it to penetrate the mulch.

Three weeks after planting, fertilize every two or three weeks with compost or manure tea (made by soaking a bag of compost in a pail of water overnight). Avoid high-nitrogen fertilizers, which produce excessive vegetative growth and soft fruit.

Except in coastal British Columbia, strawberries need protection in winter. After the ground has frozen but before the temperature drops to -7°C, cover plants with eight to 15 centimetres of straw, old hay, evergreen boughs or dead leaves. In early spring when the trees start to leaf out, remove the mulch, work in 2.5 to three centimetres of compost, apply fertilizer and replace the mulch around the plants, but don't cover them. If plants are blooming when a late spring frost strikes, cover them with straw or blankets; frost damage to flowers reduces or eliminates fruit production.

best dayneutrals

- 'Tristar' Hardy, medium-small plants produce runners and delicious medium-sized fruit with flavour ranking with that of the best June-bearing varieties.
- 'Tribute' Vigorous, hardy plants yield firm, medium-sized, good-tasting fruit. Fruit is larger than 'Tristar', but not as strong in flavour. Trials at Cornell University in New York showed that under good conditions, 'Tribute' produced two pounds of fruit per foot of row in its first year of planting, three pounds in its second.
- 'Seascape' Hardy and very productive. Firm, good-tasting fruit is larger than that of 'Tribute' and 'Tristar', but not as flavourful.
- 'Hecker' High yield, good hardiness; fruit with good texture and flavour.
- 'Fern' Medium-high yield, good hardiness; fruit with good texture and flavour, but weak vegetative growth.
- 'Selva' Hardy, with high yields of berries that are large but inferior in quality and taste to other dayneutrals.

harvesting

Fruit sets three to five weeks after blossoms appear. The harvest is shorter the first year because you've removed the first six weeks' worth of flowers. In the second year, the plants tend to bear heavily in the spring, slow down during hot weather and pick up again in the fall.

Harvest dayneutrals only when the berries are fully red and ripe; that's when flavour is most intense. Pick every couple of days so berries don't spoil. Removing the hulls when picking greatly speeds spoilage.

Even if you don't plan to use them, pick substandard berries so they don't rot and encourage disease. To avoid spreading disease through the patch, harvest good and substandard berries separately. Try not to touch ripening berries and leaves.

diseases and pests

Disease is more of a problem for commercial growers than home gardeners. To reduce the potential, avoid planting where tomatoes, peppers, eggplants, potatoes or raspberries have been grown in the past three or four years. Water plants in the middle of the day so leaves dry quickly, keep well weeded and mulched, and regularly remove and dispose of any rotting fruit.

Leaf scorch A fungal disease; infected leaves have irregular purplish blotches that become brownish in the centre. Edges of leaves dry and look burned.

Leaf spot A fungal disease; infected leaves have small, round, purple spots that develop grey or light brown centres.

Powdery mildew White patches of fungus on the lower leaf surface cause leaf edges to roll up; leaves eventually die.

Slime mould A primitive form of fungus that appears in warm, wet weather in spring and fall, and generally disappears in hot, dry weather. Appears as jelly-like masses or crusty structures of grey, white, purple or yellow.

Grey mould or botrytis fruit rot A fungal disease prevalent in long periods of wet weather. Flowers become brown and dry; fruits develop soft, light brown areas, become covered with a grey dust.

Leather rot Appears as a darkened spot and spreads until the entire berry is brown, leathery and rough. Infected berries have an unpleasant smell and taste.

Verticillium wilt Outer leaves wilt, turn reddish with upturned margins; stems develop black areas.

Black root rot A fungal disease; roots of plants turn dark brown. Aggravated by heavy, poorly drained soil.

Red stele A fungal disease aggravated by cool, wet soil. Stunted plants may wilt. Identified by a reddish core in the roots.

Tarnished plant bug Brownish, six-millimetre-long adults and greenish nymphs suck on stem tips, buds and fruits, injecting a toxin that produces a nubby, deformed berry with a clump of seeds at the end. Hand-pick. Spray or dust with rotenone or pyrethrum only as a last resort.

Strawberry bud or clipper weevil Dark-reddish beetles, three millimetres long with reddish snouts, cut the stems of blossoms causing them to wilt, drop off or hang by a thread. Keep patch weeded; control using same measures as for tarnished plant bug.

Slugs They eat holes in berries at night, leaving slimy trails. Reduce hiding places by clearing away any debris in the area; then add your own: 15-centimetre square boards placed throughout the patch. Every morning remove the slugs that have accumulated under them. Or hand pick slugs at night.

Birds Cover patch with netting with openings no bigger than six millimetres. Suspend over plants with stakes.

new life for older beds

Dayneutral strawberry plants produce fewer and smaller berries with age, so for optimum production, renew a patch every two years—three at most. Start the new patch in a different location to help reduce disease buildup. It's easier, but more expensive, to buy new, disease-free plants, but a new plot can also be started with runners from the original plants. This is more challenging with dayneutrals because they produce fewer runners than other kinds of strawberries.

In the spring of the second year, allow plants to produce some runners. This will decrease fruit production somewhat. Make sure the little plantlets at the ends of the runners have contact with the earth by placing a stone on the runner next to each plantlet. Once the daughter plant has rooted, cut it from the runner, transplant it to the new location, water well and mulch. Some plants may not survive the shock of being transplanted, but the success rate is good if the rootballs are moved with plenty of soil around the roots and disturbed as little as possible.

For vigorous plants that produce more berries the following year, try this method: root plantlets still attached to the mother plant in eight-centimetre soil-filled pots buried in the ground to their rims. Once rooted, cut the runner joining mother and daughter and transplant the daughter plant, without the pot, in another location. This method ensures minimal root disturbance. Do all transplanting well before fall so plants develop a good root system for winter survival.

If your strawberry patch starts to run down over the years, it may be because diseases have become established. It's best to buy new plants and start over again. Never try to renew a dayneutral patch by shearing off the tops of plants after flowering, as with other varieties.

classic strawberry fool

SERVES 6 TO 8

A traditional English dessert, a fool is an amalgam of fruit purée and cream—surely one of the best things that can happen to fresh, summer berries.

4 cups (1 L) or 1 1⁄2 lb. (680 g) fresh, ripe strawberries
1 cup (250 mL) granulated sugar
2 tsp. (10 mL) fresh lemon juice
3 cups (750 mL) whipping cream
1 tsp. (5 mL) pure vanilla extract

1 Inspect berries carefully, discarding any that are heavily bruised or spoiled. Remove stems and wash. Place in a large, heavy-based saucepan over low heat.

2 Over low heat, stir and mash fruit against the bottom and sides of the pan with a wooden spoon to release the juice. Continue gently stirring and mashing for about 20 to 30 minutes. Add sugar all at once and stir to dissolve into the berries. Simmer for a few minutes until completely dissolved. Stir in lemon juice. Transfer mixture to a bowl, cover and refrigerate until ready to serve.

3 Using a blender, food processor or food mill, purée the fruit, in batches, until smooth.

4 Whip cream until stiff peaks form. Stir in vanilla extract until well blended. Using a rubber spatula, gently fold the berry purée into the cream—be careful not to overmix. Spoon into tall parfait glasses and serve immediately.

crème fraîche

Many strawberry lovers swear by the simple for total perfection: fresh, ripe, home-grown berries with cream and perhaps a modicum of sugar. It's difficult to argue with that. But you could try strawberries with homemade crème fraîche. Widely available in Europe, crème fraîche is difficult to find here, but you can make a very good approximation of the thick, ultra-rich, slightly tangy cream by combining 1 cup (250 mL) whipping cream with 2 tablespoons (25 mL) buttermilk in a glass bowl. Cover and let stand at room temperature (around 21°C) for 8 to 24 hours, or until thick. Give it a good stir, cover and refrigerate. Use within 10 days—if it lasts that long!

fragole al balsamico (strawberries with balsamic vinegar)

SERVES 4 TO 6

Emilia Romagna, the region in Italy that produces balsamic vinegar, is also the source of dozens of unconventional ways to enjoy it. Here's a refreshing combination: the lemon zest and mint aren't traditional, but they help to heighten the flavours. Prepare the recipe just before sitting down to dinner to allow time for the flavours to develop.

5	cups (1.25 L) ripe strawberries
3	tbsp. (45 mL) balsamic vinegar
	Zest of 1 lemon, grated and finely chopped
20-25	mint leaves, washed, dried and chopped
2-3	tbsp. (25-45 mL) extra-fine sugar

1 Wash and hull strawberries. Slice them into thirds and place in mixing bowl. Add balsamic vinegar, mix well and let berries marinate for about 25 minutes.
2 Add lemon zest, mint and sugar, mix well and serve.

champagne strawberries

SERVES 6

Simple to make and simply magnificent to eat.

	Juice of 1 small lemon
	Juice of 1 small lime
4	tbsp. (50 mL) mild-tasting honey
4	cups (1 L) or 1 1⁄2 lb. (680 g) fresh, ripe strawberries, washed and hulled
	Bottle of chilled champagne or sparkling white wine

1 In a small saucepan set over medium heat, combine lemon and lime juices and honey. Stir until honey dissolves.
2 Place strawberries in a bowl. Pour warm sauce over berries and stir to combine. Refrigerate 30 minutes, or until well chilled.
3 Divide berries among 6 stemmed dessert dishes. Pour champagne over each and serve.

summer

Not too long ago our vegetable intake was limited to peas, carrots, green and yellow beans, potatoes and corn. How tastes have changed! After the Second World War, Italian and Portuguese immigrants helped us fall in love with garlic and gradually persuaded us to try eggplant, zucchini, the marvellous paste tomatoes, and broccoli. Recently we've gone a step further and are cooking the pleasantly bitter rapini, a broccoli lookalike delicious sautéed in olive oil with masses of garlic. Other immigrants from around the world have introduced us to hot chilies, cilantro, lemongrass and bok choy. Supermarkets are widening their horizons, too, stocking tomatillos, okra and dandelion greens. But as this chapter shows you, most of these formerly "exotic" vegetables will grow happily and successfuly in our own Canadian backyards.

Beautiful, versatile, unbelievably nutritious

beans

recipes

purple snap beans
with couscous

white bean soup
with swiss chard

green & yellow beans
with sesame seed sauce

Beans are a delightful staple of the summer garden. With little effort, plants yield quantities of fresh, crisp pods unequalled by supermarket produce. Left to dry on the plants, pods produce a rainbow of coloured beans that provide delicious healthy soups, stews and chilies throughout the year.

The common bean (*Phaseolus vulgaris*) originated in South and Central America. Bean seeds found in archeological sites in Peru and Mexico have been dated at 8000 and 5000 BC respectively. During the 16th century, the conquering Spaniards took bean seeds back to Europe and Asia. At first they were grown as ornamental plants in Europe, but eventually they became the mainstream food crop they are today. And no wonder—fresh or dried, beans are high in food value, from the vitamin-rich fresh beans to the nutrition-packed dried variety. Dried beans eaten with grains or dairy products provide all the essential amino acids a person needs for a day.

Beans are typically divided into three categories: string or snap beans, picked when the pods are young; shell beans, harvested when the seeds are full size but still fresh; and dry beans, picked when the pods are papery and the seeds are dry inside. All beans are edible when left to dry on the plant, but not all varieties have good flavour when dried. BY HEATHER APPLE

GARDENER'S TIPS
- Fresh beans are a good source of vitamins A and C, provide potassium and are low in calories.
- Dry beans are an almost perfect food—low in fat, high in fibre, rich in B vitamins and a good source of protein. Their complex carbohydrates have less effect on blood sugar than other starchy foods, making them well-suited to people with diabetes.
- To test beans for dryness, put a few in a tightly capped jar and set it in the sun. If no drops of moisture appear, beans are dry.

Native people grew beans as a staple food, along with corn and squash. Beans often grew up corn stalks. Opening page: 'Slender Wax', a yellow bush bean. Opposite page: purple-podded 'Blauhilde', top left, and 'Royalty Purple Pod', bottom right.

growing

First, decide what type of bean you wish to grow. Bush or pole beans, to eat fresh or to dry for winter? Bush beans grow 45 to 60 centimetres tall and as wide, yield an early crop—in 50 to 60 days—and bear heavily for three weeks or so; successive plantings are necessary for a steady supply. Pole beans require vertical support. They start bearing at 55 to 65 days andusually require only one successive planting.

Beans won't grow in cool weather and are susceptible to frost. Plant at least one week after the last spring frost, when the soil reaches 15°C to 18°C. Low temperatures may cause the seed to rot. Plant in full sun in well-drained soil, in an area protected from the wind but with good air circulation.

Before planting, dig compost or composted manure into the bed. Dust seed with an inoculant containing a nitrogen-fixing bacteria called Rhizobium; this bacteria lives in nodules on the plants' roots and helps plants utilize the nitrogen available in the air. Buy a product containing Rhizobium for beans—different types are available. If your seeds have been treated with a fungicide (which turns them bright pink), don't use the inoculant; the fungicide will kill the bacteria. And don't use a high-nitrogen fertilizer with inoculated plants. If you do, plants will produce many leaves but few pods.

Plant seeds of bush beans 2.5 centimetres deep and five centimetres apart. Establish rows 45 centimetres apart, or, to make better use of garden space, plant two rows 15 centimetres apart with 45 centimetres between the double rows. Keep soil moist during germination. When seedlings develop leaves, thin to 15 centimetres, keeping the most vigorous seedlings. Push soil or mulch against the stems to keep plants upright.

Plant pole beans with the same spacing and thinning. Before you plant, install a trellis, fence or poles for the beans to climb on. If you use a fence, plant seeds 7.5 centimetres away from it; both sides of the fence can be planted. Plant six to eight seeds around poles, thin to four plants 15 centimetres apart. Seedlings may need help at first to reach the support. Pole beans twine counter-clockwise (you can see this if you look down on the plant from above) and that should be kept in mind when twirling young plants around a support—they break or fall off if you twine them in the wrong direction.

Beans need adequate moisture, especially around flowering time. During hot weather, water when the top centimetre of soil is dry. Mulch after the soil has warmed up. When plants start to flower, work compost or organic fertilizer into the surface of the soil; don't disturb the shallow roots. For pole beans, fertilize every three to four weeks, as long as plants flower.

diseases and pests

To help keep plants healthy, rotate bean crops so they grow in the same spot only once every three years. Destroy infected plants and do a good fall cleanup. Weed or harvest beans when plants are dry; control weeds and avoid overcrowding to provide good air circulation.

Mexican bean beetle Spiny yellow larvae and copper beetles like ladybugs with 16 spots skeletonize leaves. Hand-pick; squish yellow-orange eggs.

Aphids Tiny green and black aphids infest new growth, spreading viral diseases. Wash off with a jet of water from the hose; use insecticidal soap.

Cutworms Fat, grey to brown grubs chew off tender seedling stems at ground level. Search in the soil around the base of cut-off seedlings and destroy. Protect stems with foil collars.

Viral diseases Leaves develop light and dark green patterns, and may become curled and stunted.

Anthracnose Plants develop dark brown, sunken spots on leaves, pods and seeds; spots may later develop pink centres. Plant resistant varieties.

Rust Reddish-brown circular lesions form on leaves and pods; leaves turn yellow and drop off. Plant resistant varieties.

Grey mould Dark green lesions on leaves turn to velvety grey, hair-like mould; they also form in pods.

White mould Dark green lesions increase in size, and affected leaves turn brown.

harvesting and storing

Harvest snap beans when the pods are firm and crisp and the seeds inside are small. To avoid pulling branches off, hold the stem with one hand and the pod with the other, and pull the pod. Pick every few days or plants will stop producing. To avoid spreading disease, never pick when the plants are wet.

Harvest filet beans, which are slender baby beans, before the pods reach .5 centimetre in diameter; pick at least every other day.

Pick shell beans when seeds are plump but the pods still soft. Leave beans for drying till they're papery and the plant has begun to die; then pull it up and allow pods to finish drying in a sheltered spot—spread out on screens or hung up. If the weather is wet, pick the pods as they dry to prevent them from getting mouldy. If plants haven't started to die back before frost, pull them up—most will mature. Let the pods dry thoroughly before shelling or threshing. To thresh, spread pods on a tarpaulin or in a large box, and knead them. The beans settle to the bottom and the pods rise to the top. Allow beans to dry until they can't be dented with a fingernail. Store in large, glass jars in a cool, dark place.

Small holes in dry beans indicate bean weevils. Put beans in a jar in the freezer for several days to kill the unappealing yet harmless pests.

a guide to beans

Tender snap beans may be green, yellow or purple; some have streaks. They grow to finger length or as long as a yard, and some are flat. Good varieties include 'Kentucky Wonder', 'Blue Lake Pole' and 'Romano Pole', a green Italian heirloom bean. 'Blue Lake Bush' has a particularly

fine flavour. 'Jade' is tender, sweet and a rich green. 'Provider' is the earliest. Good varieties of yellow or wax beans are 'Beurre de Rocquencourt', 'Goldkist', 'Rocdor' and, in particular, 'Dragon Tongue'—a beautiful old variety with flat pods streaked with bright purple. Purple-podded snap beans (which turn green when cooked) have ornamental plants with pretty, light purple flowers. They tend to have fewer problems with insect pests. Good varieties are 'Royal Burgundy' and 'Purple Queen'.

Filet beans are green varieties of bush snap beans harvested while still small—often bite-sized. Filet beans aren't good candidates for canning or freezing.

Shell beans are a gourmet food rarely available in North America unless you grow them yourself. They're easier to grow than lima beans, but you shell and prepare them the same way. They're easily canned or frozen for winter use. 'Cannellini' is a white variety.

As well as the traditional kidney, navy and pinto beans, there are literally hundreds of dry bean varieties to choose from. 'Midnight Black Turtle Soup' and 'Black Coco' are rich, flavourful, black, soup beans.

lean on me

The vines of pole beans need support. Before you plant seeds, install a support of some kind. Ideally it should be at least 180 centimetres tall. Use trellising or make a fence with chicken wire or nylon netting strung between sturdy supporting poles set 240 centimetres apart. Thin three-metre-tall saplings were often used on traditional farms, and make attractive and serviceable poles today.

Other options: hang strings from an overhead support, or tie three or more poles together to form a teepee. Use more poles if you want to create a great place for children to play. For example, 12 poles, each three to five metres long, can be lashed together to create a teepee two to three metres in diameter. Leave a wide enough gap between two of the poles so kids can enter to play, or you can enter to harvest.

Dry beans grow in a dazzling array of colours and often mottled, striped or streaked designs.

purple snap beans with couscous

SERVES 4 TO 6

Vary this fresh-tasting bean and grain dish with whatever fresh beans and herbs are in season—for herbs, basil, mint, parsley, chervil and oregano all work well. To add extra flavour and texture, toast the pine nuts, following the method described for sesame seeds in the recipe following.

1 1/2 cups (375 mL) quick-cooking couscous
2 1/2 cups (625 mL) vegetable or chicken broth
2 tbsp. (25 mL) extra virgin olive oil
2 small white onions, sliced thinly
1 lb. (500 g) purple snap beans, washed and trimmed
2 tbsp. (25 mL) chopped flat-leaf parsley
2 tbsp. (25 mL) chopped fresh mint
1/3 cup (75 mL) pine nuts
2 tbsp. (25 mL) lemon juice
Salt and freshly ground pepper

1 Place couscous in a large mixing bowl. Bring broth to a boil and pour over couscous. Stir once or twice and let stand for 10 minutes, or until couscous is tender and broth is absorbed.
2 Meanwhile, heat olive oil in a skillet and sauté onions until golden, about 5 minutes. Add beans and stir-fry, along with the onions, until beans are tender, about 10 minutes (less if beans are particularly skinny).

3 Add parsley, mint, pine nuts, lemon juice, and salt and pepper to taste. Combine ingredients well, then transfer bean mixture to the couscous and toss together gently.

white bean soup with swiss chard

SERVES 4 TO 6

The cooking time for this great-tasting soup—almost a meal in itself—depends on the freshness of the dried beans. Don't add salt to the beans' cooking water; it toughens them and causes them to split open. The cheese-toast embellishment originated with Italian peasants, who traditionally saw it as a way to use up dried bread—it's like a giant crouton that softens as you eat the soup.

2 cups (500 mL) dried white kidney beans or navy beans, soaked overnight in water to cover
1 tbsp. (15 mL) olive oil
8 oz. (250 g) mushrooms, finely chopped
3 cloves garlic, minced
1 onion, chopped
1/2 tsp. (2 mL) freshly grated nutmeg
6 cups (1.5 L) chicken broth
1 lb. (500 g) Swiss chard, washed, stemmed and chopped
Salt and freshly ground pepper
8 slices country-style bread
3 cups (750 mL) ricotta cheese
3/4 cup (175 mL) grated Pecorino Romano cheese
1/4 cup (50 mL) chopped flat-leaf parsley

1 Drain and rinse beans, and place in a large saucepan. Cover with 2 in. (5 cm) of water. Bring to a boil; reduce heat to simmer and cook 1 1/2 hours, or until beans are tender, skimming foam that rises to the surface. Drain beans, discarding cooking liquid.
2 Wipe saucepan clean. Pour in olive oil and heat over medium heat. Add mushrooms, garlic, onion and nutmeg; cook 5 minutes, stirring often, or until vegetables are softened. Stir in cooked beans and chicken broth. Bring to a boil, reduce heat to medium-low and cook 20 minutes. Add Swiss chard; cook 2 minutes, or until wilted. Season to taste with salt and pepper.
3 Preheat broiler. Spread ricotta cheese on bread and top with grated Pecorino Romano. Broil 2 minutes, or until cheese is golden.
4 Ladle soup into bowls. Place a piece of cheese toast in centre of each serving, and sprinkle with parsley. Serve extra toast on the side.

green & yellow beans with sesame seed sauce

SERVES 4

The wonderfully savoury sauce gives steamed beans a slightly Asian flavour. Buy rice wine—called mirin—in health-food stores or supermarkets that stock Japanese or Chinese items. Goes well with grilled ginger shrimp or teriyaki chicken.

1   lb. (500 g) fresh yellow and green
    snap beans, washed and trimmed
1/3 cup (75 mL) white sesame seeds
1/4 cup (50 mL) soy sauce
1   tbsp. (15 mL) granulated sugar
1/4 cup (50 mL) rice wine

1 Cover beans loosely in a steamer set over boiling water and steam until tender, about 10 minutes. Plunge into ice water and drain thoroughly. Set to one side.

2 Meanwhile, in a heavy, dry skillet, toast sesame seeds over medium-high heat until golden, stirring to prevent burning. Once seeds are toasted, transfer to a mortar. Add 1 tbsp. (15 mL) of the soy sauce and, using a pestle, pulverize the mixture to form a smooth paste. Add sugar, rice wine and remaining soy sauce, and combine well.

3 Using a rubber spatula so you get all the mixture, transfer to a small saucepan set over medium heat. Bring to a gentle boil, reduce heat and simmer 2 minutes, or until mixture thickens.

4 Transfer beans to a serving platter and drizzle with the hot dressing.

Today's snap beans are yesterday's string beans without the string, which has been bred out of the newest varieties.

Luxury berries easy to grow in your garden

blackberries and RASPBERRIES

recipes

classic summer berry pudding

raspberry sorbet

blackberry fool

One of my greatest pleasures in summer is wandering through my raspberry patch, snacking on sweet, sun-warmed berries, knowing I can eat to the bursting point and still have lots left for freezing, jams and pies. But most people have to buy their raspberries at the market, in tiny boxes at exorbitant prices. Blackberries too—if they can find them. Since both must be hand-picked and can be stored for only a couple of days, they're luxury items.

Red raspberries are the most familiar, but there are also yellow, black and purple raspberries. The yellow ones, a variation of the red, have a sweeter, milder flavour. Black raspberries are a different species, with a mild-tart flavour. Purple raspberries are a hybrid of the red and black. Blackberries are close cousins of raspberries. Some varieties have a similar erect growth; others have long, trailing, often thornless vines. Collectively called brambles, all these berries belong to the genus *Rubus*.

Phytochemicals called flavanoids give berries their colours, but also help protect against chemical reactions in our bodies linked to heart disease, cancer, cataracts, Alzheimer's disease, osteoarthritis and immune deficiency. Research also strongly suggests that flavanoids help strengthen blood vessels and keep joints healthy.

BY HEATHER APPLE

GARDENER'S TIPS
▪ Raspberries contain vitamins C and A as well as fibre, and are higher in vitamin E than any other fruit.
▪ Blackberry plants need 2.5 to 5 centimetres of water a week while setting fruit, but don't let foliage stay wet. Drip irrigation is a good watering method.
▪ For a long and varied harvest of raspberries, plant an early red variety like 'Nova' and the fall-bearing yellow 'Goldie'.

berry varieties

Red Raspberries
- 'Canby' Mid-season; thornless; large, delicious berries highly resistant to viruses and aphids. Sensitive to root rot. Zone 5.
- 'Nova' Productive, disease-resistant plants yield flavourful fruit ripening early- to mid-season. Zone 4.
- 'Autumn Bliss' Superior size, flavour and yields. Resistant to powdery mildew. Zone 4.
- 'Double Delight' Very hardy; bred in Manitoba. High yields. Zone 3.

Yellow Raspberries
- 'Honey Queen' High yields of juicy, mild fruit from July to late August. Zone 3.
- 'Goldie' Good flavour, yield and disease resistance. Zone 5.

Purple Raspberries
- 'Royalty' Widely considered the best purple. Zone 5.

Black Raspberries
- 'Jewel' Considered by many to be the best of the black. Zone 5.

Blackberries
- 'Darrow' Wild blackberry taste. Zone 5.
- 'Ebony King' Sweet. Zone 5.
- 'Black Satin' Sweet. Semi-erect, thornless vines. Zone 6.
- 'Chester' Hardiest trailing blackberries; thornless; large, sweet fruit. Zone 5.

Blackberry-Raspberry crosses
- Loganberry Large, tart berries. Zone 7.
- Tayberry Juicy, deep purple, slightly tart. Long prickly canes need support. Zone 6.

growing

Full sun, shelter from wind and good air circulation are crucial. Brambles planted in heavy, poorly drained soils are susceptible to disease. Rich loam and a slightly acidic pH of 6.0 to 6.5 are ideal. Sloping land is best and north-facing slopes conserve moisture.

Wait at least four years before planting where crops subject to verticillium wilt (tomatoes, peppers, potatoes, eggplant and strawberries, fruit trees, flowering quince) have been grown.

Prepare the site at least a year before planting. Remove perennial weeds and dig a row 90 to 120 centimetres wide; adjust the pH level with limestone or sulfur, and incorporate compost or composted manure. To increase drainage, mound the soil 15 to 20 centimetres high and plant one cane per hill.

In spring, soak the roots in a pail of water for a couple of hours before setting out. Dig holes one and a half to two times the size of the root balls and mix in more compost or composted manure. Make a small, cone-shaped mound in each hole and over it fan out the plant's roots evenly. Fill so the soil is two centimetres higher than the level at which the plant was growing. Press soil down gently and water with a diluted solution of liquid seaweed fertilizer. Cut the cane back to 15 centimetres.

Space red and yellow raspberry canes 60 centimetres apart, and black and purple ones 90 to 120 centimetres apart. Plant erect blackberries 60 to 90 centimetres apart, and trailing blackberries 1.8 metres apart, farther apart on the West Coast, where they grow vigorously. Water regularly with a soaker hose or drip irrigation, especially during blossoming, fruit ripening and flower development. Unless August is very dry,

reduce water in late summer and fall so canes can harden off for the winter.

Weed by hand to avoid damaging the canes' shallow roots. After one season's growth, apply a deep mulch to keep weeds down and conserve moisture. Always apply mulch when the soil is moist.

training and pruning

Heavy wires strung between crossbars are effective supports for raspberries and trailing blackberries. Pruning techniques vary, but all brambles need their old canes cut to the ground after they finish bearing. Each year brambles send up new shoots, which bear fruit the second year and then die. Fall-bearing raspberries (sometimes called everbearing) produce a crop in summer and a second late in the season on the tips of new wood. The following year they produce berries on the lower portion of the same canes.

Single-crop raspberries In early spring, prune away the tips of canes taller than 1.5 to 2 metres. In summer, cut all canes that have borne fruit to the ground.

Fall or everbearing raspberries Cut canes to the ground after the summer crop. In fall, cut off the tips only—the rest of the cane will bear next summer's crop.

For both the above types, rows should be no wider than 60 centimetres.

Black and purple raspberries To produce maximum yield, prune off the tips of first-year canes at 90 centimetres. In early spring, cut these branches back to 30 centimetres. After the summer crop, cut back to the ground.

Erect blackberries Prune off tips of first-year canes at 1.2 metres. In early spring, cut back side branches to 40 centimetres. After fruiting, cut back to the ground.

Trailing blackberries The long vines need to be tied to a support. In a mild climate, tie the canes up as soon as they're long enough and fan out vines for maximum sunlight. Where blackberries are marginally hardy, let canes grow along the ground the first year and mulch for winter. In spring, tie them to the support before they leaf out. By the third year the stiffer canes won't bend as easily. If winter protection is necessary, prune off the tips of first-year canes once they reach 60 centimetres to encourage side branches close to the ground; cover these in winter.

pests and other problems

Buy certified disease-free plants whenever possible. Never plant wild canes in your garden or get canes from friends—you risk introducing diseases or pests. Black raspberries are particularly susceptible to disease.

Keep brambles well weeded, space 15 centimetres apart and avoid overhead watering. Cut back canes as soon as they finish bearing and do a good fall cleanup. Inspect regularly and destroy canes that show signs of diseases or pests.

Crumbly berries Could mean poor pollination, water stress, viral diseases, and deficient nitrogen, phosphorus or iron. Check the plants' health, water regularly and use compost.

Mosaic virus Mottled green and yellow-green leaves, stunted canes, small, crumbly fruit. Spread by aphids.

Leaf curl virus Leaves are darker than normal, often wrinkled, small and curl down at the edges. Fruit is small and crumbly. Destroy infected canes and those immediately adjacent.

Verticillium wilt Soil-borne fungal disease. Leaves wilt and drop, canes become bluish, remain stunted and die. Poor drainage with cool soil encourages verticillium wilt.

Anthracnose Grey spots with purple borders on young canes. Bark may crack, green fruit dry up and ripe fruit turn brown. Purple or brown spots on leaves.

Botrytis cane wilt Brownish areas appear and fruits can be covered with grey mould. Provide good air circulation, and avoid overhead watering and high nitrogen fertilizers.

Cane borer Adults lay eggs between two sets of rings around cane. Larvae feed on cane pith. Tips wilt and drop off. Destroy wilted tips below the lower cut as soon as the rings appear.

classic summer berry pudding

SERVES 6

A beautiful summer dessert popular in England when ripe berries are plentiful. Use any combination of red summer fruits: raspberries, blackberries, black and red currants, strawberries or black cherries. Make in the morning or the night before you intend to serve it.

8 slices stale, crustless white bread, sliced 1/2-in. (1-cm) thick (use good-quality, homestyle bakery bread)
1 1/2 lb. (750 g) assorted soft berries, washed, hulled and pitted if necessary
1/2 cup (125 mL) sugar (or to taste)

1 Line the bottom of a 4-cup (1 L) pudding basin or soufflé dish with 1 or 2 slices of bread. Line the sides of the dish with more bread as needed, cut to shape if necessary so pieces fit closely together. Set aside.

2 Place prepared fruit in a wide, heavy-based pan and sprinkle with sugar. Bring to a boil over low heat and cook for 2 to 3 minutes, stirring once or twice gently, just until sugar is completely dissolved and juices from fruit begin to run.

3 Reserve 2 tablespoons (30 mL) of juice. Then carefully spoon fruit and remaining juice into the prepared dish. Use remaining bread as a lid for the pudding.

4 Place a heavy plate that fits inside the dish on top of the pudding; weigh down with a filled jar or can. Transfer pudding to refrigerator and allow to chill for 8 hours or overnight.

5 When ready to serve, remove weight and plate. Cover dish with a serving plate and invert to unmould the pudding. Use reserved juice to colour any bits of bread that may need it. Serve with thick pouring cream, whipped cream, crème fraîche or thick yogurt.

Summary berry pudding is a simple, old-fashioned favourite that almost everyone's English grandmother made on cool summer mornings for the day's supper. Almost any combination of fresh-picked berries can be used. Right: 'Royalty' is widely considered the best of the purple raspberries.

raspberry sorbet

SERVES 6

An easy sorbet that doesn't require special equipment. Serve in quartered (or halved, if small) ripe cantaloupe. The flavour and colour contrast is beautiful and dramatic.

1	lb. (500 g) fresh raspberries, rinsed
1 1/4	cups (300 mL) water
6	tbsp. (90 mL) clear honey
2	tbsp. (30 mL) framboise liqueur (optional)
	Fresh raspberry or mint leaves

1 In a blender or food processor, purée raspberries. Rub through a sieve to remove seeds. Mix the purée with water, honey and liqueur, and pour into a sturdy, freezer-proof container with a lid. Cover and freeze for about 6 hours or until firm.
2 Chill glass serving plates. Scoop sorbet into cantaloupe pieces with a melon baller. Garnish with raspberry or mint leaves and serve.

blackberry fool

SERVES 6

A little fancier than the standard fool, which consists of only fruit and cream, this dessert is special enough for company and can be made the day before. Also wonderful with fresh raspberries. Look for mini bottles of fruit liqueur if you don't want to invest in a full bottle.

6	cups (1.5 L) fresh blackberries, rinsed, drained
2/3	cup (150 mL) sugar
1	tbsp. (15 mL) lemon juice
3	tbsp. (45 mL) pear, plum or other fruit liqueur
2/3	cup (150 mL) thick, plain yogurt, drained
1	cup (250 mL) heavy cream
8	*langue de chat* or ladyfinger biscuits

1 Reserve 18 berries for decoration. In a blender or food processor, purée remaining blackberries, in batches if necessary. Rub the mixture through a fine sieve to remove seeds.
2 Combine purée with sugar in a heavy saucepan and slowly bring to a boil. Lower heat and simmer, uncovered, until well thickened. Remove from heat and pour mixture into a heatproof bowl. Let cool, stirring frequently. Cover with plastic wrap and refrigerate until completely chilled (4 to 6 hours).

3 Stir lemon juice and liqueur into chilled mixture. In a separate bowl, whisk yogurt until smooth. In another bowl, whip cream until soft peaks form; then fold into yogurt. Carefully fold cream mixture into berry mixture to create a marbled effect; then transfer to individual serving glasses or one large bowl for serving. Refrigerate, covered, for at least 4 hours or overnight. Decorate with reserved berries and serve with *langue de chat* or biscuits.

Sweet or sour, spring or summer, cherry trees brighten the garden

cherries

recipes

pickled cherries

sour cherry cobbler

duck breasts with cherries

Gardeners right across Canada can grow cherries, though not every species is suited to every region. The genus is diverse, ranging from the chokecherry, which grows well into the boreal forest of northern Canada, to the prized sweet cherry, restricted to milder regions such as British Columbia's Okanagan Valley and Ontario's Niagara region.

When I think of edible cherries for the home garden, two species stand out: the sweet cherry (*Prunus avium*) and the sour, or tart, cherry (*P. cerasus*), which taste exactly as their names imply. Sweet cherries are grown largely for the fresh market and for cakes and cookies, while sour cherries are used almost exclusively for pies and preserves.

Sour cherries are hardier than the sweet varieties and dominate the acreage devoted to cherries in Canada, mainly in response to demand by the processing market. The 'Montmorency' sour cherry, for example, grown extensively in Ontario, covers 10 times the acreage of its sweet cousin, 'Hedelfingen'. Most varieties of either species tolerate temperatures down to -25°C quite nicely. In regions with colder winters—including Alberta, my home turf— sour varieties are the best bet. But don't be afraid to experiment with out-of-zone trees. I've seen plenty thriving where they were supposedly not hardy enough to survive. BY JIM HOLE

GARDENER'S TIPS
- 100 grams of cherries (about 10) contains 11 mg of vitamin C. Cherries are also rich in bioflavanoids and ellagic acid.
- The fruit of an early-ripening mulberry tree grown near a cherry tree may keep birds away from the ripening cherries.
- Aluminum pie plates and strips of white cloth distract birds from sour cherries, but they don't work as well with sweet cherries.

growing

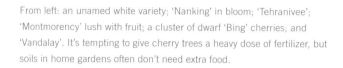
From left: an unamed white variety; 'Nanking' in bloom; 'Tehranivee'; 'Montmorency' lush with fruit; a cluster of dwarf 'Bing' cherries; and 'Vandalay'. It's tempting to give cherry trees a heavy dose of fertilizer, but soils in home gardens often don't need extra food.

Early spring's cooler temperatures allow trees to root more rapidly than they would in soaring summer temperatures. However, container-grown trees can be planted throughout the summer and into early fall, provided they're watered often to get roots established. Plant less hardy varieties in spring or summer rather than fall.

Valleys or ravine bottoms are poor locations; higher spots on slopes are ideal. Never plant where water stands for any length of time; trees root poorly in boggy soils and can drown. Sandy, loamy soils with good moisture retention and drainage are best. Roots must have ample room to grow. Dig a hole four times as wide as the tree's root ball and deep enough to accommodate, but not bury, the entire root ball. The base of the trunk should be level with the ground. The sides of the hole should be gently sloping, like the sides of a dish, rather than steep and vertical.

It's tempting when planting cherry trees to give them a healthy application of fertilizer, but backyard soils are variable and fertilizer may not be necessary. For low-fertility soils, apply a starter fertilizer (10-52-10). Avoid heavy applications of high-nitrogen fertilizers at all times. Keep the dose light; reapply two or three times in early spring and summer in the first year to encourage vigorous, but not excessive or "soft" growth.

A little pruning each year keeps cherry trees clean and healthy. Early spring, before buds swell, is the best time since there are fewer diseases floating around that could infect the cut branches. For maximum fruit production, all branches should be wide-angled to the trunk, or U-shaped. Upright or V-shaped branches often snap under the weight of a heavy load of fruit.

Broken, dead or diseased branches should be removed as soon as possible. Horizontal branches (often called "scaffold" branches) capture light better than vertical ones. Eliminate "stacked" branches—or branches growing directly over each other—but don't cut off healthy branches except to improve overall fruit productivity. If you must prune large branches, leave about one centimetre of

wood protruding from the trunk. On most trees, you'll see a thick ridge of bark between the trunk and the branch; cut about five millimetres beyond this ridge.

winter care

Thick plastic or cloth trunk wraps, put on in late fall and removed in spring, stabilize trunk temperatures and reduce damage. Screens and light, organic mulches help delay premature root warming and early bloom. Keep mulch about five centimetres away from the trunk, and a couple of centimetres deep is plenty.

pests and diseases

The greatest threat to cherry trees is rodents. To protect the trees, cut the grass around the cherries a little shorter than usual in fall to reduce the winter food source for mice. Always surround trees with a wire cylinder or a plastic tree guard.

Birds are also a threat, to the crop, not the health of the tree. Cast netting over the trees (difficult with large varieties) or try decoys that imitate bird predators although they get uneven results. It's probably best just to let the birds eat a few.

Black knot A fungal disease that causes large, black, warty growths, each containing millions of contagious spores. Be on the lookout for black growths and immediately prune out affected branches eight to 10 centimetres below the knot. Black knot can kill the tree. Place pruned branches in sealed plastic bags and remove them from your yard.

Shot hole fungus Causes round holes in leaves. Usually more annoying than debilitating, but severe defoliation can cause die back. Spraying is rarely warranted in drier regions but, if necessary, use benomyl or sulfur spray, starting at petal fall and increasing applications if the weather is moist and cool.

Iron deficiency Pale leaves with prominent veins. A problem on the Prairies, iron deficiency is common in cherries grown in alkaline soil. Regular applications of chelated iron help, but in very alkaline soil no amendments help.

Low fruit set The source is usually a lack of pollination. To set fruit, sweet cherries generally require cross-pollination—another sweet cherry variety growing close by and in bloom at the same time for pollination by bees and other insects. Not all varieties cross-pollinate; check with your nursery for compatible varieties.

Self-fertile sour cherries pollinate their own flowers without difficulty, but they don't pollinate sweet cherries. Recently considerable effort has gone into breeding self-fertile sweet cherries; successes include the variety 'Stella'.

June drop A tree that suddenly drops great quantities of fruit alarms gardeners, but it's just the tree's way of self-thinning an excessive fruit load and promoting its own long-term health. Sometimes abnormally cool June weather causes more fruit drop than usual, but it doesn't harm the tree.

harvesting

Cherries tend to ripen in mid to late summer, depending on the variety. When fruits start colouring, it's time to taste them: if they're tart or sweet but not bitter, and the flesh comes off the pit easily, start picking—but be gentle. Don't drop them into baskets or stack them more than a few layers deep. Bruised fruit deteriorates rapidly, infecting undamaged cherries.

cherry varieties

Sweet Black
- 'Bing' Highly rated for flavour, with large, firm, round, dark red fruit, its main drawback is that fruit tends to split after a shower. Harvest in mid-July.
- 'Stella' The first self-fertile sweet cherry, it has large, heart-shaped black fruit; somewhat susceptible to splitting. 'Compact Stella', a dwarf variety, is also self-pollinating.
- 'Hedelfingen' These sweet/sour cherries have deep red-black skin and dark red flesh. Harvest last week of July.
- 'Van' Self-pollinating, it produces firm, round, black fruits slightly smaller than 'Bing'. Harvest mid-July.

White
- 'Vega' Large, white fruit with a red blush is rather tart for a sweet cherry unless harvest is delayed beyond normal midsummer picking time.

Sour
- 'NorthStar' Excellent for pies, the reddish-black fruits ripen in late July but are sweeter if harvest is delayed a couple of weeks, which allows more sugar to accumulate, although fruit may not be as firm.
- 'Montmorency' One of the best sour cherries, its medium-sized, round, red, tender fruits are excellent for jams, jellies and other preserves.
- 'Carmine Jewel' A new introduction from Saskatchewan. Fruits are three to four centimetres in diameter with dark red skin and flesh; perfect for pies, jams, jellies and juices.
- 'Nanking' One of the most popular hardy cherries; pale pink blossoms are followed by red, tart-sweet fruit in late summer.

Chokecherries
- 'Boughen's Golden Chokecherry' Large clusters of small (seven- to eight-millimetre), bright-yellow cherries, excellent for jelly and wine. Chokecherries require cross-pollination.

pickled cherries

MAKES ABOUT 4 PINTS

Pickled cherries are a wonderful addition to antipasti platters and cheese courses, and are great served instead of gherkins and silverskin onions with patés.

2   lb. (1 kg) sour cherries
2   cups (500 mL) white wine vinegar
2   cups (500 mL) red wine vinegar
2 1/4 cups (560 mL) light brown sugar,
      lightly packed
1   heaping tbsp. (17 mL) pickling salt
6   cloves
6   dried juniper berries, crushed
      Zest of 1 lemon, cut into fine strips
      2-in. (5-cm) piece of cinnamon,
      broken into pieces

1 Sort through the cherries, discarding any that are bruised or otherwise damaged. Trim the stems to about 1 centimetre. Rinse and dry thoroughly. Have ready four sterilized pint jars.
2 Using a needle, prick the cherries several times, then pack them into jars to about 2.5 centimetres below the rim.
3 In a stainless-steel saucepan, combine the vinegars, brown sugar, pickling salt, cloves, juniper berries, lemon zest and cinnamon. Bring to a boil over high heat, stirring to help dissolve sugar and salt. Reduce heat and keep liquid at a simmer for 10 minutes.
4 Pour hot vinegar mixture over cherries, making sure each jar gets a bit of lemon, cloves, cinnamon and juniper berries.

5 Wipe rims clean and fix the lids. Store in a dry, dark cupboard. They'll keep for about a month. (Alternatively, after adding hot liquid to cherries in the jars, seal according to preserving jar manufacturer's directions and process jars in a water bath for 10 minutes.)

All it takes is one rodent-friendly winter—lots of fall moisture followed by heavy snows that protect mice from predators—to damage trees and reduce crop yields. Protect trees with wire or plastic cylinders.

sour cherry cobbler

SERVES 4 TO 6

One of summer's finest comfort desserts.
Serve with good-quality vanilla ice cream
or whipped cream.

1   lb. (500 g) sour cherries, pitted and
    halved
2   tbsp. (30 mL) unsalted butter
1/4 cup (60 mL) water
1   cup + 1 tbsp. (250 mL + 15 mL)
    granulated sugar
1   cup + 1 tbsp (250 mL + 15 mL)
    all-purpose flour
1 1/2 tsp. (7 mL) baking powder
1/2 tsp. (2 mL) salt
3   tbsp. (45 mL) chilled, unsalted butter
    Approximately 3/4 cup (175 mL) milk

1 Preheat oven to 425°F (220°C). In a
stainless-steel saucepan combine the
cherries, 2 tbsp. (30 mL) butter and the
water over medium-high heat. Bring to
a boil, then remove from heat. Blend
together 1 cup (250 mL) sugar with 1
tbsp. (15 mL) flour. Add to the cherries
in the saucepan, stirring all the while to
prevent lumps. Return mixture to a
boil, reduce heat and cook for a minute
or two until slightly thickened.
2 Transfer cherry mixture to a shallow,
4-cup (1-litre) baking dish. In a mixing
bowl, sift together the remaining flour,
sugar, baking powder and salt. Cut 3
tbsp. (45 mL) of chilled butter into
pieces and add to dry ingredients,
cutting it into the flour mixture as for
pastry-making. When mixture resembles coarse meal, add a portion of the
milk; stir with a fork until flour mixture resembles a thick batter, adding
more milk gradually as needed (you
may not need to use it all).
3 Use a large spoon to drop spoonfuls of
the batter all over the fruit. Bake in the
preheated oven for about 25 to 30 minutes until golden brown. Serve just warm.

duck breasts with cherries

SERVES 4

Start preparations for this simple yet
sumptuous entrée the day before you plan
to serve it so the duck breasts have time to
marinate. Serve with crisp potatoes and a
green salad that includes a few bitter
greens such as arugula or frisée.

4   duck breasts, trimmed, rinsed and
    patted dry
2   shallots, minced
2   garlic cloves, minced
2   sprigs fresh thyme
1   cup (250 mL) Beaujolais or other
    light red wine
2   tbsp. (30 mL) extra virgin olive oil
1   cup (250 mL) chicken stock
1 1/2 lb. (750 g) sweet cherries, pitted
2   tbsp. (30 mL) sherry vinegar
    Salt and freshly ground black pepper

1 Score the skin of the duck breasts
four or five times with a sharp knife.
Place breasts skin side down in a shallow baking dish. In a mixing bowl,
combine the shallots, garlic, thyme and
red wine. Pour mixture over the duck
breasts, cover with plastic wrap and
refrigerate for about 8 hours or
overnight.
2 Preheat oven to 200°F (100°C).
Remove breasts from marinade and pat
dry with paper towel. Strain marinade
and reserve. In a heavy frying pan, heat
the oil over medium-high heat. Add
duck breasts, skin side down, and sear
over high heat for 2 to 3 minutes on
each side (longer, if you prefer) until
golden brown. Transfer to the oven to
keep warm while you prepare the
sauce.
3 Add chicken stock to the frying pan,
scraping up any browned bits. Add
reserved marinade and bring to a boil.
Boil quickly for a few minutes to
reduce mixture and thicken slightly.
Add cherries, vinegar, salt and pepper
to taste; stir and cover loosely to simmer for 6 to 9 minutes, until cherries
are beginning to soften.
4 Remove duck from the oven and
serve immediately with the sauce.

An acquired taste that's worth cultivating

chicory

"Take the bitter with the sweet"—what good advice! Europeans have long enjoyed the bitter but sophisticated flavour of chicories, appreciating the interest they add to salads and their ability to stimulate digestion. Fortunately, North American supermarkets are increasingly offering selections from the *Cichorium endivia* species, including frilly endive and escarole, and from the *C. intybus* species, which includes Italian dandelion greens, striking red radicchio and Belgian endive. Chicory also has a wild relative—the beautiful blue-flowered plant that proliferates along roadsides across Canada.

Chicories can be roughly divided into three groups. The leafy types are eaten raw or cooked as greens. The heading types form heads similar to romaine lettuce, with outer leaves wrapping around a lighter inner heart. The rooting chicories are grown for their roots, which are cut up, dried and ground for use as a coffee additive or as a healthier, caffeine-free alternative. But all are cool-weather crops. Start seeds indoors in early spring or outdoors in summer so plants mature in the cool days of fall.

BY HEATHER APPLE

GARDENER'S TIPS
- Chicory is rich in vitamin A, calcium, potassium, magnesium and iron. And it's good for your digestion.
- If chicory seems too bitter, soak in lukewarm water, then cold.
- The expensive blanched witloof can be forced at home. In fall, cut tops off unharvested plants and move roots to trays of damp sand. Leave dormant a month, then plant upright in pots, covering each with an inverted pot. In another month, you should have delicious, pale yellow cones of leaves.

growing

Choose a sunny location with good drainage and fertile soil. Chicories do best in cool weather, so although some varieties tolerate heat, most are grown as spring or fall crops. Spring crops are sown mid-April, preferably using fast-maturing varieties so they can be harvested before hot weather. To decide when to plant fall crops, take the variety's number of days to maturity, add 10 more days, then count back from the date of your first expected fall frost.

Seeds can be sown directly in the garden. Work in lots of compost and plant seeds three millimetres deep, 2.5 centimetres apart. Keep seed bed moist until germination. As the leaves of the seedlings begin to touch, thin to 25 to 30 centimetres apart. Thinnings can be used in salads.

For best results, start plants in individual cell packs or five-centimetre pots. Plant three millimetres deep, two to three seeds per container, later thinning to the strongest seedling. If seedlings are grown indoors, place under grow lights or in a southern window. Before they're planted outside, harden off by gradually introducing them to direct sunlight and cooler temperatures. Hardened plants will survive a light frost.

Plant outdoors 25 to 30 centimetres apart. Dig a hole three times the size of the root ball and add compost. Firm the soil around the plant, then water. When the soil surface dries out, water deeply. Rapid, continuous growth is necessary for good quality. In areas where slugs aren't a problem, a 10- to 15-centimetre layer of mulch of straw, hay, or shredded leaves conserves moisture, keeps the soil cool and controls weeds. Midway through the plants' growth, carefully dig some compost or organic fertilizer into the soil around them.

pests and diseases

Chicories are relatively immune to pests and diseases. Don't overcrowd the plants, keep well weeded and watered. Always clean up well in fall and wait three years before planting chicories in the same place.

endive and escarole

The attractive frilly leaves, sturdy texture and sharp taste of endive (*Cichorium endivia*) adds interest to salads. The leaves of escarole, also called Batavian endive, are thinner, milder and more tender than those of endive. The leaves in the centre of the plant are especially good.

Although spring and fall crops do best, sowing new seed every three to four weeks until mid-July (mid-August in coastal British Columbia) provides a steady supply throughout the season if the plants are kept well watered. Harvest

individual leaves at any time or harvest the whole plant by cutting the entire head just above ground level.

Blanching turns the leaves a creamy colour and gives them a milder taste. Seven to 10 days before harvest, when the centres of the plants are dry, draw the outer leaves around the plant and tie with strips of cloth to keep the sun from reaching the inner leaves.

'Neos' endive (55 days) has medium-sized heads with extra-frilly leaves. 'Salad King' (95 days) has large heads 38 to 43 centimetres across.

'Nataly' escarole (50 to 55 days) is heat-tolerant, grows under challenging conditions and is suitable for spring, summer or fall crops.

'Full Heart Batavian' escarole (80 to 85 days) adapts to a wide range of growing conditions. Both it and 'Nataly' have pale, blanched centre leaves.

radicchio

Deep red leaves with prominent white veins make tender-textured radicchio (*Cichorium intybus*) a striking addition to the salad bowl. (It's the plant often grown in darkness for witloof, a gourmand's delight.) It's less uniform than other vegetables, and not all plants form good heads or do so at the same time. While older varieties such as 'Red Treviso' are difficult and demanding to grow—foliage has to be cut back, then heads allowed to resprout—the newer ones form heads sooner.

In areas with hot summers, spring and fall crops are usually the best. However, successive sowings throughout the season often yield good results. New varieties can handle temperatures in the high 20s to low 30s C, with occasional high 30s as long as they are well watered. When the plant is in the seedling stage, nighttime temperatures below 10°C can cause bolting, so start early crops inside and don't plant out until the nights are warm enough. Radicchio is fairly frost hardy and, in areas with only moderate frosts, can be harvested all winter.

When the head is firm, as with iceberg lettuce, it's ready to harvest. It will keep for up to a month in a perforated plastic bag in the refrigerator.

Radicchio comes in two shapes. The round chioggia varieties—'Indigo', 'Carmen' and 'Chioggia Red Preco No. 1', for example—mature in about 75 days, are heat-tolerant and fairly easy to grow. Although the tall, cylindrical kinds can sometimes be a bit trickier, 'Early Treviso' (80 days) and 'Fiero' (80 to 85 days) are quite dependable.

chicory varieties

Leafy Types
These varieties are at their mildest three to five weeks after planting and become more bitter as they mature to their full size of 30 to 45 centimetres. To harvest, remove individual leaves or cut the entire plant.

■ 'Italian Dandelion' (65 days), also called 'Catalogna Special', 'Dentarella', 'Cicoria Catalogna' and 'Radichetta', is not a true dandelion. The plant has deeply notched, dark green leaves with tender white stems. 'Red Dandelion', also called 'Italico Rosso', is similar but has red stems and mid-veins.

■ 'Cicoria San Pasquale' (70 days) resembles 'Italian Dandelion' but has broader, more deeply cut leaves.

■ 'Italian Dandelion' (green and red varieties) is very hardy; in coastal British Columbia, it can be planted mid-July to early August and harvested throughout the winter. In mild areas, fall crops can be covered with mulch for harvest in the spring.

Heading Types
These are best grown as a fall crop and can be eaten raw or cooked. 'Greenloaf', 'Sugar-loaf' and 'Bianca di Milano' all mature in 75 to 80 days.

■ 'Bianca di Milano' is fairly winter hardy in coastal B.C. if protected from rain.

Root Chicories
■ 'Magdeburgh' (100 days), also known as 'Cicoria Siciliana', has green dandelion-like leaves that can be eaten raw or cooked. In early June, and in fall dig up the roots. Roast and grind to use as a coffee substitute or added to fresh-ground beans.

belgian mussels

MAKES 4 DINNER SERVINGS
(6 TO 8 APPETIZER SERVINGS)

Belgian endive and Dijon mustard provide
the punch in this lovely mussel dish. Be
sure to have plenty of crusty bread on
hand to mop up the sauce.

1   tbsp. (15 mL) extra virgin olive oil
2   tbsp. (30 mL) butter
1   large leek, white part only, halved
     and sliced
3-4 small cloves garlic, halved
1   tsp. (5 mL) dried thyme
1   cup (250 mL) dry white wine
2   tbsp. (30 mL) Dijon mustard
4   lb. (1.8 kg) mussels, scrubbed
     and debearded
2   cups (500 mL) Belgian endive,
     julienned
1   large carrot, peeled and coarsely
     grated
1/2 cup (125 mL) 10% cream
     Freshly ground pepper, to taste

1 Heat oil and butter in a soup pot over
medium-high heat. Add leek, garlic and
thyme; sauté, stirring continuously,
until leek softens, about 5 to 10 minutes. Do not brown.
2 Stir in wine and mustard, bring to
boil, then reduce heat and simmer for
5 minutes. Add mussels, endive and
carrots to pot. Stir to mix thoroughly.
Cover pot and cook mussels until they
open, about 5 to 6 minutes.
3 Transfer mussels to bowls using a
slotted spoon. Add cream to mixture in
pot and heat through on low for 5 minutes. Add pepper. Pour sauce over mussels. Serve immediately.

minestrone with white beans & italian dandelion greens

MAKES 4 DINNER SERVINGS
(6 TO 8 APPETIZER SERVINGS)

Spinach is often added to minestrone soup
to provide colour and flavour. In this recipe,
sharp-tasting Italian dandelion leaves, a
type of chicory, are the green of choice.

2   tbsp. (30 mL) extra virgin olive oil
1   small onion, chopped
1   large potato, peeled and diced
1   large carrot, sliced vertically, then
     horizontally
1   small fennel bulb, chopped
1   small zucchini, sliced vertically, then
     horizontally
2   small cloves garlic, minced
1/2 tsp. (2 mL) each dried oregano, basil
     and thyme
1/4 tsp. (1 mL) red pepper flakes
1   bay leaf
4   cups (1 L) vegetable stock
2   cups (500 mL) canned tomatoes
     with juice
1   19 oz. can white (cannellini) beans
3   cups (750 mL) torn Italian dandelion
     leaves
     Salt and pepper, to taste

1 Heat oil in a large saucepan over
medium-high heat. Add onion, potato,
carrot, fennel, zucchini and garlic;
sauté for about 8 to 10 minutes.
2 Stir in dried herbs and spices. Add
stock and tomatoes. Bring to a boil;
then reduce heat, cover pan and simmer for 25 to 30 minutes or until vegetables soften.
3 Add beans and leaves. Simmer soup
for another 10 minutes. Season with
salt and pepper; serve immediately.

Chicory's pleasantly
bitter taste has become
a familiar element in
salad greens, especially
in the dwarf mixtures
sold by the kilo in
greengrocers. But small
heads of chicory are
also good halved,
brushed with garlicky
olive oil, and grilled on
the barbecue.
Torn or julienned leaves
add a pleasant sharp-
ness to soups or pasta.

radicchio, green bean & cherry tomato salad with hazelnuts

SERVES 4

A crunchy, colourful summer salad with lively flavours. It pairs nicely with simply prepared grilled fish or chicken.

Salad

1/4	cup (60 mL) whole hazelnuts
2	cups (500 mL) green beans, topped and halved on the diagonal
2	small heads radicchio
1	medium bunch watercress
2	cups (500 mL) cherry tomatoes, quartered

2-3	oz. (50-75 g) chèvre (goat cheese), crumbled
	Freshly ground pepper, to taste

Vinaigrette

2	tbsp. (30 mL) white wine vinegar
2	tbsp. (30 mL) maple syrup
1	shallot, chopped
	Pinch of salt
2	tbsp. (30 mL) hazelnut oil (or substitute 2 tbsp. extra virgin olive oil)
2	tbsp. (30 mL) extra virgin olive oil

1 Place hazelnuts in a dry skillet over medium-high heat; toast for 8 to 10 minutes or until they begin to brown. Wrap hazelnuts in a tea towel and rub to remove skins. Coarsely chop peeled nuts and set aside.

2 Meanwhile, cook beans in a small pan of boiling, salted water until just tender, about 3 to 5 minutes. Drain, rinse with cold water and drain again.

3 Prepare vinaigrette: place first four ingredients in a blender. Purée until smooth. With motor running at the purée setting, slowly add oils and blend until emulsified. Reserve.

4 Tear 12 leaves from radicchio. Wash, dry and set on 4 plates to form cups. Tear remaining radicchio into pieces, trim stems from watercress and wash and dry leaves.

5 Toss radicchio, watercress, green beans, cherry tomatoes and hazelnuts in a salad bowl with the vinaigrette. Spoon salad into radicchio cups; top with chèvre and pepper.

The sweet sunshine of late summer

corn

recipes

corn & cucumber relish

barbecued corn with chipotle butter

corn fritter cakes

Sweet corn, field corn, cornmeal, popcorn—in its approximately 7,000-year history, corn in all its forms has never ceased to be in demand. Tastes may change, but corn has remained a staple worldwide.

Developed by Amerindian farmers from a Mexican wild grass plant called teosinte (*Zea mexicana*), hundreds of varieties of maize (*Zea mays*) were growing in the New World by the time Christopher Columbus arrived. But sweet corn is relatively modern, probably developed in the Andes around AD 1000. Until the introduction of 'Golden Bantam' in 1902, most sweet corns were white-kernelled. The deep yellow 'Golden Bantam' was an immediate hit, but it's been eclipsed by sweeter, tastier hybrids with larger cobs and better resistance to insects and disease.

In 1950, scientists discovered the "supersweet" gene (s2), which produces corn that contains little sucrose (corn sugar) but lots of fructose (fruit sugar), and retains its sweetness longer after harvesting. It's too sensitive for our growing conditions, but "sugar enhanced" corns (se in catalogues) from the 1960s, are easy to grow, produce huge cobs with tender, crunchy kernels and do fairly well in cold soils. The hybrid three-way crosses combine characteristics of s2 and se corns with excellent cold-hardiness, but kernels often discolour during cooking. BY LARRY HODGSON

GARDENER'S TIPS
- Corn is filled with fibre, and delivers folate, vitamin C, niacin and thiamin. An ear contains about 83 calories.
- Many foods come from corn: oil, starch, flour and sweeteners. It's an animal food and is used in the manufacture of some plastics.
- To keep fresh-picked corn sweet, plunge the cobs—husks and all—into icy water as they are harvested, then refrigerate.
- Any sweet corn produces baby cobs. Just grow plants 5 to 10 cm apart and harvest as soon as silks emerge.

corn varieties

Supersweet
- 'Fortune Bicolor' Good germination in cooler soils, disease-resistant; 75 days.
- 'Fortune' (yellow) Good germination in cooler soils, disease-resistant; 73 days.

Sugar Enhanced
- 'Early Peaches and Cream' Sweet, tender and juicy; 70 days.
- 'Speedy Sweet' (bicolour) Extra early, good germination in cold soils; 57 to 64 days.
- 'Silver Knight' (white) Extra early, well-filled ears; 61 to 67 days.

Three-way Hybrids
- 'Honey Select' (yellow) Very sweet, 2001 All-America Selections winner; 74 days.

container corn

Corn grows surprisingly well in containers on a balcony or patio. Use large tubs, at least 60 centimetres wide and deep. Sow seed equidistantly, about 15 centimetres apart, two or three seeds per cluster, then thin to the strongest plant per cluster. Keep soil moist and fertilize regularly: minerals quickly leach out of containers.

growing

Corn isn't difficult to grow but it needs rich, well-drained soil in full or nearly full sun. Where these conditions are lacking, it can be grown in a raised bed of soil well amended with compost. Add plenty of fertilizer or organic material to any soil: corn is a very heavy feeder. You'll need 10 centimetres of fresh compost or well-decomposed manure, or a fertilizer rich in phosphorus and potassium rather than nitrogen (4-6-8, for example) at recommended rates (these vary; read the label). Always plant corn to the north of other vegetables so it doesn't overshadow them.

Corn will not germinate in cold soil. In climates where soil warms up slowly, put down black plastic mulch at snow melt to speed up the process. Many seed suppliers treat corn seeds with fungicide to help prevent rot under cool conditions. Plant treated seed when soil temperature reaches 16°C. Wait until soil temperature reaches 21°C before sowing untreated seed of sugar-enhanced corn, usually not until early June in most of Canada.

Supersweet corn is even more cold-sensitive: wait until soil temperature reaches 24°C before sowing even treated seed. In areas with less than 70 frost-free days, or where summers are cool, start corn indoors in peat pots about four weeks before the last frost date.

The only wind-pollinated common vegetable, corn must be planted in blocks of at least four rows rather than in single rows so pollen reaches neighbouring plants. Ears won't fill out if pollination is poor. For added insurance, once the male flowers (tassels) have formed at the tops of the plants and the female flowers (silks) appear, shake the plants twice a day until the silks turn brown, allowing pollen to drop onto the silks below.

You'll get more corn in less space if you forget traditional rows and plant equidistantly: two or three seeds sown 30 centimetres apart in all directions.

In most parts of Canada, only one crop of early corn is possible. Sow seeds about three centimetres deep (two centimetres if you're planting supersweets) and water well to initiate germination. When plants sprout (four to seven days in warm soil, up to three weeks in cool soil), thin to the sturdiest plant per cluster, and keep it watered and weeded. Corn's shallow roots can be damaged by hoeing, so mulch to keep weeds down. In windy areas, especially where soil is sandy, hill up the plants' bases with 10 centimetres of soil when they're about 30 centimetres tall so they don't blow over.

pests and diseases

Insects are a minor problem in most parts of Canada. The first sign of corn borer, a type of caterpillar, is usually a small hole in the stalk surrounded by sawdust-like frass (excrement). Squash the pest by squeezing the stalk below the hole before it works its way into the ear and eats the kernels.

Corn earworm Lays its eggs on the silks; the larvae then work their way down into the husk and eat the immature kernels. The tight husks of modern corn varieties don't allow easy entry, but to be sure they stay out wrap an elastic band tightly around the tip of the ear as soon as the silks appear. Even if the corn earworm makes it into the ear, it will damage only the uppermost kernels, which can be cut off.

Raccoons, squirrels and deer are far more serious pests, usually showing up at harvest time and stealing the crop overnight. Repellents such as deodorant soap hung around plants on the outside of the patch, or baby powder sprinkled over the leaves (reapply after a rainfall), sometimes work. More drastic measures such as motion-detecting sprinkler devices or electric fencing cost more than the crop is worth and still aren't foolproof.

Diseases aren't usually a major problem in home gardens, especially if you rotate your corn crop each year (a four-year cycle is sufficient). Corn smut is a wind-borne fungus that causes a misshapen grey growth to form on the ears, usually affecting only one or two ears per patch. But a week or two of rain at the wrong time—when the silks are receptive to pollen—will ruin the crop.

harvesting

Maturity dates listed on seed packets aren't always an accurate indicator of when to harvest; sweet corn can take a few days to a week longer to mature than expected. Check a few cobs: when they're ripe, all the others of the same variety likely will be too, if growing conditions are consistent.

Peeling back the husk to check for ripeness can dry out the upper kernels. When the silks turn brown, feel the tips of a few cobs. If the husk feels loose, wait a day or two. When the cob feels full to the tip, it's time to harvest.

Sweet corn should be canned, frozen or eaten within a few hours of harvest, but supersweets and sugar-enhanced corns retain their flavour for a day or two. For optimal sweetness, immediately plunge corn into icy water as you harvest, then refrigerate. Freeze the surplus, blanching by boiling cobs for eight to 10 minutes then chilling them in cold water.

Corn plants have presence, whether grown in fields on a farm or in a single row in a home garden. But they're the most fun in fields, where you can play hide-and-seek among the stalks or pretend you're finding your way through a jungle. When planting in quantity, avoid cross-pollination by planting varieties 7.5 metres apart.

Corn is easy to freeze: Blanch whole cobs or kernels cut from cobs for a minute in boiling water, then blanch in ice water. Freeze immediately. Spread kernels on a cookie sheet and package in plastic bags. Freeze cobs separately and wrap tightly in foil or use freezer bags.

corn & cucumber relish

MAKES ABOUT 2 PINTS (1 LITRE)

Because this colourful corn relish is not processed in the traditional way but simply stored in the refrigerator, it's a little easier to make than many others. Pack it into small preserving jars if you like.

1/2   tsp. (2 mL) hot sauce (or to taste)
1/2   tsp. (2 mL) mustard seeds
1   tsp. (5 mL) salt
1/4   cup (60 mL) sugar
1   cup (250 mL) white wine vinegar
1   small cucumber (unpeeled) seeded, chopped to medium dice
1   small red bell pepper, seeded, chopped to medium dice
2   green onions, chopped
6   ears corn, or about 4 cups (1 L) of kernels
1/3   cup (75 mL) fresh coriander, chopped

1 Combine hot sauce, mustard seeds, salt, sugar and vinegar in a heavy, stainless-steel or other non-reactive pot or saucepan. Bring to a boil over medium heat, uncovered, and continue to boil for about 5 minutes.

2 Using a sharp knife, remove kernels from ears. Combine kernels with remaining ingredients in a large mixing bowl and stir to combine well. Divide between 2 pint jars. Pour hot vinegar mixture over vegetables.
3 Cover jars tightly with sterilized lids and refrigerate. Use within one month.

barbecued corn with chipotle butter

SERVES 8

Grill the ears of corn in their husks, as suggested here, or with husks removed. If you choose to grill the cobs husked, apply the chipotle butter at the table. Chipotles are large, dried, smoked jalapeno peppers, available canned in a red sauce called adobo. Look for them in the specialty sections of supermarkets and Latin American markets.

8   ears fresh corn, husks on
1/2   cup (125 mL) butter
2   green onions, chopped
1   clove garlic
3-4   chipotles in adobo sauce (or to taste)
1   tsp. (5 mL) fresh lime juice

1 Preheat grill to medium-high. Peel back husks on corn but leave attached at the bases. Remove cornsilk.
2 In a food processor or blender, combine butter, onions, garlic, chipotles (with any sauce that clings to them) and lime juice. Process until all ingredients are well blended and relatively smooth.

3 Spread chipotle butter over each ear of corn. Pull husks back over ears of corn and tie with a strip of corn husk or kitchen yarn. Soak corn in cold water for about 15 minutes; squeeze out excess water. Place corn on grill for about 10 to 12 minutes (less time if corn is without the husk), turning frequently. Serve with more chipotle butter and salt.

corn fritter cakes

SERVES 6

For these cakes, a cross between a traditional corn fritter and a pancake, you'll need corn flour. Look for it in health food stores, Latin American food shops, Indian groceries and in the specialty sections of supermarkets. Delicious plain or topped with chunks of smoked ham, smoked salmon, a spoonful of salsa or small grilled shrimp.

3   ears of corn or 1 1/2 cups (375 mL) of kernels
1   cup (250 mL) milk
1 1/2 cups (375 mL) corn flour
1 1/2 tsp. (7 mL) baking powder
1/2   tsp. (2 mL) salt
2   eggs, separated
1/4   cup (60 mL) vegetable oil
6-8   sun-dried tomatoes, rehydrated, drained, snipped into small pieces
3   tbsp. (45 mL) fresh chives, finely chopped

1 Using a sharp knife, cut kernels from ears of corn. Put 1 cup (250 mL) of kernels and milk in a blender—reserve the other 1/2 cup (125 mL) of corn. Purée for a few minutes. Place a sieve over a bowl and pour corn purée into sieve. Using the back of a wooden spoon, press mixture to release as much liquid as you can. You should get about 1 1/4 cups (310 mL), which is all you require; discard excess.

2 Sift corn flour with baking powder and salt into a different bowl. Add egg yolks and oil, and gradually whisk in the corn milk until mixture is smooth.

Add reserved corn kernels, sun-dried tomatoes and chives, and stir until well combined.

3 In a separate bowl, beat egg whites until stiff peaks form, then fold carefully into the batter. Heat a non-stick pan over medium-high heat. Ladle out a small amount of batter into pan (fin-

ished fritter cakes should be about two inches/five centimetres across) and cook briefly, just over a minute or so, until cake is cooked on the bottom. Flip over and continue to cook for another minute or so. Transfer to a plate and keep warm while you make remaining cakes. Serve with a little melted butter.

The garden's crisp, cool antidote to a sultry summer

cucumbers

recipes

sautéed cucumbers
with cream & parsley

cucumber salad with
mint & dill

cool cucumber soup
with mint & chives

When you bite into a freshly picked cucumber on a hot summer day, you're following a long tradition. Early travellers always carried cucumbers on caravans across a desert to quench their thirst. There's truth in the phrase "cool as a cucumber": the vegetable is 96 per cent water and its interior temperature is 11°C cooler than the outside air.

Along with squash, pumpkins and melons, the cucumber (*Cucumis sativus*) is a member of the gourd family. It's native to India, where it has been grown for more than 3,000 years. Cucumbers eventually made their way to the Roman Empire, where the Emperor Tiberius was said to have eaten 10 a day. In the 16th century, Spanish explorers carried them to the Americas, where they were cultivated by the indigenous people.

Harvest cucumbers when they're slim and dark green. Large fruit tends to be seedy, tough and bitter. If the vines bear more than you can use at one time, pick them anyway; otherwise the plants will stop producing. Don't tug the fruit off the plant; use a sharp knife to cut through the small stem that joins the cucumber to the vine, being careful not to cut into the cucumber itself.

BY HEATHER APPLE

GARDENER'S TIPS
▪ Cucumber flesh provides little nutrition, but the skin is an important source of silica, which helps strengthen the body's connective tissues—bones, cartilage, tendons and ligaments.
▪ Cucumber seeds won't germinate at temperatures below 10°C, and they rot without sprouting in cool, damp soils.
▪ While the small, immature fruit of many regular varieties can be used for pickles, it's best to plant special pickling types.

The slender, plastic-wrapped cucumbers sold in supermarkets need highly controlled greenhouse conditions and aren't easily grown in the home garden. Right: 'Lemon' can be eaten like an apple, pickled or sliced for salad. Middle: the cucumber beetle, which can carry bacterial wilt and mosaic virus.

growing

Cucumbers are a tropical plant and grow best when days and nights are warm. Start seeds indoors three or four weeks before planting outdoors; don't start earlier or the vines become too straggly to transplant well. Plant seeds one centimetre deep, three to each eight-centimetre pot. Cucumbers hate having their roots disturbed: use peat pots, which can be planted directly into the garden, and hold planted pots at 21°C to 24°C till the seeds sprout. As soon as they germinate—usually in about a week—move the seedlings to a sunny southern window or under grow lights. Thin to the best seedling per pot by cutting off the other seedlings at soil level; pulling out weaker seedlings disturbs the roots of the chosen plant.

Gradually acclimatize the seedlings before planting outside. Cucumbers are extremely susceptible to frost; even cool nights cause blossoms to drop. Don't plant out until the soil has warmed up and the nights have lost their chill.

Cucumbers like loose, rich, well-drained soil in a sheltered location with full sun. Let vines sprawl over the ground or train them up a trellis. Using a trellis saves garden space, keeps the fruit off the ground, improves air circulation and, in varieties with long fruit, produces attractive, straight cucumbers instead of curved ones. Make the trellis 1.5 to two metres tall and have it in place before planting the seedlings. Initially it may be necessary to tie the vines to the trellis. Dig holes 30 centimetres wide and 30 centimetres deep; space 30 centimetres apart with a trellis and 60 centimetres without. Half fill each hole with compost and top with garden soil and a handful of balanced fertilizer. Set seedling in the hole so it rests in about 2.5 centimetres below soil level. Firm the soil around the roots and create a raised rim of earth around the depression to hold water. Make sure the peat pot's rim is completely buried or torn off. Keep soil moist but not soggy until the plant puts out new growth. Cold water may set back plants; use lukewarm. A floating row cover helps keep temperatures steady and protects plants from cucumber beetles. Spread it loosely over the bed and secure edges with poles or pieces of wood. Once flowering starts, remove the cover to let in pollinating insects.

Except in areas with very short summers, plant a second crop by sowing seeds directly into the garden after the last frost and when the soil feels warm. If the soil is heavy and damp, use raised beds. Prepare holes as above, planting seeds one centimetre deep, five or six per hole. Water well. Thin to the best seedling per hole.

A steady supply of water is essential for a good crop of cucumbers; without it they may be bitter and deformed. Give plants a deep soaking at least once a week in mid-morning, never late in the day. In areas with hot summers, mulch with 13 to 15 centimetres of old hay, straw or partially decomposed leaves to help control weeds, keep the soil moist and cool, and keep the fruit of unsupported plants off the ground. A month after planting, feed every three weeks with compost tea.

pests and diseases

To help keep cucumber pests under control, clean up plant debris and weeds at the end of the season. Be on the lookout for the following specific pests.

Cucumber beetle Adults are yellow-orange with black spots or stripes. They eat small holes in the leaves and flowers and can carry bacterial wilt and mosaic virus. The white larvae feed on roots and stems. Protect plants with row covers and mulch. Use rotenone or pyrethrum as a last resort.

Squash bug Brownish-black adults emit a bad odour when crushed. Adults and nymphs suck sap from plants, causing light-coloured areas that turn brown. Place flat boards through the garden for adults to hide under overnight, then crush bugs first thing in the morning. Crush yellow and brown egg clusters found under leaves.

Squash vine borer White caterpillars with brown heads bore into the base of stems, causing the vine to wilt. Masses of green excrement exude from the holes. Slit stem, remove borer and pile earth over the damaged stem to encourage rerooting.

To help control the following diseases, don't plant cucumbers melons or squash

in the same place for three years. Destroy infected plants. Don't use high-nitrogen fertilizers. Avoid watering late in the day and don't handle plants when leaves are wet. Make sure the patch has good air circulation and and don't plant in cold, wet or poorly drained soil. Plant disease-resistant varieties.

Bacterial wilt Causes foliage to wilt quickly. To identify, cut open a stem near the base of the plant and squeeze; you're looking for sticky white sap. Cucumber beetles spread the disease.

Cucumber mosaic virus The leaves curl, turn yellow and die. Fruits become pale green and warty. Control aphids and cucumber beetles, which spread the disease.

Other diseases, such as angular leaf spot, leaf blight, anthracnose and fusarium wilt, cause spotting or discolouration of the leaves and may affect the fruit and cause the plant to wilt.

cucumber varieties

- Cucumbers vary in size, shape, thickness of skin and flavour. Some have a bitter taste that may give people indigestion. Compounds called cucurbitacins cause the bitterness, and while their concentration may slightly increase if plants receive insufficient water, bitterness is for the most part genetically controlled. The term "burpless" is often used in seed catalogues to describe varieties with thin skins and a mild, bitter-free flavour.

- Among the varieties of regular cucumbers, 'Sweet Slice' is a high-yielding, thin-skinned, bitter-free cucumber resistant to many diseases. The 25- to 30-centimetre-long fruit is crisp, juicy and sweet, and can be eaten without peeling. 'Marketmore 86' has slightly shorter vines than regular cucumbers, and can be spaced more densely to get a higher yield in small spaces without using a trellis. The 20- to 23-centimetre-long cucumbers are dark green, crisp, bitter-free and sweet, and have tolerance to some diseases. 'Amira', with 10- to 15-centimetre-long fruit, is a bitter-free Middle Eastern cucumber. It's very productive, has an excellent taste and a thin skin that doesn't need to be peeled.

- Oriental cucumbers are long, thin-skinned and bitter-free. They're best grown on a trellis so the long fruit grows straight. 'Orient Express' produces heavy yields of crisp, crunchy cucumbers and is resistant to many diseases. Harvest the fruit at 30 centimetres for pickles, salads or cucumber slices. 'Japanese Long Pickling' grows 30 to 45 centimetres long and four centimetres in diameter. The dark green fruit is crisp, very mild and easy to digest. It's excellent for slicing, salads and pickles.

container cukes

- You don't need a vegetable garden to enjoy home-grown cucumbers. Plant regular varieties in large containers and train them up a trellis, or grow smaller bush varieties in a container without a trellis. 'Salad Bush' produces heavy yields of smooth, 20- to 25-centimetre-long cucumbers on 60-centimetre plants. 'Bush Pickle' has 75-centimetre vines that produce medium green, white-spined fruits 10 to 13 centimetres long. Use them for pickling.

- Check container-grown cucumbers daily and keep the soil moist but not soggy. Don't allow soil to dry out; feed with compost tea once a week.

sautéed cucumbers with cream & parsley

SERVES 4

Cucumbers are wonderful cooked and served as an accompaniment to grilled chicken or fish.

2 cucumbers, peeled
3 tbsp. (45 mL) butter
1/4 tsp. (1 mL) salt
1/4 tsp. (1 mL) white pepper
1/4 tsp. (1 mL) dry, hot English mustard
1/3 cup (75 mL) whipping cream
3 tbsp. (45 mL) fresh parsley, chopped

1 Slice cucumbers in half lengthwise. Using a small spoon, scrape out seeds. Cut cucumbers into thirds across the width, then slice into half-inch (one-centimetre) julienne strips.
2 In a large non-stick skillet, melt butter over medium heat. Add cucumbers, salt, pepper and mustard. Sauté, stirring occasionally, about 10 minutes, or until cucumbers are softened and slightly translucent. Add cream and stir to coat cucumbers. Reduce heat and cook about 2 minutes, until sauce is thickened. Add parsley and serve immediately.

cucumber salad with mint & dill

SERVES 6

Great with baked ham and a cheese-and-potato gratin.

1/4 cup (50 mL) sour cream
1/4 cup (50 mL) plain yogurt
1 tbsp. (15 mL) mayonnaise
1 clove garlic, finely minced
   Juice of 1 lemon
2 tbsp. (30 mL) each fresh dill and fresh mint, finely chopped
   Salt and white pepper
2 cucumbers, peeled

1 In a mixing bowl, combine sour cream, yogurt, mayonnaise, garlic, lemon juice, dill, mint, and salt and pepper to taste. Blend thoroughly.
2 Slice cucumbers in half, lengthwise. Using a small spoon, scrape out seeds. Slice cucumber halves lengthwise into quarters. Chop quarters into bite-sized chunks. Add cucumbers to the dressing and toss together until well coated.

cool cucumber soup with mint & chives

SERVES 4 TO 6

Every once in a while in the heat of summer you'll crave the coolness of creamy cucumber soup. Adding fresh mint and chives elevates the flavours immeasurably. The soup is an elegant precursor to a spicy, grilled main dish.

1/2 cup (125 mL) sour cream
1/2 cup (125 mL) plain yogurt
1 cup (250 mL) buttermilk
1/4 cup (50 mL) fresh lime juice
1/2 cup (125 mL) packed fresh mint leaves
2 cucumbers, peeled
1/4 cup (50 mL) chopped fresh chives
   Pinch cayenne
   Salt and freshly ground white pepper

1 In a blender or food processor, combine sour cream, yogurt, buttermilk, lime juice and mint; process until well combined. Halve cucumbers lengthwise, remove seeds and coarsely chop. Add chopped cucumbers, 1 cup (250 mL) at a time, processing until smooth after each batch.
2 Pour mixture into a chilled soup tureen. Stir in chives, cayenne, and salt and pepper to taste. Refrigerate soup in tureen, covered, for several hours before serving.

Cucumbers can become slightly bitter if plants don't receive enough water, but bitterness is for the most part genetically controlled. Varieties with thin skins and less cucurbitacins, which cause bitterness, are described as "burpless" in most catalogues. 'Marketmore', the bitter-free variety seen on the opening page, grows on shorter vines than many cukes, making it useful in a small garden. Right: sautéed cucumbers with cream and parsley are a delicious example of how versatile cucumbers can be in the kitchen.

A magical plant that's fragrant, healing and edible

lavender

recipes

sooke harbour house
lavender honey ice
cream

lavender blueberry soup

lavender hill butter

Few scents are as universally recognized as lavender. A member of the mint family, and indigenous to the Mediterranean region, lavender has long been believed to have magical powers: North African women of the Kabyle tribe used it as protection from mistreatment by their husbands, while in Tuscany it was thought to shield children from "the evil eye," writes Cathy Wilkinson Barash in her book, *Edible Flowers*. The conquering Romans took lavender to England, where it quickly became a popular strewing herb used to freshen indoor air and add scent to linens. For centuries, its fragrance has graced sachets, soaps, perfumes and potpourris. It was among the herbs brought to America by settlers, who used the flowers as a freshener as well as an antiseptic and healing agent. Shaker communities throughout the United States supported themselves by selling medicines made with home-grown lavender. Today, lavender oil continues to be used as a naturopathic remedy for everything from burns to headaches, while lavender flowers are often used as unique flavouring in foods such as ice cream and soup.

By itself, a stalk of lavender isn't much to look at. Its grey-green foliage is often skimpy and unremarkable in colour; the flowers, from pink or white to palest blue and deepest purple, can be lanky and small. Seen en masse, however, lavender is stunning. The scent alone is captivating. BY LAURA LANGSTON

GARDENER'S TIPS
■ The scent of lavender is said to repel black flies and aphids.
■ Lavender has long been linked with the laundering of linens. The name lavender is derived from the Latin word for "to wash."
■ To make lavender sugar: layer 225 grams fruit sugar and 60 grams fresh lavender flowers in a glass jar. Close jar and keep in a warm place two weeks, shaking occasionally. To use, sieve sugar and discard flowers.

About 30 species of lavender exist, with more than 100 cultivars, and in most cases it's difficult for anyone but an expert to tell them apart. Some are more intensely scented, and others have slightly differentiated leaves. Many varieties are hardy enough to grow in most parts of Canada.

how to grow

Lavender has a reputation for being hard to grow from seed, sometimes taking a month or more to germinate, says Conrad Richter, vice-president of Richters Herbs in Goodwood, Ontario. Sow seeds in late winter, about three millimetres below the surface of a light starting mix. Keep the flats moist and warm—about 18°C. If the seeds haven't germinated in three or four weeks, moisten the soil in the seed flat or pot and put it in the freezer for a week, or in the fridge for up to three weeks, then return it to a warm environment. If germination is spotty, start another batch, water the flat and put it in the freezer for two weeks before bringing it into the warmth. Once the seedlings appear, they need another eight weeks of growth before they're ready to transplant. And usually they don't bloom until the second year of growth.

English lavender grown from seed isn't always true to its parent. Some growers recommend propagating by cuttings instead of seed, but Richter disagrees, although he concedes that lavender seeds vary. For example, in one batch of seeds there may be some natural genetic variations. "If you're after only one or two plants, or you're growing a hedge and you want absolute uniformity, cuttings might be a better choice," he says.

One relatively new variety that germinates fairly quickly, blooms the first year if started early indoors and is highly consistent is an English lavender called 'Lavender Lady'. Declared an All-America Selections winner in 1994, 'Lavender Lady' grows 20 to 25 centimetres tall and flowers abundantly. In Victoria, where I garden, I treat it as an annual because it doesn't survive the winter, but it reaches more than 30 centimetres in one season. " 'Lady' is a nice modification," says Richter, "but it's not as winter hardy as other English lavenders."

At The Herb Farm in Norton, New Brunswick, Joyce Belyea has successfully grown lavender from seed, but she usually propagates her plants by taking tip cuttings from young stems in spring and rooting them in light soil mix with plenty of perlite. The cuttings root in two or three weeks if kept warm—about 18°C—and in indirect light. Belyea also layers plants to propagate them. "I liberally cover the lower branches of my lavender with lots and lots of soil in the fall," she says. "As I do that, I give them a little tug so they're loosened, but not completely detached, from the mother plant." Many of the branches have rooted by spring, and Belyea pulls them off the parent plant to pot them or plant in the garden.

Lavender prefers a sunny exposure and light, dry, well-drained soil. Belyea suggests raised beds filled with gritty soil that's not too rich. A slightly alkaline soil is preferable over a soil that's extremely acidic. Lavender also needs good air circulation. Crowded plants invite fungal diseases. When planting en masse, space plants 45 to 60 centimetres apart. It's important to water the plants well in the first year, while they become established. After the second year, lavender is reasonably drought-tolerant. There's no need to fertilize, says Richter, though he recommends applying a light dressing of manure every couple of years. "If I use fertilizer, I apply it early in the season," Belyea says. "I feed my rooted cuttings with 10-52-10 before transplanting, and I might feed them with 20-20-20 once a week for a month. But after that, nothing."

pruning

More important than fertilizing is pruning away the dead wood in spring. Even though lavender plants take several years to reach maturity, they should be trimmed back vigorously while they're still young. Regular pruning encourages the plants to bush out, and spring is the time to give lavender a hard trim. In Ontario, Richter likes to wait until he sees new growth from the base of the plant. Then he cuts away the old wood and removes about a third of the old

Although we seldom see lavender growing in gorgeous scented blue ribbons as in some parts of France, Canada has its share of commercial gardens, such as The Herb Farm in Norton, New Brunswick, owned by Joyce Belyea. All but French and Spanish lavenders are surprisingly hardy here, although they require a winter mulch outside Zone 5.

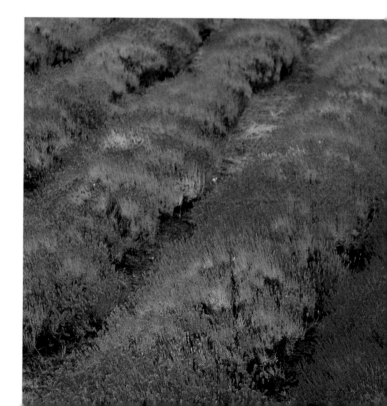

foliage, allowing the new growth to come from the base and from the remaining branches. Belyea also prunes in the spring, and gives her plants another shearing in the fall to help them retain their shape.

wintering over

Don't believe people who tell you to dig up your lavender and winter it indoors. It's not recommended for most varieties—in fact, lavender benefits from several months of dormancy. The exceptions are French and Spanish lavenders, both tender perennials that must be brought in over winter. Both make great houseplants, however, with their aromatic, resinous leaves.

Lavender is surprisingly hardy and can withstand below-freezing temperatures; the hybrid lavandins or intermedias are usually slightly hardier than English lavender. Richter gardens in Zone 5, and of the lavandins, 'Provence', survived in his garden when some of his English varieties didn't. But lavender won't tolerate extreme temperature fluctuations or too much moisture.

Mulching is necessary if you live in a colder zone or where there are high winds. Snow can act as insulation, but it's often not enough to protect plants. It's best to mulch after the ground is frozen in fall, but before the first heavy snowfall. In New Brunswick, Belyea mounds soil up around the base of her plants like a collar, filling in spaces with compost or dead leaves. She puts evergreen branches over the plants, creating a dome over them that allows snow to filter through. In most cases, however, even 15 centimetres of mulch around the base of a plant helps protect roots from temperature fluctuations in spring.

In Victoria, where we usually have wet, mild winters, mulching isn't recommended because it encourages moisture retention. In my area, it's crucial to plant lavender in a sandy, well-drained spot and allow plenty of circulation.

harvesting

Harvest when the lowest blooms on each spike have just opened, and the top blooms are still closed. Cut in the morning, just after the dew dries, leaving some green growth above the woody growth. With new plants, leave two-thirds of the overall plant intact. Even if you're planning to use just the flowers, cut some of the stem as well to leave the plant looking more uniform. Unwanted stems can be used to perfume fires, linen closets or dresser drawers.

Lavender is common in dried flower arrangements and other craft projects. To dry, tie lavender and hang upside down, or place in a single layer on a muslin-covered frame, turning once so both sides dry. Either way, leave stems in a cool, dry spot away from direct light. "Give them lots of time to dry," says Joyce Belyea, "and when they're crisp, put them away in a box. Never store them in plastic."

To store flower buds separately, gently rub the dried flowers from the stems and store them in covered boxes or paper bags.

healing lavender

Versatile lavender oil, now available at many health food stores, is an indispensable part of my medicine chest. It's a natural antibiotic, antiseptic, antidepressant, sedative and detoxifier. Useful for treating burns and scalds, it promotes healing and prevents scarring. It also relieves the itch of insect bites, helps alleviate headaches and insomnia and is especially soothing when used in the bath or as a massage oil. It's one of the few essential oils that can be used directly on the skin without being diluted.

lavender in the garden

Lavender does especially well in rockeries. It can also be used successfully to edge a path or garden bed, and some of the smaller varieties do well in containers. A classic pairing is lavender with rosemary. I like lavender with white flowers, and have several plants in my rockery that bloom at the same time as shasta daisies. In my herb garden, lavender contrasts attractively with white and pink hollyhocks. My favourite combination, however, is the border of lavender backed by white cosmos and three violet-red 'Roseraie de l'Hay' rose bushes.

Lavender is so quickly identified with the perfume industry that some people don't realize it's also edible. Lavender flowers are sweet, floral and intense; a few go a long way. Lavender jelly is delightful on warm scones. Lavender can also be used to flavour cookies, cakes, chocolate, ice cream and soups.

sooke harbour house lavender honey ice cream

MAKES ABOUT 1 QUART (4 LITRES)

Fredrique and Sinclair Philip run Sooke Harbour House, an internationally known inn outside Victoria, and this ice cream is sometimes featured on their menu.

1 1/2 cups (375 mL) whipping cream
1 1/2 cups (375 mL) homogenized milk
1   vanilla bean, slit down the centre (or 1 tsp./5 mL vanilla extract)
7   large egg yolks
1/4 cup (50 mL) granulated sugar
1/4 cup (50 mL) clear honey
2   tbsp. (30 mL) fresh lavender flowers, stems removed, broken into small pieces (if fresh lavender is unavailable, use 1 tbsp./15 mL dried, organic lavender)

1 Pour whipping cream and milk into a saucepan with the vanilla bean or vanilla extract and scald just below the boiling point for about 3 minutes. Remove from the heat and discard the vanilla bean.

2 Combine egg yolks and sugar in a large bowl and place over a pot of simmering water, or bain marie. With a wire whisk, whisk the yolks and sugar over low heat until thick. Slowly add the scalded milk/cream mixture to the yolk mixture, and whip to blend and thicken. Thickening will take 4 or 5 minutes. To test if the mixture is ready, coat the back of a wooden spoon, and make a line through it; if the line doesn't fill in quickly, it's thick enough.

3 Let the mixture cool to room temperature, then refrigerate for 3 hours. Process in an ice cream machine, according to manufacturer's directions. When the ice cream is close to completion, but while the machine is still running, pour in the honey and lavender flowers. Remove the ice cream from the machine and spoon into a container. Cover loosely and freeze for at least 3 hours. Take the ice cream out 15 minutes before serving to allow to soften.

lavender blueberry soup

MAKES ABOUT 4 QUARTS (41/2 L)

A recipe from *Edible Flowers*, by Cathy Wilkinson Barash, and attributed to John Ash, culinary director of the Fetzer Vineyards in Hopland, California.

16   cups (4 L) fresh or frozen blueberries
1   cup (250 mL) red wine
3   cups (750 mL) water
1 1/2 cups (375 mL) honey, or to taste
1/2 cup (125 mL) orange juice concentrate
2 1/2 tbsp. (35 mL) dried lavender flowers
     Juice and rind of 3 medium lemons
2   cinnamon sticks
1   tsp. (5 mL) freshly ground black pepper
1/2 tsp. (2.5 mL) ground cloves
1   tsp.(5 mL) salt
     Crème fraîche, fresh blueberries, lavender flowers

Place all ingredients in a stock pot. Bring just to a boil, reduce heat and simmer 10 minutes. Garnish with a dollop of crème fraîche and a sprinkling of fresh blueberries and lavender flowers. Serve hot or cold.

lavender hill butter

MAKES ABOUT 1/2 CUP (125 mL)

This is the best herbal butter for grilled lamb chops—but it's equally good with fresh fish such as rainbow trout, snapper or sole. Or try it tossed with grilled vegetables, or stirred into steamed rice. Be sure to choose the freshest lavender—preferably organic—for this recipe; otherwise, it may be too strong. If you can find lavender honey, so much the better.

2   shallots, minced
2   tbsp. (25 mL) Champagne vinegar or white wine vinegar
2   tbsp. (25 mL) honey
1/2 cup (125 mL) softened butter
2   to 4 fresh lavender flower heads, minced (or 1 tsp./5 mL dried lavender flowers)
     Salt and freshly ground white pepper

1 In a bowl, combine shallots, vinegar, honey, butter and lavender flowers. Cream together until well blended. Season to taste with salt and pepper.

2 Spread a piece of plastic wrap on a clean, dry surface. Using a rubber spatula, arrange the butter along the length of the wrap. Partially cover with half of the wrap and roll back and forth with your hands until it begins to take the shape of a log.

3 Wrap tightly at both ends and refrigerate until well chilled. Slice thinly and place on hot lamb before serving. Keeps for about a week in the refrigerator.

Pruning away dead wood is an important part of lavender care in spring, and it should be started while plants are still young. Vigorous pruning encourages plants to become bushy and thick, with no straggly, bloom-free branches. Save trimmings for sachets or to toss into the fireplace.

For good fruit, make them think they're in the tropics

melons

recipes

melon with parmesan
& prosciutto

mexican melon salad

melon lassi

If you've ever tasted a freshly picked, ripe melon, you know just how sweet and deliciously scented it can be. Commercially produced melons are usually harvested about a week before full maturity, which is when they produce the most sugar, and this is as good a reason as any for growing your own melons. Growing your own also gives you the widest possible choice. I love to experiment with new types, unusual forms, odd colours and different flavours.

I think the main reason most Canadians grow melons, however, is the challenge—something you try when you find growing other things too routine. Just about anyone can grow lettuce or tomatoes, but there's a certain satisfaction and cachet in being able to say you grow your own honeydews or watermelons. Although melons are better suited to hot climates—Georgia and Arizona—than to Canadian gardens, it is possible to grow them practically anywhere in this country. Even in my Zone 4 garden situated on a cool, north-facing slope, melons do fairly well, although some years are better than others. Generally I get a really good crop every two years. Most gardeners in Canada should plant cultivars needing fewer than 75 days to maturity. The number of days listed on seed packets or in catalogues indicates results under ideal conditions. I add 20 days to be more realistic. BY LARRY HODGSON

GARDENER'S TIPS
▪ Cantaloupe-type melons contain potassium, vitamin A and folate, and are considered natural laxatives. Honeydews, on the other hand, contain only a modest amount of potassium and few other nutrients. A cup of any melon delivers about 60 calories.
▪ One melon plant normally produces two or three melons, four in a good year.
▪ Try growing catnip or nasturtiums in the melon patch to deter cucumber beetles. Or save onion skins from the kitchen and toss them around the growing plants.

Melons are native to Asia and Africa, and thrive in long hot summers. If you can fool them into thinking that's where they live, they'll reward you with plenty of sweet fruit. Left: 'Apollo'. Opposite: 'Summer Flavour 800', a pollinator watermelon, and a yelow-fleshed variety. Large photo, opening page: 'Dorado'.

growing

Melons are long-season plants that thrive in heat. Growing them in Canada requires not only effort but also deceit—you have to trick the plants into believing they're growing in the tropics. If they even suspect they're growing in Prince Edward Island or Alberta, you've lost them.

It's how long and warm the summers are that matters. The prime growing areas for melons in Canada are southern Ontario and in the central valleys of British Columbia. Prairie growers in areas where summers are relatively long won't have too difficult a time. In coastal areas of British Columbia, the Atlantic provinces and parts of Quebec, however, temperatures rarely reach the 24°C to 35°C that melons like.

Don't let that discourage you. With a little work, you can extend your summer and even make them warmer, giving your melons the conditions they require. To grow good melons you need full sun, good drainage and moderately rich soil. A good garden loam of nearly equal parts sand, clay and silt is best, but sandy soils

with plenty of organic matter are suitable. Clay soils hold too much water and remain too cool for melons. They grow best with a pH of about 6 to 7. Rather than try to modify your soil's true nature, create raised beds and fill with good organic soil. Or plant melons in mounds 30 centimetres high and 60 centimetres wide. Like raised beds, mounds heat up faster than the surrounding soil.

Start seeds indoors three weeks before the last frost date (no more), three seeds to each peat pot. Seeds need 24°C to 32°C to germinate. I find placing them on top of a fluorescent light fixture, such as a grow light, gets the temperature just right, or use an ordinary heating pad to provide bottom heat.

About the same time you start the seeds, begin to prepare the garden. Cover the planting area with plastic mulch to warm soil, or use cloches or water teepees if you're setting out plants in individual spots. Biodegradable, black plastic mulch (it converts into starch as the season advances) is widely available; there's also a product called infrared transmitting (IRT) mulch, which lets in even more heat. Meanwhile, seeds indoors begin to sprout in three to seven days. Move them to a bright, sunny spot, or close under fluorescent lights. Normal indoor temperatures (about 18°C to 24°C) are adequate, and seedlings no longer need bottom heat. Thin by cutting out the weakest seedlings, leaving only one per peat pot. Don't overwater. Acclimatize seedlings about a week before planting out: place in a warm, protected spot for a few hours the first day, bringing them indoors at night. Gradually increase exposure.

Deciding when to plant out is critical. In many areas, the air never does warm up appreciably, so trust the soil temperature instead. If it's warm to the touch (at least 21°C), go ahead, spacing plants about 60 centimetres apart. If you plant in rows, leave about two metres between the rows. If you prefer beds, make them 150 centimetres wide by at least 150 centimetres long, spacing plants 60 centimetres apart. You can also grow melons up a south-facing wall, attaching the stems to a sturdy trellis. Keep melons at least three metres away from relatives such as squash or cucumbers: cross-pollination can result in bitter-tasting melons.

If air temperatures cool off in your area (under 18°C) keep cool air off your plants. with a floating row cover. Another option is a "greenhouse" of UV-resistant plastic supported by flexible branches or metal hoops available at garden centres. Keep plants well watered through the beginning of the summer, but as the fruit forms allow soil to dry out between waterings. Don't bother fertilizing—melons are not heavy feeders and dislike nitrogen-rich fertilizers. If foliage yellows, spray with diluted liquid seaweed. If you don't mulch, cultivate cautiously: melons are shallow-rooted.

When bright yellow flowers appear, decide whether to hand-pollinate—necessary if plants are under cover or if constant rain at flowering time discourages bees. Use a small paintbrush to pick up a bit of yellow pollen from a male flower (attached to the vine with a slim stem, with no rounded ball at its base), then dust it over the stigma projecting from the centre of a female

flower (with a rounded ball at its base, the future fruit). Male flowers are plentiful; female ones are few.

pests and diseases

Apart from a bit of mildew and leaf-spot at the end of the season, which doesn't seem to harm the fruit, I've never had major problems with insects and diseases. But I'm careful to grow only disease-resistant melons and I use floating row covers early in the season, which help keep insects at bay. I also rotate my vegetables, never planting melons where I grew them, squashes or cucumber in the previous four years.

Spray insects with insecticidal soap, repeating every three to four days as needed. For insects that come out at night, try diatomaceous earth, a white powdery product derived from fossils: apply over soil, stems and both sides of leaves and stems. Reapply after rain.

harvesting

Even if melons start to form weeks apart, all the fruit on the one plant tends to ripen at the same time. Slip some straw under fruits to keep them clean, and turn them slightly as they ripen so all sides are exposed to the sun.

Melons grown on a trellis need extra support. Make a sling out of old pantyhose, attach it to the trellis, then nestle the fruit in it.

Now comes the hard part: deciding when to harvest. True melons change to their final colour when ripe. If in doubt, lift the fruit and twist it slightly: it will slip right off the stem if it's ready. Watermelons aren't so easy—usually the tendril nearest the fruit turns brown when the fruit is ripe. Allowing the plants to dry out the week before harvesting helps improve flavour. Melons are ready to eat as soon as they're harvested.

melon varieties

True melons are botanically known as *Cucumis pepo*, a category that includes a range of sweet-flavoured fruits, usually round to oblong and with or without ribs or netting. The flesh can be any colour from green to orange. Here are the main categories:

- Cantaloupe A hard-shelled melon rarely grown in this country. What Canadians call cantaloupes are really muskmelons.
- Charentais A small grey-green melon, often with darker green ribs. Its flesh is usually deep orange, sweet and highly aromatic.
- Galia A large melon with a greenish rind heavily overlaid in netting, and sweet, green, aromatic flesh. Galia seeds sold in North America are usually a cross between Galias and muskmelons—true Galias are a long-season crop, best in hot climates. Varieties such as 'Passport' are adapted to short-season areas.
- Honeydew A smooth-skinned, yellow to white melon with sweet, unscented, white to orange flesh. Short-season varieties are available.
- Crenshaw Like a large honeydew, with a yellowish rind and pale green to somewhat orange flesh.
- Muskmelon This common melon is also the earliest and easiest to grow in areas where summers are short. Its netted skin is usually ribbed, and the salmon-coloured flesh has a sweet taste. Some varieties have the typically musky scent that gave the fruit their name, but most have little odour.
- Other true melons include such tropical types as casaba melons and Persian melons (both *C. melo*), and horned melons (*C. metuliferus*), none of which are of interest in short-season climates.
- Watermelons (*Citrullus lanatus*) belong to a different genus entirely. They have smooth rinds in a variety of colours; from light green or nearly black to striped, and come in many shapes from round to distinctly oblong. The sweet, crunchy flesh is usually red and punctuated by numerous flat, black seeds, but yellow and orange strains exist, as well as seedless ones. As the name suggests, the flesh is more than 93 per cent water.
- Finally, the so-called bitter melon (*Momordica charantia*) looks more like a cucumber than a melon, and is best treated as one.

Bananas and peaches may sweeten further on the kitchen counter, but not melons. They produce not one iota of sugar after they're picked. When they're ready for picking they begin a process called "slipping": a circular crack gradually appears around the stem where it joins the fruit, and a gentle tug should free the ripe melon.

melon with parmesan & prosciutto

SERVES 6

An unbeatable combination of sweet, juicy melon, slightly bitter greens, nutty Parmesan and silky prosciutto. Make sure the cheese is at room temperature.

1   bunch arugula, washed and dried
1   muskmelon or cantaloupe, peeled and sliced thinly
1/2   lb. (250 g) Parmesan (Parmigiano-Reggiano is preferable) shavings or rough chunks
1/2   lb. (250 g) paper-thin slices of prosciutto
     Freshly ground black pepper to taste
1/2   cup (125 mL) extra virgin olive oil

Arrange arugula, prosciutto and melon slices on six plates. Toss cheese shavings or chunks on melon; give each serving a good, coarse grinding of black pepper and a generous drizzle of olive oil. Serve immediately.

mexican melon salad

SERVES 6

Colourful and a delight for melon lovers, this lovely fresh-tasting fruit salad can be made with any melon combination.

3   cups (750 mL) bite-sized chunks watermelon
1 1/2 cups (375 mL) bite-sized chunks muskmelon or cantaloupe
1 1/2 cups (375 mL) bite-sized chunks honeydew melon
1/4   cup (50 mL) fresh lime juice
1/2   cup (125 mL) fresh mint leaves, torn in small pieces
1-2   tbsp. (15-30 mL) granulated sugar

In a large bowl, combine watermelon, muskmelon, honeydew and lime juice. Sprinkle with mint and sugar; stir together. Cover and chill for 30 minutes before serving.

melon lassi

SERVES 4

A lassi is a refreshing, East Indian yogurt shake. Enjoy one for breakfast or as a cooling and delicious complement to a spicy dinner. Any type of melon can be used.

3   cups (750 mL) plain yogurt
3   tbsp. (45 mL) liquid honey
1 1/2 cups (375 mL) melon chunks
1/2   cup (125 mL) ice water
     Fresh mint

In a blender, combine all ingredients except mint, and process until mixture is frothy. Serve over ice; garnish with mint sprigs.

Melons used to be grown in beds filled with fresh horse manure to generate good bottom heat, but now that manure is less available many gardeners use solar power: they cover the planting area with black plastic to warm the soil. Above: 'Earli Dew'.

A southern belle migrates north

okra

recipes

okra with shrimp & rice

pickled okra
with fresh dill

spinach & okra soup

When I think of okra, I dream of mouthwatering Cajun and Creole cuisine, filled with the flavours of shrimp and crayfish, sweet potatoes, peppers, southern peas and tomatoes. Okra's slippery texture is ideal for thickening the delicious soups and stews, called gumbos, that are a mainstay of southern cuisines. But this very consistency makes it a "love-it-or-hate-it" vegetable. While aficionados treasure its delicate flavour and thickening ability, detractors find it downright slimy.

Okra (*Abelmoschus esculentus*) is a heat-loving tropical annual that originated in Africa, was introduced to southern Europe by the Moors, and probably brought to North America during the slave trade. Reminiscent of its relative the hibiscus, it has beautiful creamy-yellow flowers five to eight centimetres wide, with deep crimson throats. The fruits are the ridged seed pods, which can be green, white or red.

Okra is usually thought of as a southern crop, but plant breeders have developed short-season varieties that tolerate cooler temperatures. While northern yields are modest compared with those of the South, in a warm summer a few plants will be more than enough to delight okra lovers. BY HEATHER APPLE

GARDENER'S TIPS
- Okra is a good source of potassium and vitamin C, and also contains vitamin A, calcium, niacin and protein—and only a few calories.
- The leaves of okra are also edible, and highly nutritious—they contain iron, and calcium as well.
- To speed up the gemination of seed sown directly in the garden: freeze seeds in ice cube trays and then plant the cubes.

growing

Start seeds indoors four weeks before the date you'll move plants outside—after all danger of frost is past and the soil has warmed up. Soak them overnight in tepid water, then plant three seeds six to 13 millimetres deep in each five-centimetre pot. Plan on three to six plants per person, depending on your family's level of enthusiasm for okra.

Keep soil temperature at 21°C to 27°C during germination, which takes five to eight days. Grow the seedlings in a warm place with lots of light. They grow very slowly—after three weeks they may be less than nine centimetres tall, but the roots will be well developed. At this point, thin to the healthiest seedling in each pot by snipping off the unwanted plants. Transplant the seedlings to 7.5-centimetre pots, being careful not to disturb the roots, and water with a high-phosphorus fertilizer. Gradually accustom the seedlings to direct sunlight and outside temperatures before transplanting.

Plant the seedlings outside only after danger of frost is well past, the average night temperature is at least 13°C and the soil has warmed up to 18°C to 21°C. Seedlings planted too early fail to thrive and may even slowly die in cool weather. Seedlings planted later, in more optimum conditions, easily surpass premature plantings.

Choose a warm, sunny location that's well drained and sheltered from the wind, but with good air circulation to discourage fungal diseases. Dig the soil deeply and fertilize well; a pH of 6.0 to 8.0 (somewhat acidic through neutral to slightly alkaline) is ideal. When planning your garden, keep in mind that in northern climates, okra plants reach heights of 100 to 120 centimetres; similar varieties grown in the south reach 240 centimetres or more. Dwarf varieties grow 75 to 90 centimetres tall.

Plant seedlings 60 centimetres apart. Dwarf varieties can be planted 30 centimetres apart, or could be grown in containers. Dig compost or composted manure into each hole and water in the seedlings with a high-phosphorus fertilizer. Keep the seedlings well watered, but not soggy, until they're well established.

Sometimes seedlings started early indoors grow well for a while, but "dampen off" shortly before they're to be set outside—the stem rots at the place where it contacts the soil, and the plant dies. If this occurs, sow some additional seed directly into the garden at the same time as transplanting seedlings outside. Soak seeds overnight, then plant in moist soil 60 centimetres apart, using three seeds per hole; thin later to a single seedling. Keep soil warm with a plastic row cover, but remove the cover once the seeds germinate unless it has slits to allow for ventilation. Depending on the weather, one planting method may do better than the other; using both increases your chances of a good harvest.

Water established plants regularly so growth is fast and succulent. Don't over-fertilize, especially with a high-nitrogen fertilizer, or the plants will produce luxuriant vegetation and few pods. When the first pods appear, side dress with compost and water with compost or manure tea (made by soaking a bag of compost or composted manure in a pail of water overnight). Repeat midway through the remainder of the growing season.

pests and diseases

In northern climates, okra is seldom bothered with diseases or pests, but the following sometimes attack.

Japanese beetles Shiny metallic blue or green beetles with copper wing covers skeletonize the leaves by chewing between the veins. Hand-pick or use rotenone.

Corn earworms Green, yellow, pink or brown caterpillars feed on leaves. Brown or grey adult moths lay eggs on the undersides of leaves. Hand-pick, or use Bt (*Bacillus thuringiensis*) twice, at three- to five-day intervals.

Flea beetles Shiny black beetles jump around rapidly when disturbed. They chew tiny holes in the leaves, not usually a problem on large plants but they can quickly destroy seedlings. For serious infestations, use rotenone or diatomaceous earth.

Aphids They suck out plant juices, causing distorted, yellow leaves and branch tips. Dislodge them with a strong spray of water every few days, or spray with insecticidal soap, being sure to get the undersides of leaves.

Stinkbugs Shield-shaped green, brown or grey bugs that give off an unpleasant odour when crushed. They suck the plant's juices, resulting in wilted new growth and hard, distorted fruits. Hand-pick. Keep garden weeded and clean up debris in fall.

Verticillium and fusarium wilt Fungal diseases that cause yellow, wilted bottom leaves. Cutting a stem reveals a brown ring inside. With fusarium wilt, only part of the plant is initially affected, but eventually the plant dies. Plants with verticillium wilt rarely die, but fruit production is poor. To control, rotate crops.

Bud drop Caused by hot, dry air, sudden changes in temperature or poor drainage. Pods fall off when soil temperature is lower than 21°C and air temperature lower than 24°C.

harvesting

Begin harvesting short-season varieties two to 2 1/2 months after planting. Pick the pods when they're small, bright green and tender, usually five to 7.5 centimetres long, but some varieties, such as 'Burgundy', are tender to 15 centimetres or longer. Don't allow pods to ripen fully or they will become tough and fibrous. Some varieties have irritating spines on the pods and leaves; wear gloves and a long-sleeved shirt to pick. Cut pods with scissors or a sharp knife just above the cap, taking about 2.5 centimetres of stem. Handle carefully; injured pods ooze mucillaginous juice and the wounds become discoloured.

Pods ripen a few at a time. Pick every two or three days to keep the plants productive, and store unwashed pods in a perforated plastic bag in the refrigerator until you have enough for a recipe. Cut large, tough pods and put them on the compost pile—leaving them on the plant could cause it to stop producing. Plants bear until the first frost, or until the soil and air temperatures become too cool.

okra varieties

- Canadian gardeners should choose varieties specially bred for a short season and cooler climates. 'Cajun Delight', a 1997 All-America winner, is considered by many to be the best choice for northern growing. Seedlings mature in 50 to 55 days after planting in the garden, depending on the weather. Other recommended varieties are 'Annie Oakley', 'Clemson Spineless' and 'Green Best'. 'Lee' is a dwarf variety suited for containers or small gardens. 'Burgundy' produces striking plants with deep-red stems, branches and pods. The pods turn green when cooked.

growing in cool, short seasons

- By using structures to create a mini-climate, gardeners can provide okra with the approximately 3 1/2 months of the warm growing conditions plants require.
- One option is slitted plastic row covers. The row covers are simply thrown over the plants, or supported with wire hoops.
- Cold frames to protect plants can be made from old storm windows. On cold, cloudy days, cover the top with heavy clear plastic. Consider height of mature plants; growing dwarf varieties may be best.
- Put up structures well before planting time to warm the soil. Start plants early indoors or sow seed directly into the ground. To provide a season long enough to ripen pods, plants need to move outside when there are still light frosts.
- Set out seedlings on a warm, sunny day. Leave row covers on day and night; the slits provide ventilation. If using cold frames, covers must be partly or completely removed when the sun comes out or the plants will quickly cook. Until the weather warms up, add protective covering, such as old blankets or burlap sheets, at night. Put them on in late afternoon to hold in heat.
- During summer, leave the tops off the cold frames and remove row covers.

Prompted no doubt by the green pod's slightly hoary exterior and somewhat viscous interior, a friend of mine once said, "I would never eat anything that needed a shave and a Kleenex as badly as okra…" That comment notwithstanding, okra remains one of the foundation vegetables of African and Southern U.S. cooking. It lends its own particular charms to many savoury dishes, but it definitely loses its appeal if overcooked.

okra with shrimp & rice

SERVES 4

Brazilians have a way with okra. One of their favourite dishes combines fresh okra, tomatoes, garlic and toothsome, fat shrimp. Quick, simple and delicious.

1	large onion, chopped
1/3	cup (75 mL) olive oil
3	cloves garlic, finely chopped
1	hot chili, finely chopped (use rubber gloves when handling hot chilies, and avoid contact with your face)
1	28-oz. (796 mL) can whole, peeled plum tomatoes, drained; reserve juice
1	tsp. (5 mL) granulated sugar
1	lb. (500 g) fresh okra, trimmed and sliced into thirds
	Salt and freshly ground black pepper
1	lb. (500 g) uncooked jumbo shrimp, shelled and deveined
	Cooked rice
	Chopped coriander

1 In a large skillet, sauté onion in olive oil over medium heat until softened, about 5 minutes. Add chopped garlic and chili, and cook 5 more minutes.

Roughly chop tomatoes and add to skillet with half of reserved juice and sugar. Add okra, and stir gently to combine; continue to cook until the mixture begins to thicken, about 10 to 12 minutes. Season with salt and pepper to taste. (If sauce gets too thick, add some of the reserved tomato juice.)
2 Nestle shrimp in sauce and cook until they're just pink and beginning to curl, about 5 minutes (be careful not to overcook). Serve over cooked rice and sprinkle with chopped coriander.

pickled okra with fresh dill

MAKES 2 PINTS

Pickled okra is a perfect accompaniment to cold meats, cheeses or grilled sandwiches, or serve as an appetizer with Creole or Cajun-style dishes.

1	lb. (500 g) tender young okra, no longer than 2 in. (5 cm)
2	hot green peppers
2	heads fresh dill
2	large garlic cloves, peeled
1	cup (250 mL) water
1	cup (250 mL) white vinegar
6	whole black peppercorns
1	tsp. (5 mL) mustard seed
1	tbsp. (15 mL) salt

1 Wash okra and hot peppers and snip off stem ends. Sterilize two pint jars. Place 1 head of washed dill in each jar. Add 1 hot pepper and 1 clove garlic to each jar. Pack okra into jars. In a small stainless-steel or other non-reactive saucepan, combine water, vinegar, peppercorns, mustard seed and salt. Bring mixture to a boil; remove from heat.
2 Pour mixture over okra. Seal jars and let stand in a cool, dark place for two weeks. (Pickled okra can be eaten after 24 hours, but flavour is better after two weeks.)

spinach & okra soup

SERVES 6

Inspired by a Caribbean soup called callaloo (which refers to the leaves of the taro plant), this dish uses readily available spinach to combine with okra, coconut milk and crabmeat (optional) to make a terrific meal in a bowl.

1	tbsp. (15 mL) olive oil
1	large white onion, chopped
4	cloves garlic, finely chopped
1 1/2	lb. (680 g) spinach (or bok choy or Chinese spinach), washed, drained and stems removed
1 1/2	cups (375 mL) okra, sliced 1/2 in. (1 cm) thick
1	whole hot chili
3	cups (750 mL) unsweetened coconut milk (if using canned, shake can well before opening)
1	lb. (500 g) canned crabmeat, drained well, or frozen, picked clean of any cartilage or shell (crab is optional)
	Salt and freshly ground black pepper

1 In a large, non-reactive stockpot, gently warm oil over medium heat. Add onion and garlic, and sauté until onion is soft and translucent, about 5 minutes. Add spinach (or bok choy) a bit at a time and stir-fry briefly. As the greens soften slightly, add more. Add okra, hot chili and coconut milk; stir to combine. Cover and simmer gently over low heat until mixture is thick and creamy, about 30 minutes. Remove whole chili from soup. Purée half of mixture in a blender or food processor, then return it to the pot. Return mixture to a gentle simmer, and add crab, if using. Stir gently and cook 5 to 10 minutes more. Season to taste with salt and freshly ground pepper.

Juicy, sun-kissed fruit from trees that look good in your garden

peaches and PEARS

recipes

red pears & blue cheese with watercress

pickled peppery peaches

pear & almond tart

Picture a magnificent row of fragrant blossoms gracing your walkway each spring. Imagine the delights of plucking blush peaches or golden pears right off your own trees and carrying a heaping basket into the kitchen. Think about a bubbling pan of pear crisp or a peach pie fresh from the oven made with fruits from your own garden.

Although peaches and pears are challenging to grow (peaches, unfortunately, are not reliably hardy outside the warmer parts of Canada), the rewards can be great. Expect peach trees to be productive for 15 to 20 years. Pear trees will bear fruit for decades if well cared for. A single peach tree is sufficient for the home garden because it's self-pollinating, but at least two pear trees of different cultivars must be planted together to ensure successful cross-pollination and fruit set. 'Bosc' and 'Bartlett' are ideal companions.

BY MARIBETH FITTS

GARDENER'S TIPS

■ Peaches and pears deliver vitamins C and A and potassium. Pears also contain some folate and are higher in calories than peaches: about 97 for a medium pear compared to 42 per peach.

■ In the nursery, look for trees 14 to 17 millimetres in diameter and 1.5 to two metres tall. They should be free of gumming, an indicator of fungal canker, with several well-feathered, supple side branches.

growing

Both species, especially peaches, are at the northern limit of their range in southern Canada. Outside of southwestern Ontario, the Niagara Peninsula, the Annapolis Valley in Nova Scotia, some areas in the Okanagan Valley and coastal British Columbia, the risk of peach mortality increases. At 23°C or lower, bud death can occur. Even at slightly higher temperatures, peach trees are vulnerable, so a protected site is desirable.

Pears can be grown in a wider range of climates. The northern limit extends from London to Kingston and up to the Bruce Peninsula in Ontario, most of Nova Scotia and southern New Brunswick, southwestern Alberta and along the south coast of Newfoundland. Even so, pears sometimes lose flower buds when late spring frosts occur. Make sure there is sufficient room for the mature size of your tree. Farmers plant fruit trees four to five metres apart. Full sun is important for fruit development and ripening.

Peach trees need deep, well-drained soil, as they have little tolerance for wet feet. Pears are more tolerant, but heavy clay or extremely sandy soils are the least desirable. Pears grafted onto dwarf quince rootstock need soil similar to that for peaches.

Before planting, test the soil for deficiencies and to determine fertility and pH status. If the pH is less than 6.5, dig lime into the planting area long before planting. Well-rotted manure or compost can be added, provided it's incorporated the previous fall. Spring is the best time to find decent nursery stock. The trees should be planted with the soil line at

about two centimetres below the graft unions. You don't need to trim the roots of nursery trees when planting, and a fertilizer high in nitrogen isn't advisable.

Early in the second and subsequent springs, however, apply a balanced fertilizer around the drip line of each tree containing about 40 grams of nitrogen for each year of growth. For example, a five-year-old tree needs 200 grams of 10-10-10 fertilizer. Neither peaches nor pears should be fertilized any later than the end of June, as this may compromise their winter hardiness.

Weed control is very important in the first few years after planting, as weeds compete with young fruit trees. Keep the area around the trees well mowed and hand-pull grass and weeds close to the trunks. Straw mulch works well, but watch out for rodents.

Pears shouldn't be left to ripen on the tree. They'll develop brown centres and soft flesh. Pick when stems swell where they attach to the twig, and the fruit begins to turn colour.

Trees need at least three centimetres of water each week, through rainfall or irrigation. Make sure to soak the soil.

About the third year, peaches of eating quality will start to develop. Pears, however, take five or six years. Because fruit buds for the next year are established in late summer or fall, the amount of blossom and fruit set will often reflect the growing conditions of the previous summer.

Despite losing a number of fruitlets early in the season, the result of June drop, every year peach and pear trees generally set more fruit than they can support. Both species need to be hand-thinned beginning in mid-June, once fruits start to develop; if it isn't done, fruits won't reach their full size, and the tree may become so heavy with fruit the branches snap off. For peaches, thin the fruit to about 15 centimetres apart. Pears should be thinned to about one fruit per spur (fruiting stem).

diseases and pests

There will be considerably more disease and insect pressure if the trees are growing close to commercial plantings of fruit trees. Wet growing seasons increase susceptibility to diseases, while hot, dry weather is conducive to more pests.

Peaches Oriental fruit moth (larvae bore into ripening fruit) and aphids can be problems. Brown rot is the most common fungal disease, but peach leaf curl can eventually kill the tree if left uncontrolled.

- Apply lime sulfur spray when the tree is dormant to help reduce leaf curl.
- Use soap sprays to control aphids.
- Apply a sulfur spray just before and after blossom, and again when symptoms are noticed, to minimize brown rot. Also practise good sanitation around the tree, such as removing mouldy fruit.

Pears They're subject to a number of the same pests as apples, including codling moth and oblique-banded leafroller. Soft-bodied insects, such as psylla and mites, sometimes feed on the tree, making it and the fruit quite unsightly. Pear scab can render the fruit inedible.

- To reduce pear scab, use a combination of sulfur sprays and make sure leaf litter is cleaned up in fall.
- Soap sprays keep pear psylla at bay.
- To reduce the numbers of codling moths, regularly remove dropped fruit.
- Prune infected parts of the tree to prevent the spread of fire blight.

Four-footed animals can also be major pests to young fruit trees. Rabbits, deer and voles love to munch on newly planted trees. Deter by wrapping trunks with plastic tree guards or painting with a mixture of latex paint and thiram fungicide (animals don't like the taste). Commercial formulations available include Skoot and Rabbit Repell. High fencing may be necessary if deer are prevalent.

pruning

Nursery trees should be pruned shortly after transplanting, with a central-leader shape the most desirable. Prune the leader down to one to 1.5 metres. Remove all broken or weak side branches and shorten the rest, leaving about seven main branches, with the first side shoot branching out at least 25 centimetres below the top of the tree.

In the second and subsequent years, pears should be pruned in late winter or very early spring, before budbreak. With peaches, wait until the buds are swelling or close to blooming so you can see what tissue is alive. For both peaches and pears, prune out any dead, broken or weak wood. Also remove any strong, upwardly growing branches that are competing directly with the central leader. Then eliminate crossing side shoots by pruning out one of the overlapping branches. Finally, remove side branches that are close to the ground or growing up from the roots.

pear picks

There are a number of new varieties available, but many of the old familiar names are still the most reliable and winter hardy, according to Ken Slingerland, tender-fruit specialist with the Ontario Ministry of Agriculture and Food. They are generally grafted by the nursery onto standard 'Bartlett' rootstock, or sometimes on dwarf quince rootstock.

'Bartlett'	'Anjou'
'Bosc'	'Giffard'
'Flemish Beauty'	'Clapp's Favourite'

peach picks

A variety of early, mid-season and late peach cultivars can be selected to extend the harvest season for as long as a month.

Early
'Brighton'	'Harrow Diamond'
'Garnet Beauty'	

Mid-season
'Harrow Fair'	'Redhaven'

Late
'Cresthaven'	'Madison'
'Harcrest'	'Vanity'

Pears marry well with blue cheeses and nuts in a salad, or broiled with Gorgonzola and served as an appetizer. Peaches steeped in port are a simple dessert treat.

4 Just before serving, toss watercress with vinaigrette and distribute dressed greens on individual plates. Crumble cheese over the greens, then arrange the pears, followed by the walnuts. Serve immediately.

pickled peppery peaches
MAKES 2 PINTS (1 LITRE)

Wonderful with ham, sausage or any rich meat, this easy recipe uses just a few peaches, although you could double the amount. Choose slightly underripe peaches so they retain their crunch. Don't worry about peeling them; just use a coarse towel to rub off most of the fuzz. Because this isn't a traditional canning process, the finished product must be kept in the refrigerator.

1   cup (250 mL) white wine vinegar
2   tbsp. (30 mL) granulated sugar
2   tbsp. (30 mL) black peppercorns, coarsely cracked
4   small to medium-sized peaches, left whole

1 Have ready two sterilized pint jars, lids and seals. Using a whisk, combine vinegar, sugar and peppercorns in a mixing bowl. Stir until sugar is completely dissolved.
2 Pack peaches into pint jars. Add vinegar mixture until it comes 3/4 of the way up the peaches. Cover with lids and turn jars upside down a few times to distribute liquid evenly. Refrigerate, giving the jars the same upside-down treatment once or twice a day. After about a week, peaches will be ready to serve. They'll keep for about two weeks in the refrigerator.

red pears & blue cheese with watercress
SERVES 4 TO 6

Few foods complement each other as well as pears and blue cheese. In this colourful salad, fresh watercress provides a pleasant peppery counterpoint to the sweet pears and pungent cheese. Bring cheese to room temperature before using.

Vinaigrette
1/4   cup (60 mL) extra virgin olive oil
2   tbsp. (30 mL) fresh lemon juice
1   tbsp. (15 mL) Dijon mustard
1   tsp. (5 mL) granulated sugar
1   tsp. (5 mL) salt
    Freshly ground black pepper, to taste

Salad
1/2   cup (125 mL) walnut halves
2   bunches watercress, rinsed and dried thoroughly
2   'Red Bartlett' pears, unpeeled, cored, quartered and sliced
1/2   lb. (225 g) Gorgonzola cheese (or your favourite blue)

1 To make the vinaigrette: In a large bowl, whisk together oil and lemon juice. Whisk in mustard, sugar, salt and pepper. Adjust seasoning. Reserve.
2 Preheat oven to 350°F (180°C). Scatter walnuts in a single layer on a baking sheet; toast for about 10 to 12 minutes—no more, or the walnuts will burn.
3 Meanwhile, pick through watercress, discarding any tough bits, then transfer to a wide mixing bowl.

pear & almond tart

SERVES 6 TO 8

This is a simple, classic tart with few ingredients. It's important to roll the pastry as thin as possible—it will puff up when baked. You can make six or eight individual tarts instead of one large one, and use fresh peaches, apricots or apples in place of the pears.

1/2 pkg. (375 g) frozen puff pastry, thawed
1/2 cup (125 mL) ground almonds
3 pears, peeled, cored and thinly sliced
3 tbsp. (45 mL) unsalted butter, melted
3 tbsp. (45 mL) sugar

1 Roll out pastry very thin, about 1/8 in. (3 mm), and about 10 to 11 in. (25 to 28 cm) in diameter. Wrap pastry over the rolling pin and transfer to a fluted tart shell. Use a fork to prick the pastry in a few places. Refrigerate for 20 minutes.

2 Preheat oven to 425°F (220°C). Sprinkle pastry shell with almonds and arrange pear slices in a concentric pattern, ending with a few in the centre. Brush or drizzle with butter and scatter sugar over the surface.

3 Bake for 30 minutes until light golden brown. Serve warm with unsweetened whipped cream or vanilla ice cream.

Sweet or hot, they're loved by gardeners and cooks

peppers

recipes

grilled peppers
with cheese

peperonata

pepper & eggplant
spread

When Christopher Columbus arrived in what he believed to be the Orient, he was served a pungently hot dish that he assumed was seasoned with black pepper, a spice so costly in his time it was literally worth its weight in gold.

Columbus had actually landed in the Caribbean and the dish wasn't spiced with black pepper (*Piper nigrum*), but with the little green fruits of the totally unrelated *Capsicum annuum*. However, the "pepper" misnomer stuck.

Members of the nightshade family, peppers are believed to have originated in central South America, and by Columbus's time they'd spread to Central America, the Caribbean and what's now the southwestern U.S. Columbus took seeds back to Europe, while Portuguese and Spanish explorers carried them around the world. There are peppers to suit every taste, from mild, sweet bell peppers to incendiary habaneros, in a rainbow of colours—green, yellow, orange, white, red, purple and chocolate brown—to please both gardeners and cooks.

Many varieties require a long, warm growing season, but plant breeders have produced a number of sweet and hot short-season varieties that, with proper growing techniques, give good yields throughout most of Canada. BY HEATHER APPLE

GARDENER'S TIPS
▪ Peppers are low in calories and rich in vitamin C, potassium and amino acids. Red ones are an excellent source of vitamin A. Research suggests that peppers, especially hot ones, help prevent blood clots and lower cholesterol.
▪ Peppers with thin skins are ideal for drying.
▪ Capsaicin, the chemical in hot peppers that gives them their heat, has been used experimentally to treat chronic pain because it short-circuits pain messages to the brain.

peppers in pots

A number of dwarf, ornamental peppers can be grown in containers. The bottom of the container must have several drainage holes; cover with 2.5 centimetres of coarse gravel, or use screening or landscape fabric. Fill the container with equal parts compost and high-quality potting soil, then place in full sun in a sheltered location. Plant out seedlings at the same time as they would be planted in the garden. Keep containers moist but not soggy. Fertilize every other week with a diluted fertilizer mix or compost tea.

- 'Dainty Sweet'—Pointed peppers change from green to yellow to purple to red as they mature.
- 'Marbles'—Small hot peppers turn yellow, purple, orange and flame red as they mature.
- 'Thai'—An heirloom variety with tiny, red, cone-shaped fruits. Ripe peppers are incendiary!
- 'Varengata' (also know as 'Varingata') or 'Variegata'—White, lavender, purple and green variegated foliage; purple peppers ripen to bright scarlet.
- 'Super Chili'—Short, spreading plants bear up to 300 super-hot peppers that mature from light green to orange to red. Use fresh, dry or pickled.
- 'Prairie Fire'—The tiny, pungent fruits of this prostrate, fan-shaped plant mature from chartreuse to cream to yellow to orange to red.
- 'Pretty in Purple'—Leaves are purple or variegated purple and green. Masses of small, pungent peppers ripen from purple to yellow to orange to scarlet.
- 'Fruit Basket'—Low, spreading plants are ideal for hanging baskets. The sweet fruits mature to golden orange.

growing

Start seeds eight to 10 weeks before seedlings are to be planted outside, a week to 10 days after the last spring frost. Plant four seeds per pot in five-centimetre pots filled with a light, water-retentive potting soil mix that's been well watered. Plant seeds 0.5 centimetres deep, and put the pots in a warm place, covered loosely with plastic. Germinate at 27°C to 30°C, using an electric heating pad underneath or lights above to create warmth. Seedlings sprout in one to two weeks.

During germination, keep the soil moist but not soggy; use warm water. As soon as seedlings germinate, remove the plastic. Daytime temperatures should be 20°C, 15°C at night. Peppers require lots of light to grow—tall, leggy plants produce poorly. Grow lights are best; or put seedlings in a sunny, southern window with supplemental lighting in the evenings and on cloudy days.

Once seedlings have developed their first set of true leaves, choose the best plant in each pot and cut off the rest. Give a diluted fertilizer when the second set of leaves appears, then feed every other week with half-strength fertilizer.

As plants begin to outgrow the pots, transplant into 10-centimetre containers, spaced for optimum light. Seedlings may need transplanting into larger pots before planting out.

Two weeks before planting, harden off seedlings by gradually increasing the amount of sun exposure over two weeks. Don't put the peppers outside if the temperature falls below 15°C.

Pepper plants produce poorly if planted out too early, so wait until the soil has warmed to 18°C. Help speed warming by loosening the soil and covering it with plastic, or by making raised beds.

Plant in a sunny, sheltered location in rich, organic, well-drained soil. Set plants 45 centimetres apart with rows 60 to 90 centimetres apart. Dig a hole for each plant three times the size of its root ball and mix in compost. If soil is poor or if you're short on compost, sprinkle fertilizer into the hole and mix well. Bury up to the first leaves—the plant will grow roots along the buried part of the stem. Water in with lukewarm water. Pinch off the tiny fruits so they don't drain the plant's energy. Cover soil with plastic or place flat stones around the plant's base to soak up the sun's heat; the stones warm the soil at night. Cover young plants with a floating row cover until they start to flower; remove when the temperature under the cover reaches 30°C.

In hot summers, add mulch once the temperature is consistently hot. Soil temperatures under 10°C or over 30°C stunt roots and affect growth and yield.

Make sure plants receive 2.5 centimetres of water a week. Each month, gently dig compost into the soil around the plants. Low nitrogen results in pale leaves and few flowers, but fertilizers high in nitrogen result in bushy, fruitless plants. Stake tall plants for support.

Above: green and red cayenne peppers. The redder they get, the hotter they are. Thin skins make them ideal for drying. 'Super Cayenne II' is a long tapered variety that turns red in 75 days.

harvesting

Most peppers start off green and mature to their true colours. Pick the first fruits as soon as they reach full size, leaving later fruits to ripen fully; otherwise plants will stop producing. Cut off with scissors or a knife, and include a bit of a stem.

Green peppers hold a week or two in the refrigerator, red peppers about a week. Peppers freeze well, chopped or halved. Thin-walled peppers, such as cayenne, dry well whole or cut in half.

If frost threatens, pull up the plant and hang it upside down in a warm, dry place. Strip off leaves as they yellow. The peppers will ripen in a couple of weeks.

pests and diseases

Temperatures below 13°C or above 30°C cause blossoms to drop. Consistently low night temperatures (13°C to 15°C) result in small, misshapen fruit. In hot areas, choose varieties resistant to blossom drop caused by heat, such as 'Ace'. In cool areas, plant early varieties.

Sunscald Blistered areas form on the fruit if the plant is suddenly exposed to direct sunlight. Keep plants well fed to encourage leaf cover. Do not prune.

Blossom end rot The blossom end of the fruit looks water-soaked; the area enlarges and turns black and leathery caused by water stress or calcium deficiency. Water deeply and regularly; dig a sprinkling of ground limestone or wood ashes around plants.

Cutworms Caterpillars cut off the stem near the soil surface. Place a collar—half a toilet roll, strips of newspaper, plastic or metal—around the stem and insert 2.5 centimetres into the soil.

Aphids Tiny green insects suck the juices from plants and spread viral diseases. Wash off with a shower of water.

Anthracnose Spots appear on ripe fruit, merging into large areas. Leaves and stems may also be affected.

Bacterial spot Wart-like raised spots with slightly sunken centres appear on fruit. Spots form on leaves, which may fall off. Blossoms may drop.

Verticillium and fusarium wilt Foliage yellows and parts of the plant wilt, eventually threatening the entire plant.

To deal with disease, use prevention: provide good air circulation; space plants well apart and weed regularly. Water early in the day. Don't work around plants when leaves are wet. Don't plant tomatoes, potatoes, eggplant in the same place for four years. Destroy affected plants.

Grilled peppers with cheese are a great side dish or filling for tacos or tortillas. Most peppers are green in their unripe stage and mature to yellow, orange, red or chocolate brown, their mature colour. The mature peppers have fuller flavour than green ones, and all freeze well chopped or stuffed.

grilled peppers with cheese

SERVES 6

A smoky pepper appetizer perfect with crusty bread. Also good as a side dish, or a colourful filling for soft tacos or tortillas. *Queso fresco*, a mild, slightly salty cheese, is sold in plastic tubs in food stores that carry Latino products. You can also use farmer's or cottage cheese.

1   large white onion, thickly sliced
1   tbsp. (15 mL) olive oil
     Salt and freshly ground pepper to taste

4   fresh Anaheim (or Poblano) chili peppers
2   red bell peppers
2/3   cup (150 mL) packed fresh coriander leaves
1/2   cup (125 mL) sour cream
2   large cloves garlic, roasted
1/2   cup (125 mL) *queso fresco* (see above)

1 Lightly grease grill; preheat to medium-high.
2 Hold onion slices together with a water-soaked toothpick; brush both sides with oil. Season with salt and pepper. Grill for about 5 minutes; set aside.

3 Grill whole chili peppers for about 6 minutes and whole bell peppers for 15 to 20 minutes or until softened and lightly charred. Place peppers in a paper or plastic bag, seal and let cool. Wearing rubber gloves, peel and seed peppers. Cut into strips and set aside.
4 In a blender or food processor, combine coriander, sour cream, garlic and cheese. Blend until coriander is finely chopped. Using a spatula, scrape mixture into a medium-sized saucepan set over medium heat. Add reserved onions and peppers; heat gently for a few minutes. Serve warm.

peperonata

SERVES 4 TO 6

Capture the vibrant flavours of summer-ripe vegetables with this classic Italian dish. In Tuscany, potatoes would be added and in Sicily, green olives. Delicious with roast pork, veal or grilled sausages, on pasta, in sandwiches or as part of an antipasti table.

1/4	cup (60 mL) olive oil
3	cloves garlic, chopped
2	large red onions, sliced
2	large red bell peppers, cut into strips
1	large green bell pepper, cut into strips
1	large yellow or orange bell pepper, cut into strips
2	large ripe plum tomatoes, peeled, seeded, roughly chopped
1/4	cup (60 mL) chopped flat-leaf Italian parsley
2	tbsp. (30 mL) balsamic or red wine vinegar
	Salt and freshly ground black pepper to taste

1 In a large, heavy-bottomed skillet, warm olive oil over medium heat. Add garlic and onions; cook, stirring occasionally, for 10 minutes or until softened.

2 Add peppers; stir to coat with oil, adding more olive oil if necessary. Cook, stirring occasionally, for 20 minutes or until vegetables are tender and beginning to brown.

3 Stir in tomatoes, parsley, vinegar, salt and pepper. Cook 10 minutes longer, stirring occasionally. Serve at room temperature.

pepper & eggplant spread

SERVES 4

This spread is packed with flavour, thanks to the slow-roasted eggplant. Roast over a grill, a gas flame or in the oven. Delicious with a selection of raw vegetables, or with grilled pita or other flatbread. Drizzle with a little more extra virgin olive oil before serving, if desired.

1	medium eggplant
1	each, red, orange and yellow bell pepper, seeded, chopped
1-2	jalapeno or other hot chili peppers, seeded, chopped
3	tbsp. (45 mL) extra virgin olive oil
4	cloves garlic, thinly sliced
	Salt and freshly ground black pepper to taste
1	tsp. (5 mL) cumin
1/2	tsp. (2 mL) lemon juice

1 In the oven, roast eggplant at 400°F (200°C) for about 30 minutes or until eggplant softens and flattens, turning occasionally, charring it on all sides. To grill, randomly pierce the eggplant, then place directly over a hot fire, about 10 to 15 centimetres from the coals. Turn to cook on all sides, until skin is charred, about 45 minutes to one hour. Allow to cool after cooking.

2 Next, sauté bell and chili peppers in olive oil over medium heat. Once softened, add garlic, salt, pepper and cumin; mix well and remove from heat when all vegetables are quite soft.

3 Working over a bowl, remove eggplant skin and discard, allowing any juices to collect in the bowl. Roughly dice flesh and add to bowl. Return peppers to heat and add eggplant and juices. Cook for a few minutes until all ingredients are well incorporated and mixture begins to thicken.

4 Using a blender or food processor, lightly blend the mixture; don't purée. Add lemon juice; adjust seasoning if required. Serve warm or at room temperature.

Add character to your vegetable patch with a zesty Mexican fruit

tomatillos

recipes

mushrooms
in salsa verde

tomatillo & chicken
enchiladas

tomatillo & avocado salsa

Exotic-looking tomatillos are a bit deceptive: inside papery lantern-shaped husks nestle slightly sticky green fruits that resemble small green tomatoes. The two names even sound similar. But the similarities end there. The flavour of slightly immature tomatillos is sour with a hint of lemon and fruitiness. The texture is different, too: tomatillos are seedy but solid, without the juicy cavities of tomatoes.

Tomatillos (*Physalis ixocarpa*) are one of the traditional ingredients in Mexican cooking, along with chilies and cilantro. Some English translations of Mexican recipes substitute green tomatoes for tomatillos, but for authentic-tasting dishes, don't interchange them. The fruit grows on sprawling 90- to 120-centimetre-tall annual plants, and of the nearly 100 species of *Physalis*, most native to Central and South America, the few available to gardeners are often misnamed in seed catalogues. Sometimes they're incorrectly called husk tomatoes or ground cherries, two names more accurately applied to *P. pruinosa*, also referred to as Cape gooseberry or strawberry tomato. Cape gooseberry plants bear small, yellow fruits enclosed in papery husks, similar to tomatillos but sweeter. A close relative to the tomatillo is Chinese lantern (*P. alkekengi*); its papery, bright orange husks, like miniature glowing lanterns, are often dried for bouquets. BY HEATHER APPLE

GARDENER'S TIPS
■ Tomatillos may be small but they're packed with nutrition—one medium-sized fruit contains 91 mg of potassium, 4 mg of vitamin C, 3 mg folic acid and 39 IU of vitamin A.
■ The papery husk around a tomatillo is really an enlarged calyx: as the fruit matures it fills the calyx and splits it open.
■ When buying tomatillos, select hard ones, like unripe tomatoes, with dry husks.
■ The Cape gooseberry may be a close relative, but it's not interchangeable with tomatillos in recipes.

timing is everything

- The yellow flowers of tomatillos keep producing fruit right up until fall frosts. As the fruit grows, the enveloping husks change colour from green to tan and become increasingly filled, splitting open as the fruit reaches maturity. The fruits change colour from green to pale yellow or purple, depending on the variety, and continue to ripen and sweeten for a week or so after they're picked.

- Tomatillo fruits are picked at different stages of maturity, depending on their intended use. For making salsa, pick them when they're sour—they're still green and don't yet fill the husks. For eating fresh, or for making preserves, allow the fruit to mature fully.

growing

Tomatillo plants are prolific; two produce enough fruit for the most serious salsa lovers. Start seeds indoors when you start tomatoes—about six weeks before the date of the last expected frost. Fill five- to eight-centimetre pots with starter mix and plant three seeds per pot, three millimetres deep.

Germinate the seeds at 20°C. As soon as the seedlings break through the soil, usually in three to five days, place pots under grow lights or in a sunny window. Bright light is essential or the plants become weak and leggy. To encourage bushy plants, space pots so each plant receives good light on all sides. Once seedlings grow to 2.5 to 5 centimetres, thin to the healthiest seedling per pot. Fertilize with compost or manure tea (made by soaking a bag of compost or composted manure in a pail of water

overnight) or half-strength fish emulsion once a week if you're using a soilless mix, or every 10 to 14 days if growing in potting soil. When the seedlings begin to get root-bound, transplant to 10-centimetre pots.

After the danger of frost has passed and the soil has warmed up, harden-off the seedlings by gradually introducing them to direct sunlight and cooler outdoor temperatures. If a late frost threatens, bring them inside for the night.

Plant hardened-off seedlings in a sunny, well-drained site. Dig a hole several times larger than the root ball and work in lots of compost or composted manure. Plant about 90 centimetres apart. After transplanting, keep the plants well watered until they've recovered from the shock of transplanting. Tomatillos need little care throughout the season except for watering and weeding. Once a month, fertilize with compost or manure tea. Don't overfertilize, especially with a high-nitrogen fertilizer, or you'll get plenty of leaves and few fruits.

Tomatillos are vigorous plants and sprawl on the ground if left to their own devices. Sprawling does no harm, but to conserve garden space and make harvest-

Tomatillos have been grown in the United States since the middle of the 19th century and were traditionally used in pies and preserves, or dried in sugar and eaten like raisins. But they never caught on in Canada and even in the U.S. they gradually slipped into oblivion once homemade preserves went out of fashion. It's taken the recent interest in Mexican cuisine to put them back on greengrocers' shelves and in seed catalogues. The skin and flesh of 'Purple' turn a decorative royal shade at maturity. Store fruit in the light to intensify the purple pigment.

ing easier, grow them in tomato cages or stake them. They sometimes self-seed in all but very cold, short-season areas. To encourage this, allow some of the ripe fruit to remain on the ground in the fall. In spring, thin the volunteer plants, transplanting extras to other spots. Self-seeded plants often bear fruit as early as or even earlier than plants started indoors; however, it's best to experiment with this method first before counting on it as a source of plants.

Tomatillos are generally healthy and disease-free. They're not susceptible to tomato blight, a bonus for gardeners who have a problem with this disease.

varieties

'Toma Verde' Produces fruit 2.5 to five centimetres in diameter, well protected by a papery husk. Matures 60 to 70 days after transplanting.

'Indian Strain' A smaller, faster-maturing variety than 'Toma Verde' and other large-fruited types. Upright plants with dark green foliage; fruits add a sweet-sour flavour to salads and salad dressings. Matures in 55 days.

'Mexican Strain' Preferred for Mexican dishes because of its unique, savoury flavour; also good in pasta sauce. Matures in 65 days.

'De Milpa' A Mexican heirloom that yields small to medium-sized fruits that are less juicy than other varieties. Can be stored for several weeks strung like garlic with the husks pulled back. Fruit has a blush of purple after harvest. Matures in 70 days.

'Purple' Skin and flesh turn a decorative royal purple at maturity. Husks are green or buff. After harvesting, store fruit in the light to intensify the purple pigment. Matures in 65 days.

As fruits grow, their husks change from green to tan and split open. The fruits change colour, too, from green to pale yellow. For their sweet but distinctively citrusy taste, pick before fruit becomes too soft.

mushrooms in salsa verde

SERVES 4

Try a combination of oyster, portobello, cremini or trumpet mushrooms, and serve as a vegetarian main course with grilled tortillas or pita bread.

10 tomatillos, husked, quartered
1 fresh jalapeno pepper, trimmed and halved
2 cloves garlic
1/4 cup (50 mL) chopped fresh cilantro
1/4 cup (50 mL) chopped fresh flat-leaf parsley
3 tbsp. (45 mL) olive oil

3/4 lb. (375 g) assorted mushrooms, roughly chopped
1/4 tsp. (1 mL) salt
    Freshly ground black pepper
3 tbsp. (45 mL) mild goat cheese, crumbled

1 In a food processor or blender, combine tomatillos, jalapeno, garlic, cilantro and parsley. Purée just until smooth. Set aside.
2 Warm oil in a large skillet set over medium heat. Add mushrooms and sauté about 5 minutes, stirring occasionally. Add salt and pepper to taste and sauté another 2 minutes. Add tomatillo mixture, stir to combine well and continue to cook another 4 minutes, or until mixture thickens.
3 Transfer to a serving dish and let cool to room temperature. Sprinkle with goat cheese.

tomatillo & chicken enchiladas

SERVES 4

For a light entree, serve slightly spicy enchiladas with a cooling salad of shredded iceberg lettuce and cucumbers.

For the sauce
11/4 lb. (625 g) tomatillos, husked and quartered
1/2 cup (125 mL) water
1 large clove garlic, peeled
2 fresh chili peppers (jalapeno or serrano)
1/4 tsp. (1 mL) salt
1/4 tsp. (1 mL) freshly ground black pepper
1/4 cup (50 mL) chopped fresh coriander

For the enchiladas
4 boneless, skinless chicken-breast halves
1 cup (250 mL) chicken broth
8 corn tortillas
1 cup (250 mL) sour cream
1-2 cups (250-500 mL) shredded Monterey Jack cheese

To make the sauce
1 In a medium-sized saucepan set over high heat, combine tomatillos, water, garlic, chilies, and salt and pepper. Bring to a gentle boil, reduce heat and simmer about 20 minutes, or until tomatillos are soft.
2 Transfer the contents of the saucepan to a blender and purée the mixture until almost smooth. Add coriander and blend until smooth. Set sauce aside.

To make the enchiladas

1 In a skillet or saucepan, gently poach chicken breasts in chicken broth over medium heat (if broth doesn't cover chicken, add a little hot water), about 10 to 15 minutes. Be careful not to overcook. Remove chicken from broth and cool slightly. When cool enough to handle, shred chicken with your fingers.

2 Preheat oven to 375°F (190°C). Wrap tortillas in a clean, damp tea towel and warm gently for a few minutes in the oven. Evenly distribute shredded chicken among the 8 tortillas and add 1 to 2 tbsp. (15 to 30 mL) of the tomatillo sauce to each. Begin rolling up each tortilla from the bottom, fold in sides, and finish rolling. In a lightly greased, ovenproof dish, place enchiladas seam-side down in a single layer.

3 Pour remaining tomatillo sauce over the enchiladas and dot with sour cream. Sprinkle shredded cheese over all. Bake 6 to 8 minutes, or until cheese melts and begins to brown.

tomatillo & avocado salsa

MAKES ABOUT 3 CUPS (750 ML)

Think of this as guacamole with a difference. The tomatillos give a wonderful depth of flavour. Serve it as a side dish to grilled chicken, pork, shellfish or fish steaks, or as an appetizer with tortilla chips.

1	small white onion, finely chopped
2	slender green onions, finely chopped
3	cloves garlic, minced
2	tbsp. (30 mL) chopped fresh cilantro
1/2	lb. (250 g) tomatillos, husked and chopped
2	large ripe avocados
	Juice of 1 lime
	Salt and freshly ground black pepper

1 In a medium-sized mixing bowl, combine white and green onions, garlic, cilantro and tomatillos.

2 Halve the avocados, remove the pit and peel; chop in 1/2-in. (1-cm) chunks. Add to tomatillo mixture along with lime juice, and salt and pepper to taste. Gently mix together, and serve. If not using immediately, cover with plastic wrap and refrigerate.

How to bring out the flavour of the king of the garden

tomatoes

When it comes to tomatoes, I'm fickle. I seldom grow the same variety twice. It's not just the hope for better flavour that makes me so unfaithful—it's curiosity. A few summers ago I grew eight new cultivars that could only be described as curious: the slender yellow 'Banana Legs' was one of them. I thought I might as well throw the genetic dice into the air and have fun. All were rather vaguely advertised as tasting either "unusual" or "superlative." I break the taste of our favourite summer vegetable into five categories:

▪ Sugary includes all the cherry tomatoes with the word "sweet" in the cultivar name, like 'Sweet 100' and 'Sweet Million'.

▪ Acidic is the mouth-puckering flavour that comes from most early-maturing determinates. Good ones: 'Early Girl', 'Kotlas', 'Scotia'.

▪ Robust is the flavour most gardeners aim for. Most paste tomatoes and almost any late-ripening variety can reach this pinnacle.

▪ Different encompasses a range of unusual overtones, including spicy, like the heirloom 'Brandywine'; concentrated, like 'Currant'; or musky, like 'Tiny Tim' when it's grown indoors.

▪ Bland Low-acid is a more popular but less accurate description.

   Pretty well any home-grown tomato can also be called delicious, especially if it's complemented with basil, oregano, cilantro or chives, or brightened with a dash of salt. BY JENNIFER BENNETT

GARDENER'S TIPS
▪ One medium tomato contains 35 calories, 380 grams of potassium and 40 per cent of the average person's daily requirement of vitamin C.
▪ Plants described as determinate produce fruit at the ends of the branches and sprawl over the soil. Use cages. Indeterminates grow fruit along the stem and continue to grow and produce all season. Use a strong stake and prune to one main stem.

choosing cultivars

I've never tasted a tomato I didn't like, provided it was healthy and had ripened outdoors, on the vine. It's that process of maturing outdoors—roots in the warm, moist soil, foliage in the sun—that brings out a tomato's full flavour, whatever the variety. To harvest the best flavour from the tomatoes in your garden, choose a cultivar that ripens before the first fall frost. That means starting seeds early indoors or buying good-sized transplants in spring, and choosing cultivars that mature within your frost-free season. Huge-fruited beefsteaks advertised as tasting fabulous won't reach their potential if you have to pick them green and ripen them in the kitchen. Beefsteaks usually require 72 to 75 days from transplanting outdoors till the first fruit ripens. However, the earliest-ripening tomatoes (like 'Siberia', which needs only 54 days) generally don't match the

taste of those that require a longer season, so don't be too cautious. Grow the early types because they're early, as well as a few later ones for their full, height-of-summer flavour.

In other words, as in raising children, both nature (the cultivar you choose) and nurture (how you grow it) play a part in how a tomato turns out. A good-tasting tomato is a contented tomato, one that's had a stress-free upbringing. Plants that

don't have to struggle to survive can spend their energy creating sugars and the hundred or so components of rich tomato flavour.

disease resistance

All tomato plants need full sun, well-drained soil and freedom from disease. Some supposedly luscious heirloom tomatoes, like 'Brandywine', are susceptible to diseases, so if your garden harbours fungal diseases—and most do—you might end up harvesting better flavour from a more disease-resistant variety, whether hybrid or open-pollinated. In my own garden I've picked larger crops of blemish-free fruit from cultivars bred to resist alternaria and verticillium wilt, two of the most common diseases. Disease resistance may be described in a seed catalogue's small print, or it might be designated by an initial, such as 'A' or 'V', after the cultivar name. Last year, for instance, the large, red hybrid beefsteak 'Big Beef' did especially well for me. The fruit was large, unblemished, prolific—and delicious. Introduced in 1994, 'Big Beef' is resistant to many diseases.

growing conditions

Tomato stress can also come from setbacks like exposure to prolonged drought or cold, or even high heat, which prevents fruit from setting. You may need to protect your plants from cold at both ends of the season. In the spring, small plants fit under big plastic pop bottles that have had their bases removed; in the fall, I cover mature plants with tarps or plastic when an early frost is expected.

Supplies of water and fertilizer need to be even and adequate—not too much, not too little. I water the ground deeply with a watering can whenever the soil is dry under the top one centimetre. During a summer drought, this may mean four

Tomatoes are fast-growing, heat-loving plants. Unless you have a greenhouse or a cold frame to move young plants into, don't start seeds too early indoors. Plants become leggy and weak. A month to six weeks before the soil warms up is fine. 'Yellow Pear', above, ripening on the vine, is an heirloom tomato with a mild taste good in salads, especially paired with 'Sweet Million'.

Fully ripening tomatoes outdoors on a vine growing in the sun contributes to their flavour. 'Purple Calabash', left below, is a beautifully ridged deep-coloured fruit.

litres of water per plant twice a week. Never apply ice-cold water—if you use tap or well water, let it sit for a while to warm up. Cold water on the roots acts much like cold air on the leaves, slowing the development of plant and fruit alike. In early June, I mulch with straw or spoiled hay to hold in the soil's moisture and warmth and lessen fungus problems. (The mulch prevents soil-borne fungi from splashing up on the leaves.) The only fertilizer I use is a spadeful of compost per plant when planting out seedlings. I grow my vegetables organically, despite one experiment at McGill University, reported in 1995, which concluded that organically grown tomatoes taste no better than those grown using synthetic fertilizers. Specially formulated tomato fertilizers do a good job, but you shouldn't assume that extra fertilizer of any type will improve tomato flavour. A panel of tomato tasters in Florida came to the opposite conclusion, declaring tomatoes given the least nitrogen to be the best tasting.

favouring flavour

Having fertilized and watered appropriately, you might still notice that your tomatoes taste different from the same variety grown elsewhere. My friends and I hold a tomato party on Labour Day every year, and when we compare our harvests we notice differences from garden to garden. When a tomato is picked affects its taste—not everyone waits till tomatoes are fully ripened before picking them—but every soil and every type of water, too, subtly influence the flavour. Watering with seawater, for example, has been shown to improve tomato flavour, though it simultaneously decreases fruit size.

At harvest time, there are a few things you can do to maximize flavour. Protect the plants during brief cold periods or frosty nights, but if a long cold spell is forecast, harvest entire plants or branches, or any individual fruits beginning to ripen. Once a tomato has been picked, whether green or ripe, store it at room temperature, never in the refrigerator; refrigeration harms the tomato metabolism that creates full flavour. Green tomatoes don't need light to ripen, but they need warmth—setting them on a windowsill is fine as long as they don't get too hot. The best temperature for storing tomatoes is around 20°C. Don't slice a tomato till just before you serve it; chemicals that produce its aroma and flavour quickly dissipate into the air. Coddle those tomatoes. Think of it as prolonging summer weather, as warm and sweet as the fruit of your garden.

saving seeds

- If your favourite home-grown tomato is open-pollinated (not a hybrid), it's easy to save seeds for next year's crop. (You can save hybrid seeds too, but the resulting tomatoes may not look or taste like the parent.)
- If you intend to save seeds, it's best to grow different varieties at least three metres apart to prevent cross-pollination and keep your varieties pure. Save seeds from only the healthiest plants. Let a tomato stay on the vine till overripe. Pick it but do not wash it. Cut it in half crosswise, squeeze or scoop the pulp and seeds into a jar, and discard (or eat) the skin. Allow the jar to sit, uncovered, at room temperature for a couple of days so the mixture of seeds and pulp ferments. Then pour the mixture into a sieve, rinse it with cool tap water, spread the cleaned, wet seeds out on a paper towel or dish towel and let them dry thoroughly. Store them in labelled envelopes in tightly lidded jars kept in a cool, dark place. Tomato seeds kept dry should remain viable for several years.

the sweet science of tomato flavour

- A tomato's flavour comes from its own unique balance of acid and sugars, spiced up with essential flavour and aroma components with names like (Z)-3-hexenol, some of which develop only in the last few days of ripening. Like any chemical reaction, tomato ripening depends on temperature. A ripening temperature between 13°C and 27°C makes for best flavour; too much cold or heat at any stage takes a toll. As a tomato ripens, starch is converted into sugar, tissues soften, pigments are synthesized, essential oils and other flavour components develop and the acid content gradually lowers from about 4.2 pH to 4.6 pH. (Higher numbers mean a move toward neutral, at 7.) Tomatoes taste best if they ripen on the vine. Despite claims that some varieties are low acid, the level is fairly constant among varieties and is independent of ripe fruit colour. Tomatoes that taste low in acid are actually higher in sugars such as glucose and fructose.

During the height of the season many people boast of eating tomatoes
three times a day. Toasted tomato sandwiches with mayo and lettuce are
a favourite, for breakfast, lunch or supper.

tomato sandwiches

MAKES 4

These are best when tomatoes are at
their peak. Use a good grainy bread or
a baguette.

4   ripe tomatoes
1/2   cup (125 mL) mayonnaise
2   tbsp. (25 mL) pesto
8   slices of bread

2   tbsp. (25 mL) olive oil
       Salt and freshly ground pepper

1 Slice tomatoes thickly. Combine
mayonnaise and pesto.
2 Spread 4 slices of bread with pesto
mayonnaise. Overlap slices of tomato.
Drizzle with olive oil and season with
lots of salt and pepper. Top sandwiches
with remaining 4 slices of bread.

sea bass with tomato & olive sauce

SERVES 4

A Moroccan-inspired recipe for thick, buttery sea bass. Substitute grouper, halibut or monkfish, if desired.

1/4	cup (50 mL) chopped coriander
1/4	cup (50 mL) chopped parsley
2	cloves garlic, chopped
1/4	cup (50 mL) lemon juice
3	tbsp. (45 mL) olive oil
1	tsp. (5 mL) ground cumin
1	tsp. (5 mL) paprika
	Salt and pepper to taste
	Pinch cayenne
1/2	cup (125 mL) white wine
4	chopped fresh or roasted or canned tomatoes, puréed
4	6-oz. (170-g) sea bass fillets
1/2	cup (125 mL) cracked green olives

1 Preheat oven to 425°F (220°C). In food processor, chop coriander and parsley together. Add garlic, lemon juice, olive oil, cumin, paprika, salt, pepper and cayenne. Purée until paste-like. Reserve 2 tbsp. (25 mL) of the mixture.

2 Combine wine, tomatoes and spice mixture. Add to baking dish. Place sea bass in baking dish, skin side down. Rub remaining 2 tbsp. (25 mL) spice mixture over top of fillets.

3 Bake sea bass 15 minutes, add olives and bake 5 minutes longer, or until white juices appear. Place on serving platter surrounded by sauce.

roasted tomatoes

Roasting tomatoes gives them deep flavour, particularly if the tomatoes are not at their best. Once roasted, they can be stored, refrigerated, for up to two weeks. Use them in sauces, or mixed with other vegetables such as zucchini and eggplant. Roast any kind of tomatoes, but plum tomatoes, because of their thicker skins, work best. For a fast first course, fill roasted tomato with mozzarella cheese, bake until cheese melts, then pop on top of a salad.

6	tomatoes
1	tbsp. (15 mL) olive oil

1 Preheat oven to 450°F (230°C). Cut tomatoes in half and place cut side down on oiled baking sheet. Roast 20 to 25 minutes, depending on size and juiciness. Tomato skin should be slightly brown and cracked. Reserve for later use.

capellini with fresh tomato salsa

SERVES 4 AS A MAIN COURSE, 6 AS AN APPETIZER

Capellini or angel hair pasta is a perfect match for fresh tomato sauce. Serve as a first course or as a main dish with a salad on the side.

8	tomatoes
1/2	cup (125 mL) olive oil
1/4	cup (50 mL) chopped fresh basil
1	tsp. (5 mL) red wine vinegar
	Salt and freshly ground pepper
1	lb. (500 g) capellini
1/2	cup (125 mL) grated Parmesan cheese

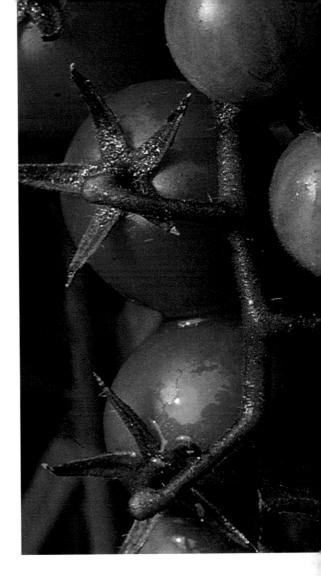

1 Cut tomatoes in half and seed them. Cut into chunks. Place in a bowl and toss with oil, basil, vinegar and seasonings. Marinate 2 hours.

2 Place pasta in a large pot of boiling water and boil 3 or 4 minutes, or until al dente. Drain and toss with tomato mixture. Serve with cheese.

fall

APPLES

GARLIC

GRAPES

JERUSALEM ARTICHOKES

KIWI

KOHLRABI

Once the sun crosses the celestial equator and the days are almost equal to the nights, we enjoy a more mellow time in the garden. The days are golden, the nights cool, and summer's crops are almost done. But the fruits and vegetables of fall are coming into their own. As you snip and pick, reflect on the past season's successes and failures. Did you have a ready supply of your favourite rosy tomatoes? Perhaps the few ears of corn you were able to raise in your small garden were admittedly delicious, but successive plantings of salad greens would make better use of the space. Mull over these considerations as you bring in the harvest, and remember that trying something new next year will add to the fun.

As Canadian as its people: no two varieties are alike

apples

My experience with apples is as a collector and a propagator. Much of my life has been spent gathering varieties I thought stood a chance of surviving in my Petitcodiac, New Brunswick, orchard, which is in Zone 4b. This has taught me that no two apple varieties are alike—each has a defining shape, a distinctive blend of sweet, tart and bitter flavours, a crisp or mealy texture, and a unique colour and pattern of spotting and striping. Of course, I've also learned there's a huge difference in susceptibility to diseases, the most common afflictions being scab, fire blight, cedar-apple rust and powdery mildew, and that disease-resistant varieties are by far the easiest to grow.

Today's apples are descendants of those brought by early European settlers and of seedlings later found naturalized across North America. Some of our best-known, such as 'McIntosh' or 'Red Delicious', are susceptible to diseases and difficult to grow without fungicides. Most modern disease-resistant apples owe their origins to Fred Hough, from the University of Illinois, who, during a severe outbreak of scab in 1943, noticed one crab apple tree was not affected by the disease. Although his plan to use the tree to develop a new strain of scab-resistant apples was met with laughter, he and several colleagues began a process whose impact is only now being appreciated. We owe him a lot. BY BOB OSBORNE

GARDENER'S TIPS
■ It may be true that an apple a day keeps the doctor away: the fruit is high in potassium and soluble fibre, and contains vitamins C, A, B_1 and B_2, as well as niacin, anti-oxidants and flavanoids.
■ One serving (a medium-sized apple, one cup of applesauce or 170mL of juice) contains 80 calories.
■ If you have a fireplace keep the prunings from your apple tree— it's one of the most fragrant of all woods.

Dwarf trees are not as vigorous as regular-sized trees, but they're much easier to pick from at harvest time. Right: 'Redfree' is juicy and mild; the yellow 'Greensleeves' crisp and tart; 'Freedom' is good for cooking and eating; and 'Spartan', a 'McIntosh' offspring, is sweet and crisp.

growing

Optimum cultural conditions help all plants stay healthy and productive, and apples are no exception. Apple trees should have a minimum of eight hours of sun a day. Trees grown in semi-shade are spindly and don't bear much fruit; sun also plays a vital role in the maturing and colouring of fruit. Plants prefer well-drained soil—moisture is necessary, but bog-like conditions suffocate roots. Rich soil is important, too. Trees rely on nutrients from the billions of micro-organisms found in decaying organic material. If you're planting a tree—bare root or potted—backfill the hole with a mixture of topsoil, compost, bonemeal, and fish or bloodmeal. For trees already planted, spread a layer of compost 2.5 to five centimetres deep on the ground below the tree's canopy every year in late fall or early spring. This mulch also helps prevent annual weeds from germinating and keeps the soil moist. Apply it several centimetres away from the trunk—excessive moisture can cause it to rot. Space dwarf-sized trees 180 to 300 centimetres apart; semi-standards 3.6 to 4.5 metres; and standard-sized trees 4.5 to 6 metres apart.

harvesting

Harvesting apples is one of the most pleasurable and satisfying tasks in the garden. When your tree bears depends on the variety of apple, on the rootstock (dwarfing rootstocks cause a tree to bear earlier than standard rootstocks) and on the conditions. Fertile soil, adequate water, ample sunshine and proper spacing all work toward early fruit production. Be sure to wait until the fruit is properly ripe. When mature, apple seeds turn from white to tan or brown. Cut open an apple to assess your crop's ripeness. Apples picked at optimum ripeness taste better and store longer.

pests and diseases

Disease-resistant varieties are still prone to insect attack. The most common pests are the codling moth and apple maggot. Pesticides help control the pests, but organic products and methods work, too. Pheromone traps, for example, substantially reduce damage from codling moths. Adult codling moths lay eggs on leaves and twigs in spring as petals begin to fall; days later, hatching larvae tunnel inside newly formed fruit. The traps, which should be in place as soon as trees start to bloom, stop the cycle: they release molecules that mimic sex attractants of the female codling moth. Males fly to the traps and are caught by a sticky lining.

Pheromone traps are also available for apple maggot flies, which also create tunnels in apples.

Another way to control apple maggots is with sphere traps. The sticky, red plastic balls are hung like Christmas ornaments, and the flies, mistaking them for fruit, get stuck to the surface. Set out traps for apple maggot flies in mid-June, or three weeks after petal fall.

Good housekeeping also helps control pests. Apple maggots, for example, overwinter in the soil after emerging from fallen fruits, so it's important to dispose of fruit rather than leaving it on the ground to rot.

choosing a hardy variety

- Apple trees sold today are reproduced by budding or grafting one or several buds of a desired cultivar to the rootstock of another variety. The rootstock is chosen primarily for its ability to impart productivity to the variety, its cold hardiness and its ability to create a standard-sized tree or dwarf-sized tree. When you buy an apple tree, choose a variety of fruit that's hardy to your area, and also a hardy rootstock—dwarfing or standard. But it's not quite this simple.

- With an average mature height of three metres, versus six metres for semi-standards and eight metres or more for standards, dwarf trees are a more manageable fit into your garden if you don't have much space. The apples are easier to pick, and you'll also have an earlier harvest—the rootstock diverts energy from stem and leaf growth to seed production.

- However, trees on dwarfing rootstocks are typically less vigorous than those on semi-standard or standard rootstocks, and tend to be shorter lived. The average lifespan of a dwarf-sized tree is 30 years; for a standard-sized tree it's 70. Dwarf trees require deep, rich soil and conscientious watering, and staking is sometimes required. In other words, they require more effort than standard-sized trees to keep them in good health. A local nursery can recommend the best rootstocks for your soil and climate. Dwarf trees for mild areas such as British Columbia, southern Ontario and southern Nova Scotia are often put on the Malling series of rootstocks from England. If you live in Zone 5 or colder, you should look for hardier rootstocks—the hardiest dwarfing rootstocks are 'Ottawa 3', 'Budagovsky 9' from Russia, and the 'P series' from Poland. Hardy standard rootstocks include 'Antonovka', 'Anis', 'Borovinka' and 'Beautiful Arcade'.

Here are some sweet, warm apple desserts—and not a traditional pie or crisp among them. This is fall comfort food at its best.

apple croustade

SERVES 6

A croustade is a rustic pastry shell used for both sweet and savoury fillings. The pastry is rolled out in a large circle, the filling placed in the middle, and the edges of the pastry are folded toward the centre, partially covering the filling.

Use your favourite pastry recipe if you wish; just make sure you have enough for about a 14-inch (35-centimetre) crust. Add a little lemon juice to the apples as you slice them to keep them from browning.

Pastry

1 1/3 cups (325 mL) all-purpose flour
1/4 lb. (125 g) butter (or 1 stick), chilled
1 tbsp. (15 mL) granulated sugar
 Pinch salt

Filling

1 1/2 lb. (750 g) apples, peeled, cored and thickly sliced
1/3 cup (75 mL) granulated sugar
2 tbsp. (25 mL) butter
1 tbsp. (15 mL) cornstarch
1/4 tsp. (1 mL) allspice
1/4 tsp. (1 mL) nutmeg (freshly grated is best)
1 egg white, beaten
 Granulated sugar for dusting
 Whipping cream, unsweetened and lightly whipped

1 To make pastry, combine flour, butter, sugar and salt in a food processor. Using an on/off motion, process until mixture resembles bread crumbs.

2 Transfer mixture to a medium-sized mixing bowl and add about 2 tbsp. (25 mL) of cold water; gently toss with a fork until mixture forms a loose ball. If necessary, add a little more cold water. Wrap ball of pastry in plastic wrap and chill about 1 hour.

3 Have an ungreased baking sheet handy. Roll dough out on a lightly floured surface to a circumference of about 14 inches; wrap it around a rolling pin and transfer to the centre of the baking sheet.

4 Preheat oven to 400°F (200°C). In a mixing bowl, combine all filling ingredients and stir together, making sure cornstarch is well dissolved.

5 Pile prepared fruit in centre of the pastry. Turn up edges of pastry so it partially covers the filling. (Edges are meant to be a little uneven.)

6 Brush pastry with egg white and dust with sugar. Bake on highest shelf in the oven 30 to 40 minutes, or until pastry is golden brown. Let cool slightly before serving warm with barely whipped, unsweetened cream.

pommes au beurre

SERVES 4

Sweet and spicy, apple slices sautéed in butter and sugar are a simple classic of the French country kitchen. They're wonderful with French toast or pancakes (don't forget the maple syrup), or piled over vanilla ice cream.

1/4 cup (50 mL) butter
2 lb. (1 kg) apples, peeled, cored and sliced
1 tsp. (5 mL) cinnamon
1/2 tsp. (2 mL) freshly grated nutmeg
3 tbsp. (45 mL) granulated sugar

1 In a large skillet, melt butter over medium heat. Add apple slices, spices and sugar. Using a metal spatula, turn apples over a few times to coat well.

2 Sauté for a few minutes on one side until fruit begins to turn pale gold, then flip fruit gently to colour the other side. Serve hot and drizzle with thick pouring cream or warm custard.

A local nursery can recommend the best rootstocks for your soil and climate. Dwarf trees in mild areas are usually grafted to Malling stock from England. Lower than Zone 5 look for 'Ottawa 3', 'Budagovsky 9' or Poland's 'P' series.

mele fritte (apple fritters) jenna

SERVES 4 TO 6

This is one of the ways apples are enjoyed in the Italian region of Lombardy. Try serving them with mascarpone cheese that's been thinned with a little whipping cream.

2   cups (500 mL) all-purpose flour
1   egg
1 1⁄4 cups (300 mL) whole (homogenized) milk
1 1⁄4 cups (300 mL) water
3   apples
     Vegetable oil for frying (enough to cover apple slices as they cook)
     Icing sugar or granulated sugar for dusting

1 Place flour in a mixing bowl, making a well in the centre. Add egg and whisk it into flour. Gradually whisk in milk and water to form a batter. Cover with plastic wrap and refrigerate for about 30 minutes.

2 Meanwhile, line a platter with paper towels and set aside. Peel, core and thinly slice each apple into 16 pieces. Remove batter from fridge. Add apple slices to the batter, turning and tossing to coat evenly.

3 In a deep, heavy saucepan, add oil to a depth of 2 to 3 inches (5 to 7.5 centimetres); heat over medium-high heat to 375°F (190°C). Add coated apple slices in batches, and fry, turning once or twice, for about 3 minutes, or until golden brown on both sides.

4 Remove with a slotted spoon to the platter, sprinkle with sugar and serve immediately.

The universal flavouring—easy to grow, easy to eat

garlic

recipes

roasted garlic purée

aioli

garlic chicken

roasted vegetables with
roasted garlic vinaigrette

Be suspicious of anyone who doesn't eat garlic, a Romanian proverb counsels. Worshipped by ancient Egyptians, chewed by strength-seeking Olympic athletes in ancient Greece and used, according to European folk traditions, to keep vampires at bay, garlic has been around for millennia. A member of the onion, or allium, family, the herb has become one of the most common flavourings in the world.

Anyone who's tasted home-grown garlic knows of its superior taste. Happily, it's easy to grow and amenable to winter storage. There are many varieties—more than 500 strains are documented. The classification system, however, is informal. Growers sometimes rename varieties, resulting in several different names for the same one, but all fall into two basic types: hard neck and soft neck. Garlic with cloves clustered piggyback-style in layers, is soft-neck (or non-bolting) garlic. Hard-neck (sometimes called rocambole) is said to be closer to wild garlic. It has large cloves growing against a thick central stalk. The stalk is generally snipped off so the plant can put its energy into bulb formation. Neither is more pungent than the other—in fact, you get a gamut of flavour in both groups—but rocambole is easier to work with in the kitchen, especially for baking whole. For braiding, and storing, some consider the soft-neck variety best. BY LAURA LANGSTON

GARDENER'S TIPS
■ Garlic may be low in vitamins and minerals, but its health benefits are impressive: it lowers cholestrol, thins the blood and as an antibiotic fights about 70 infectious agents.
■ Cooked garlic may be more appealing than raw garlic, but keep in mind that allicin, the component credited with garlic's therapeutic qualities, is destroyed by prolonged cooking.

Elephant garlic isn't garlic but a member of the leek family, the result of cross-pollination between garlic and leeks. And it isn't hardy in Canada, although purchased bulbs store well. It's also less pungent than garlic.

growing

Because garlic needs roughly 100 days to mature (small varieties may mature in 90 days), it's best to plant cloves in the fall, three or four weeks before the ground freezes, for a harvest the following year. "About the same time you plant your tulip bulbs," says Ted Maczka, who owns Fish Lake Man in Demorestville, Ontario. August is too early, he says, because the garlic grows four or five

the great healer

Pliny the Elder thought garlic cured madness and snake bites. Hippocrates treated tumours with it. Physicians in the First World War used it to kill bacteria when they dressed wounds.

Today, the humble bulb is touted as one way to lower cholesterol levels and chase away colds. Pet owners say it wards off fleas and ticks. And in Japan, soaps and lotions using deodorized garlic powder are thought to increase blood circulation to the skin.

Garlic's healing properties can be attributed to allicin, one of its key ingredients. Also the source of its odour, pure allicin was recognized as a powerhouse by Louis Pasteur. Today, at least a thousand studies have been published on the health benefits of garlic. They show it inhibits dysentery, attacks typhoid fever and slows the growth of some cancer cells. Japanese and Indian researchers are currently studying its benefits in treating tuberculosis, arthritis and diabetes. Garlic increases the flow of bile, and garlic juice is used in China to treat pulmonary tuberculosis.

Even if health isn't an issue, garlic helps in the garden. Because it masks insect-attracting scents, it helps deter insects from attacking roses, tomatoes and cabbages. A spray made of puréed garlic and chili peppers keeps away aphids and spider mites.

leaves above ground, then frost hits and kills the leaves, causing the bulb to rot.

Plant after a hard frost but three or four weeks before the ground is completely frozen. In milder climates, such as coastal British Columbia, it could be November or December. Late-fall planting allows root development. You can also plant garlic when the ground is workable in early spring: April in most parts of Canada. Yields will be smaller, since the cloves won't have developed strong roots.

Choose a sunny location with good drainage. Garlic doesn't like wet feet. It prefers rich, sandy loam with plenty of humus. Dan Jason, of Salt Spring Seeds on Salt Spring Island, B.C., recommends compost or well-rotted manure, but not too much. Soil that's too fertile produces good garlic but the bulbs may not be as pungent as you'd like.

Maczka is careful never to plant garlic where onions have grown the previous year. "Bugs from the onions could easily move to the garlic," he says. He also favours raised beds, although they may drain too quickly and need extra water.

Once the bed is prepared, gently break

the bulbs apart and loosen the cloves, being careful not to loosen the skin. Plant individual cloves base (the wide end) down, about five centimetres deep so the pointed end is about 2.5 centimetres below soil level. Jason leaves 10 to 12 centimetres between cloves so each has plenty of nutrients available, but says eight is acceptable in rich, sandy loam. If you mistakenly plant cloves upside down, yields will drop by about half because some cloves won't sprout.

Fertilizing is optional. At planting time, Maczka gives his garlic a dose of manure tea and repeats the process a few times during the growing season. Another option is to apply a balanced organic or synthetic fertilizer, such as 5-5-5 or 10-10-10.

Both growers recommend mulching garlic in fall with about an inch of hay, straw, grass clippings or leaves, unless you normally get good snowcover with no mild spells to melt it. Not only does the mulch encourage root growth during winter, it discourages weeds in spring and helps retain water. Mulching can mean the difference between getting a good crop of garlic and not getting one at all.

"We don't always get enough snowcover where I am in Ontario," Maczka says. "Sometimes we get two weeks of mild weather. The ground may be frozen solid but the mild weather warms up the top and the garlic starts growing, but eventually dies because its roots can't penetrate the frozen soil. Mulch prevents this."

Fall-planted garlic is usually the first thing to jump out of the ground in spring. If the weather is dry during the growing season, garlic appreciates a good soaking once a week and it doesn't like to compete with weeds. "The weeds can shade it and the crop will be poor," Maczka says.

Watch for flowers on hard-neck garlic. If a round bulb forms (usually in late

spring), cut it off to allow the plant to put its energy into bulb growth rather than seed formation. Maczka recommends breaking the flower heads off when they're seven to 10 centimetres above the leaves—usually in June. And don't throw them out; they're a delicacy.

Garlic may be one of the best first crops for novice gardeners. "The time I spend with garlic is probably a hundredth of the time I spend with everything else," says Jason. "Not only is it low maintenance, but in 15 years I've never had a pest or disease problem."

Jason does know gardeners, however, who've had outbreaks of grey rot, or mould, in their garlic. He says there were two probable causes: the garlic was a California variety, so not well suited to the Canadian climate, and his friends didn't practise yearly crop rotation, something Jason says is important for disease prevention.

Maczka stresses the importance of buying good seed garlic, and not planting supermarket garlic because it's mostly imported, and isn't acclimatized to our seasons. And while supermarket garlic is safe to eat, it isn't inspected for diseases such as rot or nematodes, which may infect crops. Maczka occasionally has a problem with nematodes, tiny pests that move into the bulbs in spring, swiftly turning the garlic leaves yellow. The only option is to destroy the whole plant.

harvesting

Garlic generally grows about waist high and is usually ready to harvest when one-third to two-thirds of the foliage dies back or turns yellow in mid- to late July or early August. To allow maximum bulb curing underground, don't water garlic for a few weeks before harvest.

If the soil is loose, pull the garlic by hand to avoid puncturing the bulbs; otherwise, dig the bed carefully. Loosen the soil from the roots and lay or hang the garlic to dry. Drying outdoors is tricky because the garlic may cook in the heat of the sun; it's not until weeks later when you notice a rotten smell that you realize what's happened.

Maczka layers his garlic on the ground in bunches so the leaves protect the bulbs from direct sun. Another option is to hang the bulbs in a cool, dry place like a barn or garage, or to be sure they're in the shade outdoors. In one or two weeks, when the leaves turn brown, the garlic is cured. Gently rub remaining dirt from the bulbs, being careful to keep as much skin intact as possible. Cut away the roots and tops, and the garlic is ready to store.

Don't, under any circumstances, store garlic in the refrigerator. The cloves sprout and lose flavour. Instead, keep it in open containers such as baskets or mesh bags. In a cool, dark place, bulbs should keep four to six months. Don't worry if they lose weight as the months go by; garlic continues to lose small amounts of water.

As tempting as it might be to use all your harvest in the kitchen, save some cloves for planting. Jason likes to save the biggest cloves from the biggest bulbs for his next crop. Maczka, on the other hand, prefers small and medium-sized bulbs. "I think large cloves aren't as potent for reproduction," he says. "Smaller ones are more eager to produce better-sized bulbs."

braided garlic

A coil of braided garlic is decorative as well as useful. But the rules for storing garlic still apply: hang it away from heat and light.

The ideal time to braid is when the garlic stems are half brown but still pliable—fresh garlic may develop mould because of poor air circulation around the bulbs in the braid. Soft-neck types are usually easier to work with because their stalks aren't as stiff and thick as hard-neck varieties.

You'll need 8 to 10 heads, and natural jute or raffia (not string, which may contain creosote) to tie off the finished braid.

Working on a flat surface, start with three bulbs with the stalks facing you. Braid the three stalks together once or twice, pulling on the stalks so the heads are clustered next to each other.

Lay the fourth bulb on top of the braided stalks, just below the cluster of the first three bulbs. Place the stalk of the fourth bulb with the stalk in the centre of the braid and bring the far right stalk up and over all the other stalks. Take the stalk on the left and bring it up and over all the other stalks.

Now lay another bulb below the cluster of bulbs, letting its stalk rest with the centre group of stalks. Bring the right section of stalks up and over. Continue to build the braid, adding one head at a time, always bringing the stalks up from the bottom. Like all braids, you'll have three streams, or sections, of stalks at any one time—it's much like French-braided hair. By the time you add your last head or two of garlic the braided stalks will be quite thick.

When the last head has been added, continue braiding the three streams of stalks, incorporating a few sprigs of dried herbs, if desired, until you have 10 to 12 centimetres of braid below the last bulb. Tie off the end of the braid with jute or raffia.

To mute garlic breath, eat a handful of fresh green herbs such as lovage, parsley or celery. Roasted cloves are delicious with roasted vegetables accompanying beef or pork.

roasted garlic purée

MAKES ABOUT 1/2 CUP (125ML)

A whole head of garlic cooked until soft and mellow loses its characteristic bite and becomes a mild-mannered vegetable. Combine it with goat cheese for a spread for toast or crackers, use to flavour a sauce, or beat into mashed potatoes. It keeps about a week in the refrigerator.

1	or more whole heads garlic, unpeeled
1	tbsp. (15 mL) olive oil

1 Preheat oven to 350°F (180°C). Cut off about 1/4 in. (6 mm) from top of head to slightly expose cloves. Sprinkle with oil. Wrap in a double thickness of aluminum foil. Bake 45 minutes, or until garlic is soft and slightly brown.
2 Remove base of garlic with a sharp knife. Squeeze garlic cloves into a bowl, discarding skin. Purée cloves in food processor.

aioli

SERVES 4 TO 6

A dip to serve with raw vegetables, smoked ham, hard-boiled eggs, boiled potatoes, cold roasted chicken, mushrooms, boiled shrimps, mussels or oysters—or anything you love to eat. Drinking a small glass of brandy mid-feast is supposed to prevent gastric discomfort caused by raw garlic.

2	cloves garlic, chopped
2	egg yolks
1	cup (250 mL) olive oil
1	tbsp. (15 mL) lemon juice
	Salt and freshly ground pepper

1 Combine garlic and egg yolks in food processor. With machine running, pour olive oil slowly down feeder tube until

it's incorporated and mixture thickens. Stir in lemon juice. Season with salt and pepper to taste.

garlic chicken

SERVES 4

Make ahead of time to point of baking, refrigerate and bake when needed. Serve with couscous or roasted red potatoes.

1	head garlic, separated into unpeeled cloves
4	chicken breast halves, skinned and boned
1/4	cup (50 mL) all-purpose flour
	Salt and freshly ground pepper
1	tbsp. (15 mL) finely chopped fresh rosemary
2	tbsp. (30 mL) olive oil
4	oz. (100 g) ham, thickly sliced and diced
1	red onion, thickly sliced
3	tbsp. (45 mL) brandy
2	tbsp. (30 mL) finely chopped parsley

1 Preheat the oven to 375°F (190°C). Add garlic to a pot of cold water and bring to a boil. Boil 3 minutes, drain and peel garlic cloves.
2 Cut chicken breasts into 2 halves down the centre. Cut each piece in thirds. In a shallow dish, combine flour with salt and pepper to taste, and 1 tsp. (5 mL) rosemary. Coat chicken pieces with flour mixture.

3 Heat olive oil in a large skillet on high heat. Brown chicken in batches about 1 or 2 minutes per side. Remove with a slotted spoon to a baking dish. Turn heat to medium-low. Add ham to skillet with onion, garlic and remaining rosemary. Sauté until onion is golden-brown, about 10 minutes. Pour brandy over mixture; bring to a boil.
4 Scrape contents of skillet over chicken breasts. Dish can be kept in refrigerator for up to 24 hours. Remove one hour before ready to bake. Bake 15 to 20 minutes, or until chicken is cooked through. Sprinkle with parsley.

roasted vegetables with roasted garlic vinaigrette

SERVES 6

A great side dish for a barbecue or a first course to serve with a mixture of romaine and radicchio.

1	butternut squash, peeled
2	red peppers
2	sweet potatoes, peeled
2	medium red onions
12	brussels sprouts
1	tbsp. (15 mL) chopped fresh thyme or 1 tsp. (5 mL) dried
1/4	cup (50 mL) olive oil
	Salt and freshly ground pepper to taste

1 Preheat oven to 450°F (220°C). Cut squash, peppers and sweet potatoes into 1-in. (2.5 cm) cubes. Cut onion in half and each half into 4 wedges. Cut off root end and separate onion pieces. Slice brussels sprouts in half. Place all vegetables in a large bowl.

2 In a separate bowl combine thyme, olive oil and seasoning. Toss with vegetables until coated.

3 Place all vegetables in a single layer in a roasting pan. Use 2 pans, if necessary, to keep vegetables in one layer.

4 Roast vegetables 25 to 35 minutes, stirring every 10 minutes, or until they're cooked through and browned. Toss with Roasted Garlic Vinaigrette and serve.

Roasted garlic vinaigrette

2	tbsp. (30 mL)	roasted garlic purée
2	tbsp. (30 mL)	red wine vinegar
1	tbsp. (15 mL)	chopped red onion
2	tbsp. (30 mL)	fresh lemon juice
1/3	cup (75 mL)	olive oil
2	tsp. (10 mL)	chopped fresh mint
		Salt and freshly ground pepper

1 Whisk together garlic purée, vinegar, onion and lemon juice. Slowly whisk in olive oil. Add chopped mint and salt and pepper to taste. Serve over roasted vegetables.

Hail the ancient grape, nectar of the gods

grapes

recipes

salmon in grape leaves
with verjuice butter

seedless grape tart

vineyard chicken

When grapevines come to mind, people usually imagine exotic fruit hanging from picturesque pergolas in subtropical hot spots, not vines scrambling along their very own fences. Grapes are probably the oldest cultivated fruit, and could have just as easily snared Adam and Eve in the Garden of Eden as the apple. Throughout history the fruit has been associated with revelry and joy. For gardeners who love grapes, the same can still hold true.

Grapevines are surprisingly easy to grow. Cuttings can even be rooted in a sand bucket, which is how they are sometimes started at the federal breeding station in Morden, Manitoba. Vines can spread over arbours, providing shade and a stunning patio decor. Naked, woody vines can be twisted and knotted for wreaths.

But getting the vines to produce mature fruit is another game altogether. It takes long, hot summers and lots of sunshine to produce fruit for wine, juice, jelly, or just for nibbling.

That's why southern Ontario's long sultry summers helped commercial growers harvest 47,738 metric tonnes of grapes in 1996, with nearly two-thirds going into wines, according to the Ontario Grape Growers' Marketing Board. A lesser amount, about 10,000 tonnes, is harvested annually in southern British Columbia, also mainly for wine. BY MARLENE ORTON

GARDENER'S TIPS
■ One cup of grapes contains about 12 grams of calcium, 175 mg of potassium and 92 IU of vitamin A.
■ Grape seeds have been found in the remains of Bronze Age dwellings n Switzerland and in the tombs of ancient Egypt.
■ Allow grapes to ripen on the vine. Once picked, they won't ripen further.
■ If mature-sized grapes aren't ripening, pinch back foliage-bearing side shoots to one leaf to allow more sunlight and warmth to reach the clusters.

Wild grapevines, sometimes called riverbank grapes, are commonly seen in rural areas and make a lush canopy or trellis. 'Concord' is a popular blue grape, a *labrusca* hybrid suitable for Zone 5 and warmer. It's used for jelly, desserts and juice.

varieties

Gardeners in the warmer parts of the country have their pick of many grape varieties, including 'Concord', probably the most famous blue dessert, juice and jelly grape in North America. But it needs up to 150 days to turn out beautiful fruit. For shorter-season, colder Canadian regions, two of the hardiest are 'Valiant' and 'Beta', hybrids bred from *Vitis riparia*, a native vine (nicknamed the riverbank grape) that's common to rural landscapes in southern Manitoba, Quebec and New Brunswick. Boughen's Nursery in Valley River, Manitoba, has been selling *riparia* since Ron Boughen's grandfather started the family business in 1890, but Ron prefers the hybrid 'Valiant', as does Robert Osborne, a grower in New Brunswick.

Although a clear favourite, 'Valiant' is not flawless. Last summer, for the first time, Osborne noticed powdery mildew on the fruit, the most common affliction to affect grapes in the East. (Downy mildew is more common in Western Canada.) But Osborne was able to control the mildew's spread with a homemade baking soda solution.

Most grape varieties sold in Canada come from a complicated lineage that includes cross-breeding several generations of hybrids derived from three species: *Vitis riparia* and *V. labrusca*, native American grapes known for their hardiness and berry size, and the European *V. vinifera*, a more tender vine used for wines and seedless table grapes. 'Himrod', a common seedless white table grape available at many Ontario and British Columbia nurseries, is half *vinifera* and therefore less likely to withstand severe winters.

planting

Spring is the best time to plant, in well-drained soil, in a protected site and against a sturdy support, from an elegant arbour to a garage wall. Dig a generous hole, mixing in bonemeal or well-rotted manure if the soil is poor. Plant vines at least 1.5 metres apart, at the same level they grew in the nursery.

"Some vineyards in France practically grow on gravel," says grape specialist Campbell Davidson of Agriculture Canada's research centre in Morden, Manitoba. "Grapes don't need fertile soil, but they do demand high temperatures for the fruit to ripen. They're quite drought tolerant because they have deep root systems." Ideal temperatures in September, when the fruit ripens, are between 20°C and 25°C; above 10°C at night.

training and pruning

You don't need an arbour to grow grapes at home; a simple three-wire trellis will do. Fasten three horizontal wires on fence posts or to a fence, spacing them about 40, 80 and 120 centimetres respectively above the ground. In cold areas, it's best to train the vines in a low fan shape to give fruiting buds a greater chance of snow protection (or protect with straw). Grapes close to the ground ripen faster because of the soil's warming effect.

To make a low fan shape, allow three shoots to grow and fasten them loosely to the bottom wire. In early April the following year, prune the three canes to just above the bottom wire. Retain six to eight of the emerging shoots near the bottom wire, and three of the lowest shoots on the vine—remove all others. The three lowest shoots will produce next year's crop. If you don't keep these "renewal shoots", it's impossible to keep the fan shape low. As the six to eight shoots grow upward during the summer of year two, tie them to the middle and top wires, maintaining a fan shape. Grapes will be produced in this area. The following spring, prune out everything except the renewal canes and tie them to the bottom wire. Shorten them to just above the wire, and the cycle continues.

Winter injury to buds can damage fruiting vines. Prune back to just below the middle wire, untie the canes on the bottom wire, lay the vine down and cover with straw for winter. Allow a sucker to grow to replace the trunk every three or so years to maintain the vine's flexibility.

pests and diseases

Mildew   This is considered the most serious disease for grapevines east of the Rockies. Mildew is easy to spot: with powdery mildew, spores leave a grey and white powdery trail on the leaves' upper surfaces; with downy mildew, white fuzzy blotches on the underside of leaves are the giveaway. Wet spring weather encourages downy mildew east of lake Superior, and high humidity promotes powdery mildew in hot, humid summers. Good pruning and fungicides, such as wettable sulfur, help prevent mildew. Robert Osborne, a New Brunswick grower, recommends a home-made baking soda spray: 15 to 30 milli-litres of baking soda and a few drops of dish soap in nine litres of water.

Botrytis A fruit rot seen worldwide, it generally affects varieties with tight clusters of grapes. Fruit turns dark and may split; veins show reddish-brown scars.

Cool, damp weather encourages the disease. The thick-skinned *labrusca* varieties tend to be less susceptible. Spray with sulfur fungicide.

Most other diseases and pests don't affect backyard vines. The grape berry moth, for example, is a problem among large Niagara vineyards. The phylloxera aphid creates a gall on the undersides of leaves, but the plant isn't damaged unless the infestation is severe.

when 'concord' is not enough

'Concord' is perhaps the most popular blue table grape and is often the standard against which other North American blue grapes are measured. A *labrusca* hybrid that ripens in early October and is suitable for Zones 5 and up, it's used as a dessert, juice and jelly grape. Here are other varieties with a hardier track record.

- 'Beta', blue, bred in Minnesota. A *riparia* hybrid, harvested in mid-September, used for dessert, juice, jelly. Zones 3 to 6.
- 'Eona', small, white *labrusca-riparia* hybrid. Harvested in late September, used for juice, jelly or wine. Zone 3.
- ES414, large, dark blue fruit; a hybrid of *riparia*, *vinifera* and other hybrids, bred in Wisconsin. Harvested in mid-October, used for desserts, juice or jelly. Zone 4.
- 'Kay Gray', white, bred in Wisconsin. Harvested in early October; used for dessert, juice or jelly. Zone 4.
- 'Minnesota 78', reddish purple, bred from 'Beta'. Harvested in mid-October; used for juice or jelly. Zone 3. Needs a pollinating variety nearby.
- 'Severnji', blue, bred in Russia from *V. amurensis*, a native Russian species. Also needs a pollinator. Wine, juice, jelly. Zone 4.
- 'Valiant', a *riparia* hybrid, bred in South Dakota. Matures early, from early September; used for dessert, juice or jelly. Zone 3.
- 'L'Acadie Blanc' (formerly known as 53261) is a tart, white wine grape, a cross between *vinifera* and French hybrids bred in Ontario. It didn't do well in Ontario but adapted to the Maritimes, where it was named. Harvested in mid-October in Zones 5 and up. Considered an alternative to 'Seyval', a French white wine grape hardy only to Zone 6.

salmon in grape leaves with verjuice butter

SERVES 4

Wrapping salmon in grape leaves seals in moisture and makes it easier to turn the fish on the grill. You can use vine leaves packed in brine as a substitute for fresh, but rinse first and then blanch. For a low-fat sauce, reduce butter to 2 tbsp. (15 mL) or omit altogether. Verjuice, the juice of grapes, was used in cooking centuries before wine.

3   tbsp. (45 mL) grainy mustard
3   tbsp. (45 mL) soy sauce
2   lb. (900 g) whole salmon fillet, skin on

Grapevine leaves
Freshly ground black pepper to taste

Verjuice butter:
8   oz. (250 g) seedless red grapes
1/4   cup (50 mL) softened butter
Salt and pepper to taste

1 Combine mustard and soy sauce. Spread over all of salmon. Blanch grapevine leaves in boiling water 2 minutes; drain. On a cookie sheet, overlap leaves, making a shape large enough to cover salmon. Place salmon on leaves and fold them over the sides. Lay more leaves on top to completely wrap salmon.

Tie wrapped fillet with string in 3 places.
2 Place grapes in food processor or blender and purée. Press pulp through a sieve to obtain the juice; you'll have about 3/4 cup (175 mL).
3 Preheat grill to high. In small saucepan, bring juice to boil; reduce heat and cook until 1/2 cup (125 mL) remains and juice begins to thicken. Beat in butter. Keep warm.
4 Grill salmon, with lid closed, 7 minutes per side. The vine leaves will probably burn a bit. Remove salmon from grill, untie string and remove leaves. Slice salmon into individual portions and serve with verjuice butter.

Scientists are still trying to develop a wine grape that will survive on the Prairies. A few years ago one was bred using the cold-tolerant gene of alfalfa and planted in a southern Ontario vineyard. It survived temperatures to -20°C, not quite hardy enough. But hardy vines, even if they don't bear wine-quality fruit, make fine arbours.

seedless grape tart

SERVES 6

You might think making a grape pie is a waste of time because fresh grapes taste so good. But taste this pie and you'll never think of grapes the same way again. Concord grapes work too, but they must be pitted.

2	lb. (900 g) red or green seedless grapes
1/4	cup (50 mL) orange juice
2	tsp. (10 mL) grated lemon zest
1/4	tsp. (1 mL) nutmeg
1/2	cup (125 mL) granulated sugar
1	tbsp. (15 mL) lemon juice
3	tbsp. (45 mL) instant tapioca or cornstarch
1	9-in. (23-cm) unbaked pie shell

Topping

1/2	cup (125 mL) all-purpose flour
	Pinch salt
1/4	cup (50 mL) brown sugar
1/4	cup (50 mL) butter
1	tsp. (5 mL) grated lemon zest

1 In saucepan over medium heat, place grapes, orange juice, 2 tsp. (10 mL) lemon zest and nutmeg. Bring to boil, cover and simmer 15 minutes, or until grapes are soft.
2 Preheat oven to 425°F (220°C). Place grapes in strainer over a bowl and strain juice out. Measure out 1 cup (250 mL) juice; reserve remainder for another recipe. Return grapes and 1 cup juice to saucepan. Stir in granulated sugar and lemon juice. Sprinkle over tapioca or cornstarch; if using cornstarch, first mix with an equal amount of water. Bring to boil, stirring. Cook 1 minute, or until mixture thickens. Pour into pie shell.
3 In food processor, combine topping ingredients until mixture is the size of small peas. Sprinkle topping over pie and bake 15 minutes. Lower heat to 375°F (190°C) and bake 20 minutes longer, or until pastry is golden and grape filling is bubbling.

vineyard chicken

SERVES 4

Cooking chicken on a bed of grapes produces a juicy, golden bird with a marvellous sauce. If using seedless grapes, slice in half; for grapes with seeds, slice in half and flick out the seeds with a knife.

1	3-lb. (1.5-kg) whole chicken
	Salt and freshly ground pepper
1	tbsp. (15 mL) butter
1	cup (250 mL) sliced onion
1/2	cup (125 mL) sliced carrot
1	tbsp. (15 mL) chopped fresh tarragon
8	oz. (250 g) seedless red grapes, halved

1 Preheat oven to 400°F (200°C). Season chicken with salt and pepper. Heat butter in casserole dish, suitable for both oven and stove-top, over medium heat. Brown chicken, breast side down, until golden, about 3 minutes. Turn on its side and brown another 3 minutes. Brown remaining sides. Remove chicken and drain off all but 1 tbsp. (15 mL) of fat.
2 Add onion and carrot to casserole and sauté 1 minute. Add tarragon and grapes. Return chicken to casserole, breast side up. Cover and bake 55 minutes, basting occasionally.
3 Remove chicken from casserole to carving board and cover with a tea towel to keep warm. Skim fat from casserole and scrape remaining contents into food processor. Process until smooth. Return to pan, bring to boil and simmer 1 minute, or until flavours are combined. If sauce is too thick, thin with stock or water. Season with salt and pepper. Carve chicken and serve with sauce.

A North American sunflower with delicious roots

jerusalem ARTICHOKES

recipes

jerusalem artichokes
with leeks & bacon

roasted roots

cream of jerusalem
artichoke soup

In the early 1600s, when Samuel de Champlain visited what is now Cape Cod, he watched native Americans baking knobby, white-fleshed tubers unfamiliar to him. The flavour reminded him of the globe artichoke eaten in France, and he took some back to Europe.

The vegetable became known as the Jerusalem artichoke—a serious misnomer, since it's neither an artichoke nor from Jerusalem. Although its flavour may be reminiscent of the globe artichoke, it's actually a relative of the sunflower. Popular wisdom has it that Jerusalem is a corruption of girasole, Italian for "turning to the sun"—a reference to the plant's habit of turning its sunflower-topped stems toward the light. Whatever the origin of the name, Jerusalem artichokes (*Helianthus tuberosus*) are today more appropriately called sunroots, the name originally given them by native Americans. They're also known as sunchokes.

Hardy to Zone 3, Jerusalem artichokes are a self-sufficient crop that requires little care; in fall the plants form brown-skinned tubers with crisp, white flesh and a sweet, nutty flavour. Eaten raw, they remind many of Chinese water chestnuts. Cooked, they taste like a cross between potatoes and globe artichokes. And like poplar trees and cassava, the Jerusalem artichoke is among high-carbohydrate crops now being investigated by scientists as a potential source of ethanol, a gasoline substitute. BY HEATHER APPLE

GARDENER'S TIPS
■ Jerusalem artichokes contain useful amounts of B vitamins, iron and calcium, but their greatest benefits are potassium—more than 300 mg in a half-cup—and insulin, a starch that can be eaten freely by diabetics.
■ In parts of Europe during the Second World War Jerusalem artichokes were a popular vegetable because they could be bought without a ration card.

no space?
no problem

- If you have limited garden space or are concerned about the invasive nature of Jerusalem artichokes, grow them in containers. Plant in early spring, when it's warm enough that the soil in the container won't freeze. Choose a container with a drainage hole in the bottom, and cover the bottom with a two-centimetre layer of bits of broken clay pots or large stones to provide drainage. The plants will have limited room to expand their roots in search of nourishment, so be sure to fill the container with a mixture of good soil and compost.

- A container the size of a large garbage pail holds three tubers; smaller containers will be limited to one or two. Plant tubers 10 centimetres deep and water thoroughly. Throughout the season, let the top couple of centimetres of soil dry out, and then water thoroughly until water comes out the bottom. In hot weather, check small containers daily. Feed with compost tea (made by soaking a burlap or cloth bag of compost or composted manure in a pail of water overnight) every three weeks.

- When the tops of the plants die in the fall, empty the containers and harvest all the tubers. Store a few to plant the following year and enjoy the rest. Throw the old soil on the compost pile or on a garden bed and use fresh soil in the container the following year.

growing

Jerusalem artichokes are very invasive, so choose their site carefully. The root system spreads 60 to 90 centimetres from the main stem, and the young tubers that form on the roots produce new plants the following spring. Even a thorough digging of the patch leaves a few tubers in the ground, and new plants can resprout from fragments of broken tubers.

Once planted, they'll be with you forever, so it's best to grow them away from the main garden. The 1.8- to 3.6-metre plants can be used to hide an unattractive corner of the yard, a shed or compost pile, or they can be planted along a fence. Although they grow in any soil, the largest, best-shaped tubers are produced in well-drained, loose but rich soil. They prefer full sun but also grow in light shade.

Jerusalem artichokes are available from local nurseries, mail-order seed companies, some supermarkets, and fruit and vegetable stores—not to mention from friends who may have some to spare. The older varieties have knobby tubers and are the most invasive, but recent breeding has developed smoother, easier-to-clean tubers that are less invasive. Choose tubers that are firm and free from rotten spots and store them in a perforated plastic bag in the refrigerator until the ground can be worked.

Plant them as early as you can; later planting results in low yields and small tubers. Prepare the site by removing perennial weeds (although Jerusalem artichokes will grow in a weedy or grassy spot, harvesting is much easier in weed-free areas, and the yields will be larger and the tubers bigger). Dig in compost or well-rotted manure to a depth of 15 centimetres.

Cut tubers into chunks, each with an "eye" like a potato, or leave them whole. Each tuber or part produces one plant; four or five plants yield enough Jerusalem artichokes for most families. Plant tubers 30 to 45 centimetres apart and 10 centimetres deep, in rows or clumps.

Shoots appear in three or four weeks. Weed the site when plants are 15 centimetres tall—the plants grow faster than the weeds, and their leaves help shade weeds out. Jerusalem artichokes need little care during the rest of the season, although watering during dry spells produces a better crop.

diseases and pests

Although in Canada the plants are unlikely to experience serious problems with diseases, here are a few they're subject to.

Powdery mildew A fungal disease that appears as a powdery white growth on the surface of stems and leaves. A heavy infestation may reduce yield and affect plant vigour.

Rust While this can be a serious problem in the southeastern United States, it's negligible—or nonexistent—in Canada. If it does occur, it appears as reddish-brown spots on the foliage and occasionally the stems.

Scerotonia wilt, stalk and tuber rot

Infection produces root rot, tuber rot and symptoms of wilting on the plant. The root system and tubers may rot away, and rot may extend up the stem.

The problems caused by these diseases can be reduced by controlling weeds, which may serve as hosts, and by cleaning up and destroying residues of infected crops in the fall. Purchase your first tubers from a reputable source, or get them from a friend who has a disease-free plot.

harvesting and storing

With the onset of cold weather in September or October, tubers begin forming on the long runner roots, and continue to grow until the plants blacken and die. They taste bland before a frost, but once the foliage has died and there have been a couple of frosts, they have a sweet, nutty flavour and a crisp texture. They range in size from small walnuts to apples.

Using a garden fork, start digging about 30 centimetres away from the stalk to avoid spearing the tubers on lateral shoots. The blackened stems can be left intact during the harvesting, or they can be cut off above ground level before digging begins.

You can harvest tubers repeatedly as long as the ground doesn't freeze. To keep harvesting all winter, mulch the patch with straw, hay or dead leaves. Very cold areas may need a metre or more of mulch, with mulch also extending out from the patch in all directions. If mice are likely to be a problem, add a few centimetres of soil or compost to the bed before mulching. Otherwise the mice might tunnel under the mulch and eat tubers close to the surface. Harvesting can continue throughout the winter—the tubers remain tasty until they start to sprout the following spring.

The tubers can also be dug in the fall and stored for winter eating. Some gardeners can't seem to store them successfully for more than a few weeks, others manage to keep them sweet and crisp until spring. After digging, leave the earth on the tubers and spread them out to allow the skins to dry, turning them once to dry them on all sides. This may take a couple of hours—longer if the tubers are wet. Don't leave them exposed to the air for too long, though—the goal is to dry only the skin without allowing the inside of the tuber to lose moisture. Store in plastic bags in the refrigerator, or in damp sand in a root cellar at 5°C.

Even a thorough harvesting will probably leave enough tubers or fragments in the ground to grow a good crop the following year. But the first year leave several in the ground to be sure; this shouldn't be necessary in subsequent years. In severely cold areas with little snowcover, apply a light protective mulch to ensure tubers survive over winter.

As soon as the soil thaws in the spring, remove mulch and work compost into the top four centimetres or so of soil. Never rototill the patch; this can spread fragments of tubers throughout the garden, and you'll have Jerusalem artichokes sprouting up everywhere. Never put unused tubers or thick peelings that may contain any eye on the compost pile, as these may sprout new plants as well.

jerusalem artichokes with leeks & bacon

SERVES 6 TO 8

English in origin, this satisfying casserole beautifully demonstrates the knobby, nutty versatility of its star ingredient.

2   lb. (1 kg) Jerusalem artichokes, peeled and sliced
       Juice of one lemon
1 1/4 lb. (625 g) bacon
1/2   lb. (250 g) leeks (about 2), rinsed well and sliced
1   cup (250 mL) chicken or vegetable stock
       Salt and freshly ground black pepper
1   tbsp. (15mL) butter
1 1/2 tbsp. (20 mL) all-purpose flour
1/3   cup (75 mL) freshly chopped parsley

1 Preheat oven to 400°F (200°C). Cover artichoke slices with water to which you've added the juice of the lemon. In a skillet, fry half the bacon until crisp. When cool enough to handle, cut cooked bacon in half and arrange pieces on bottom of a gratin or casserole dish. Roll up remaining bacon strips, secure each with a toothpick and fry until cooked through. Transfer bacon rolls to a paper towel to drain; remove toothpicks. Drain bacon fat from skillet.

2 Drain artichoke slices and distribute them over the bacon in the dish. Slice leeks (white and light green parts) and distribute over bacon. Add stock and season with salt and pepper. Cover and bake about 50 minutes, or until artichoke slices are tender when pierced with a knife. Remove from oven and carefully drain off stock and accumulated juices, leaving vegetables in casserole; reserve stock.

3 Add butter to skillet used to fry the bacon. Stir in flour. Gradually add reserved stock and bring to boil. Add chopped parsley to sauce and pour sauce over artichokes and leeks. Garnish each serving with bacon rolls.

roasted roots

SERVES 6

Roasting root vegetables is an easy and convenient way to cook them. Add sections of Jerusalem artichokes to the usual medley of carrots, parsnips and onions for another delicious dimension. Great with roast beef, pork, veal or lamb.

2   lb. (1 kg) Jerusalem artichokes, well scrubbed
1   lb. (500 g) parsnips, well scrubbed
1   lb. (500 g) carrots, well scrubbed
2-3   onions, peeled and quartered
1/4-1/2 cup (50-125 mL) olive oil
1   tbsp. (15 mL) herbes de Provence, rubbed between your fingers
        Salt and freshly ground black pepper

1 Preheat oven to 350°F (175°C).
2 If the artichokes are of a similar size, keep them whole; otherwise, cut them to large, uniform sizes.
3 Cut the parsnips, carrots and onions into similar-sized pieces. Add all the vegetables to a roasting pan or baking dish that's large enough to hold them in a single layer. Add olive oil, herbs, salt and pepper and toss to coat well. If necessary, add a little more olive oil to ensure all vegetables are lightly coated. Bake 45 to 60 minutes, or until vegetables are no longer hard in the centre and are beginning to brown. Adjust seasonings and serve.

cream of jerusalem artichoke soup

SERVES 6 TO 8

This dream of a soup, pale-hued yet vibrant in flavour, is courtesy of chef Chris McDonald. When it's on the menu at Avalon, his Toronto restaurant, it's served with a drizzle of white truffle oil and a few Jerusalem artichoke "chips".

2   lb. (1 kg) Jerusalem artichokes, well scrubbed
1   tbsp. (15 mL) butter
1   large cooking onion, chopped
1/2   lb. (250 g) celery root, peeled and finely sliced
6   cups (1.5 L) chicken stock, preferably homemade
1   cup (250 mL) heavy cream
      Salt, white pepper and lemon juice to taste
      Chopped Italian parsley, optional

1 Finely slice Jerusalem artichokes and place in a bowl of cold water to prevent blackening. In a large saucepan, melt butter over medium heat. Gently sauté onion and celery root until soft, about 5 minutes. Add drained Jerusalem artichokes and chicken stock. Simmer 20 minutes, or until tender. Remove from heat; allow to cool slightly and purée in a blender, a batch at a time. Purée until smooth and then pass through a fine sieve. Return soup to saucepan and reheat over medium heat. Whisk in cream. Garnish with parsley, if desired.

Jerusalem artichokes are delicious with other vegetables, as in this dish with leeks and bacon, or roasted with carrots, parsnips and onions. When eaten raw, they remind many of water chestnuts, or a cross between potatoes and globe artichokes.

Small and sweet, hardy kiwis are easy to grow

kiwi

recipes

kiwi veronica

kiwi with fennel &
gorgonzola

chicken in white wine
with kiwi

If you're like most gardeners, you've probably never thought of growing kiwis. The fuzzy store-bought fruits (*Actinidia deliciosa*) have increased in popularity over the past decade, but they're mostly imported because the vines are considered too tender to grow in most parts of Canada. But here's the good news: there are hardy species of kiwi that thrive well into Zone 3, and produce an abundant harvest in late summer or early fall.

Most of the 55 species of *Actinidia* are hardy, but only a few have been grown in North America—*A. arguta*, *A. kolomikta* and *A. polygama*. Their flowers grow in dense clusters and produce green or red-tinged, smooth-skinned fruits that can be eaten without peeling, like grapes. Their fruity-scented white flowers are attractive in early to late spring but they're nearly hidden by the foliage.

Hardy kiwis are native to China, Korea, Japan and Siberia. Russians have been working on new strains since the 1920s; almost all hardy varieties sold here are of Russian origin. Hardy as they are, hardy kiwis are susceptible to late spring frosts, which can kill flower buds that have begun to swell. Ironically, this means these types are often easier to grow in cool climates, where cold spring weather prevents precocious budding. BY LARRY HODGSON

GARDENER'S TIPS
■ Considerably sweeter and much smaller than the fuzzy grocery-store variety, the hardy garden-grown kiwis are also much richer in vitamin C.
■ *Actinidia deliciosa* is also a good source of potassium, phosphorus, magnesium, calcium and vitamin A, and it rates as one of the highest fruits for fibre.
■ Don't bother trying kiwis from seed: seeds sprout readily if sown in early summer, but plants could take five or six years to fruit and the quality of fruit is variable.

varieties

- Tara vine—*A. arguta* produces myriad fruits (some growers claim up to 45 kilograms per plant per season) of moderate size, mostly green or sometimes reddish. Although quite hardy (Zone 4 or 5), tara vine requires a particularly long season and often doesn't ripen until October or November; it tends to flower early in spring, so flower buds are sometimes exposed to frost. Wrap young plants in burlap for the first few winters. Tara vine can take eight years to fruit. The top green-fruited cultivars include 'Ananasnaja', 'Michigan State', and 'Dumbarton Oaks' (the earliest). Red-fruited but less hardy (Zone 6) is 'Ken's Redflesh'.
- Arctic beauty—*A. kolomikta* has been promoted as an ornamental, so gardeners don't realize it's perhaps the easiest of the hardy kiwis to grow for fruit. In spring, many leaves are half covered in bright silver overlaid with pink. Hardy to Zone 3 and sometimes Zone 2, *kolomikta* matures in August, making it the best choice for short-season climates. Often blooms the first year after planting. 'Krupnopladnaya', 'Sentyabraskaya' ('September') and 'Pautske' are female cultivars.
- Silver vine *A. polygama* has leaves beautifully overlaid in silvery white, but the problem is finding female specimens: none seems to be available from nurseries, although a hobby grower might be able to provide cuttings. It's too new to have been widely tested for hardiness, but it's perfectly happy in my Zone 4 garden.

males and females

With most kiwis, male and female flowers are borne on separate plants, and only the females produce fruit. The easiest way to tell the genders apart is by the nursery label; another way is to run a finger over an open flower—if it leaves a trace of yellow pollen, the flower is male. A female plant won't set fruit without pollination from a male-flowering plant, but you need only one male plant for seven to nine females. Although flowers of one species may pollinate those of another, you'll have better results if you grow male and female plants of the same species, mainly because they usually flower at the same time.

'Issai', sold as a hybrid of *A. arguta*, is a special case. Currently the most widely sold hardy kiwi, it's promoted as being self-fertile (you only need one plant to obtain fruit). However, most experts believe it's a hybrid of an unknown and less hardy species. 'Issai' is a weak grower and hardy only to about Zone 6.

choosing a site

The ideal site is a sunny or partly shady area on a slope, where cold air dissipates quickly, rather than in a valley where it tends to build up. Some protection from strong winds is advisable. Kiwis often do well in city gardens where they're buffered from bouts of wind and cold by surrounding buildings. A fence or hedge, set at right angles to the prevailing winds, can have the same effect. Rich, loamy soil is best, but even poor soil improved with plenty of organic matter will do as long as it's well-drained. Avoid heavy clay; it can lead to root rot because it's sometimes poorly drained. Soil should be slightly acidic, pH 5.0 to 6.5.

growing

Plant kiwis in spring so they'll have ample time to settle in before winter. Prepare a planting hole about as deep as the root ball and three times as wide. Mix in organic matter, and an organic fertilizer such as bloodmeal, fish emulsion or soybean meal. Centre the plant in the hollow, fill in with soil and water it well. Place plants no more than 90 centimetres apart—the closer they are, the more the lower branches from one vine will entwine the base of its neighbour, which is otherwise bare.

Mulch to keep out weeds and to help soil retain moisture. Organic mulches such as grass clippings, chopped leaves or shredded bark decompose over time and feed the plants' roots. Kiwis are heavy feeders and appreciate a yearly application of organic fertilizer, in spring.

pruning

The extent that you prune kiwis is a matter of choice. For ornamental value, vines can be left to grow as they please; multiple stems ensure the plant is fully clothed in foliage, and you still get ample fruit. If your aim is abundant fruit production, follow a pruning schedule.

The first year, eliminate all but the strongest stem, pinching or pruning

Right: the fruit of *Actinidia arguta* 'Ananasnaja' shows a reddish cast in the sun. Hardy kiwis are smaller and sweeter than the exotic, grocery store varieties, they're easy to grow and the vines are attractive additions to the garden.

out side branches. Train the stem up its support. Kiwis have twisting stems that wrap around almost any support, but if the post is more than five centimetres in diameter, attach the stem to it with wire ties or strips of cloth or pantyhose, or run a string from the bottom to the top of the post so the vine can wrap around that. (If you use wire ties, loosen them once a year so they don't cut into the bark.) Once the stem reaches the top of the support, let side branches develop.

Fruit is produced on the previous year's branches, so commercial growers prune vines heavily in late winter, removing branches that have already produced fruit to leave more room for new branches that developed the previous season. They prune again in early summer, cutting off unproductive stems to concentrate the plant's energy on its fruiting clusters. Pruning also makes it easier for growers to move through the rows of otherwise dense-growing plants at harvest time. To keep vines in home gardens looking full, prune only the older stems in late winter, and any that wander too far from the trellis during the season. Plants still produce abundant fruit,

although you may have to search for it among the lush foliage.

Be forewarned that male plants tend to be very vigorous: prune them back heavily after they bloom to keep them from overrunning their female companions.

pests and diseases

Except for crown and root rot in poorly drained soils, kiwis are surprisingly free of insects and disease. In extremely dry weather, spider mites sometimes do damage, and Japanese beetles eat the foliage, but neither problem seems to affect fruit production. Spraying with water is enough to rid the plant of spider mites. To get rid of Japanese beetles, spread a tarp under the plant and shake them off, then dispose of them by dropping them into soapy water, or simply squash them underfoot.

It's worth noting that kiwi leaves, particularly those of *A. polygama*, contain a substance cats find attractive. To avoid serious mauling by felines in the spring, surround the plants with a cage of chicken wire for the first two or three years; after that, the foliage seems to lose its appeal to felines.

harvesting

Kiwi fruits usually plump up mid-July to early August, but the flavour develops much later. You'll know they're approaching ripeness (from August to November, depending on the cultivar) when they separate easily from the stalk if pulled gently. Harvested at this point, they ripen fully off the vine, within a week or so. But don't delay your harvest: the fruits often drop off if allowed to ripen fully on the vine. They keep up to two months in a fruit cellar or fridge.

propagating

Most gardeners buy their kiwi vines already rooted and ready to plant, but you can start your own from cuttings of non-fruiting branches during the summer. Or simply let a branch trail to the ground and cover it with soil; it roots within a few weeks.

Store-bought kiwi can be substituted for home-grown in these recipes. You need to peel and dice the tropical ones, whereas the hardy kiwis may be used whole and unpeeled.

kiwi veronica

SERVES 4 TO 6

Recipes with Veronica in the title usually feature grapes, but we've used kiwi instead for a light, creamy dessert.

2   cups (500 mL) kiwi, left whole or halved
1   cup (250 mL) honeydew melon balls (or cut into 1-in./2.5-cm chunks)
1   cup (250 mL) sliced banana
1/2 cup (125 mL) light-brown sugar, packed
2   tbsp. (25 mL) fresh lemon juice
1/2 cup (125 mL) plain yogurt
1/2 cup (125 mL) sour cream, regular or low-fat
1/4 cup (50 mL) fresh mint, coarsely chopped
1/2 cup (125 mL) toasted, sliced almonds

1 In a medium mixing bowl, combine kiwi, melon and banana. Rub brown sugar through a sieve over the fruit to remove lumps. Mix well.
2 Add lemon juice, toss together, then add yogurt, sour cream and mint. Stir to coat fruit. Spoon into small glass dishes and sprinkle with almonds.

kiwi with fennel & gorgonzola

SERVES 4

The sweetness of kiwi is complemented by the piquancy of a blue cheese such as gorgonzola. You could vary the recipe by using crunchy sticks of jicama, a Latin American tuber now available in many supermarkets, instead of fennel.

2   fennel bulbs, trimmed and thinly sliced
3   tbsp. (45 mL) extra virgin olive oil
    Juice of 1 large lemon (approx. 1/4 cup/50 mL)
    Salt and freshly ground black pepper
1   cup (250 mL) kiwi, halved
1/4 lb. (115 g) gorgonzola cheese, crumbled
1   head romaine lettuce, cut in strips

1 In a large mixing bowl, combine fennel, oil, lemon juice, and salt and pepper. Let stand about 10 minutes. Add kiwi, cheese and lettuce; toss together gently and serve immediately.

chicken in
white wine with kiwi

SERVES 6

Kiwi adds its own distinctive texture and
flavour to a variation of the traditional
combination of chicken and green grapes.
Pair with boiled new potatoes tossed with
chopped fresh mint and butter.

2	tbsp. (25 mL) extra virgin olive oil (approx.)
1	tbsp. (15 mL) unsalted butter
1	large white onion, chopped
1	clove garlic, finely chopped
2	lb. (1 kg) boneless, skinless chicken breasts
1	cup (250 mL) white wine (such as a semi-dry Riesling)
1	cup (250 mL) kiwi, whole
	Salt and freshly ground pepper

1 In a large heavy skillet, heat oil
and butter together over medium-
high heat. Add onion and garlic,
and sauté until soft and golden, but
not brown. Remove pan from heat
and transfer onion mixture to a
small bowl.

2 Pat chicken breasts dry with paper
towels. Add a little more oil to the
pan, if necessary. Place chicken in the
pan and brown quickly on both sides;
transfer to a plate. Return pan to the
heat and add wine, scraping up any
bits clinging to the bottom and sides
of the pan. Place onion mixture back
in the pan, reduce heat to medium,
add kiwi, stir to combine and allow to
cook gently for a minute or two.

3 Return chicken breasts to the pan,
turning them several times to coat with
mixture. Season to taste with salt and
pepper. Bring to a gentle boil, reduce
heat to low and cook, uncovered, until
chicken is cooked through, about 10
to 15 minutes.

A European favourite finally makes its way to North America

kohlrabi

recipes

oven-braised kohlrabi gratin

kohlrabi salad

garlic butter & lemon kohlrabi

Kohlrabi is one odd-looking vegetable. Just above the ground its stem swells into a ball-shaped knob from which spindly leaves radiate, giving it the appearance of a leafy flying saucer. Kohlrabi, German for "cabbage turnip," is a member of the cabbage family, traditionally enjoyed in Germany and Eastern Europe but uncommon in North America. This is unfortunate, because kohlrabi is easy to grow and pleasant to eat. The bulbs have a crisp, crunchy texture when eaten raw and taste somewhat like a mild, slightly sweet cabbage.

Kohlrabi bulbs have white flesh and greenish white or reddish purple skin. They can be eaten raw in salads or as part of a vegetable dip platter, or cooked in stir-fries, soups or stews. The young leaves, which have a flavour similar to kale or collards are good steamed or sautéed, or in soups or stews.

Kohlrabi (*Brassica oleracea*, Gongy-lodes Group) originated in the coastal areas of the Mediterranean Basin. By AD 800, the French emperor Charlemagne ordered that it be grown in his kingdom. However, it was fed only to cattle because the royal physicians warned that it would make his soldiers bovine and unaggressive.

BY HEATHER APPLE

GARDENER'S TIPS

▪ Kohlrabi bulbs are a good source of vitamin C and potassium. The leaves are rich in calcium, potassium, iron and carotene, and have the same anti-cancer properties as other members of the cabbage family.

▪ Home-grown kohlrabi is a real treat because you can pick them while they're young and sweet (at two to four centimetres in diameter) and eat them unpeeled.

▪ Purple-skinned kohlrabi is generally sweeter than the green variety.

harvesting and storage

Most varieties are best harvested when bulbs are four to five centimetres in diameter. At that size, bulbs retain their mild flavour and crisp, non-fibrous texture. Some of the new hybrids, such as 'Express Forcer' and 'Kolibri', stay tender and mild up to 10 centimetres. Large varieties, such as 'Gigante', can be harvested up to 25 centimetres in diameter.

Harvest by pulling up the entire plant or by cutting 2.5 centimetres beneath the bulb, leaving the root behind. For immediate use, snap off leaf stems, then peel off the skin and any fibrous areas. Very small, tender bulbs can be eaten with the skin intact.

It's better to harvest and store bulbs than to leave them in the ground. Remove the leaves but not the skins from bulbs to be stored. Small bulbs keep in the refrigerator for two to three weeks, larger bulbs for up to three months in a refrigerator or root cellar.

In areas with cold winters, varieties with large bulbs can be left in the ground, covered with deep mulch—up to one metre in cold areas—and harvested throughout the winter.

To freeze kohlrabi, wash, trim and skin the roots, then cut into one-centimetre-square pieces before blanching and freezing.

pests and diseases

Kohlrabi is generally less plagued by diseases and pests than other members of the cabbage family. To avoid potential problems, keep your garden well weeded, remove and destroy any plants infected with disease and do a good fall cleanup. Practise crop rotation—members of the cabbage family should not be replanted in the same place for three to four years.

Aphids Pinhead-sized insects with pear-shaped bodies that suck juices from plants, causing leaves to curl and turn yellow; plants may stop growing. Wash off aphids with a shower of water. For serious infestations, spray twice a week with insecticidal soap.

Flea beetles Shiny, two-millimetre-long

Kohlrabi is a member of the cabbage family but is less plagued by pests and diseases than many of its relatives. Planting beds should be kept well weeded and crop rotation should be practised.

beetles that chew tiny holes in leaves, killing young seedlings and spreading disease. Cover seeded rows and recent transplants with floating row covers. As a last resort, spray with rotenone.

Cutworms Dull grey or brown, 2.5 to five-centimetre caterpillars that cut off seedlings at or just below ground level. They hide in the soil during the day and feed at night. Place a plastic or cardboard collar, such as half a toilet paper roll, around the stem of each seedling when planting.

Cabbage looper Three-centimetre-long, green caterpillars, which loop their bodies as they crawl, chew ragged holes in the leaves. Cover young plants and seeded rows with floating row covers. Spray infested plants, including the undersides of leaves, with Bt (*Bacillus thuringiensis*) every two weeks until caterpillars are under control.

Imported cabbageworm Green three-centimetre-long caterpillars that chew large holes in leaves. The adult white moths hover around plants of the cabbage family. Protect young plants with floating row covers. Spray with Bt (as above).

Cabbage root maggot White, three-centimetre-long maggots burrow into roots and stems, spreading disease. Seedlings become yellow and stunted, wilt in the heat and eventually die. Protect young plants with floating row covers, or place a collar or mat around their bases.

Blackleg fungal disease It produces small, dark, sunken spots on leaves and stems. Leaf edges wilt and discolour; the whole plant may die. Remove and destroy infected plants.

Black rot Causes yellow, triangular areas with darker veins on leaves. As rot progresses, leaves wilt and plants may die. If this is a problem in your area, plant rot-resistant 'Grand Duke'.

Club root Leaves yellow, and plants stop growing and may die. Roots swell, become club-like and eventually rot. Remove and destroy infected plants.

varieties

- 'Azur Star' (45 days) Early; blue-purple skin.
- 'Early Purple Vienna' (55 days) Red-purple skin.
- 'Early White Vienna' (50 days) Mild, succulent, white-skinned bulbs.
- 'Eder' (38 days) Hybrid; tender, white-skinned bulbs; extra-early; fast-growing.
- 'Express Forcer' (42 days) Hybrid; very early; crisp, white-skinned bulbs; tender up to 10 centimetres.
- 'Gigante' (130 days) Czechoslovakian heirloom; bulbs can reach 30 centimetres in diameter and weigh up to 13 kilograms; stays tender.
- 'Grand Duke' (45 days) Hybrid; white-skinned; good disease tolerance.
- 'Granlibakken' (45 to 60 days) Extra large; white-skinned; tender flesh with little fibre.
- 'Kolibri' (45 days) Hybrid; considered the best purple-skinned variety; stays crisp and sweet up to 10 centimetres.
- 'Kongo' (50 days) Hybrid; white-skinned bulbs form quickly; stays tender and sweet.
- 'Kossak' (85 days) Hybrid; up to 25 centimetres; white-skinned; stays sweet and crisp.
- 'Logo' (45 days) Very early; white-skinned; used in Europe for baby

vegetable production. Sow at 16°C in spring.
- 'Rapid Star' (49 days) Early; slow-bolting; tasty; white-skinned.
- 'Superschmeltz' (60 to 70 days) Eastern European; white-skinned; up to 25 centimetres.
- 'Winner' (45 days) Hybrid; white-skinned; fresh, fruity taste.

early harvest

- For an earlier crop, start seeds indoors two to four weeks before the outside temperature is consistently above 5°C. Give each seedling its own pot to minimize transplanting shock, which may result in small, tough bulbs. Use a good potting soil. Plant two or three seeds per container, later thinning to the most vigorous seedling. Make sure soil is moist but not soggy, cover containers with plastic—it doesn't have to be clear plastic because the seeds germinate in light or dark conditions—to retain moisture and place in a warm location.
- Seeds germinate in a week or less at 24°C to 26°C. As soon as they sprout, move the container to a bright location with a cooler temperature. Grow lights are ideal; otherwise, place in a sunny southern window with supplemental light on overcast days. Feed weekly with diluted fertilizer or compost tea. Make sure seedlings don't become pot-bound before they're planted outdoors.
- About a week before planting outside, start hardening off the seedlings outdoors in a sheltered location. Gradually acclimatize them to sunlight. Plant out seedlings at the same time you would normally plant kohlrabi seeds directly into the ground.

oven-braised kohlrabi gratin

SERVES 6

This comforting side dish is a good complement to roasted or grilled meats. For a vegetarian version, substitute vegetable stock for chicken stock and add a little grated cheese to the topping.

1	tbsp. (15 mL) olive oil
3	medium-sized (about 8 cm in diameter) kohlrabi bulbs, peeled and thinly sliced
2	white onions, peeled and thinly sliced
2	tbsp. (30 mL) butter
	Salt and freshly ground black pepper, to taste
1 1/4 cups (300 mL) chicken stock	

Topping

1/4	cup (60 mL) fresh flat-leaf parsley, chopped
2	cloves garlic, minced
1 1/2 cups (375 mL) dry breadcrumbs	

1 Preheat oven to 400°F (200°C). Brush the bottom and sides of a shallow ceramic or glass baking dish with olive oil. In alternating layers, arrange kohlrabi with onions, adding bits of butter and a little salt and pepper to each layer. Pour chicken stock over all and set to one side.

2 Topping: In a mixing bowl, combine parsley, garlic and breadcrumbs. Toss together to blend well. Spread over kohlrabi and press into place. Bake uncovered for 40 minutes or until topping is golden brown.

Small, tender bulbs can be eaten unpeeled and sliced as part of a crudité, or steamed lightly. Larger bulbs should be peeled and any fibrous areas removed. To freeze kohlrabi, peel and cut into squares before blanching. Kohlrabi gratin is a good complement to grilled meats.

kohlrabi salad

SERVES 4 TO 6

The ultimate in crunch, this robustly flavoured salad goes well with beef, roast lamb or pork.

2	medium-sized (about 8 cm in diameter) kohlrabi bulbs, peeled and grated
2	large carrots, peeled and grated
1 1/2	red bell pepper, seeded and finely chopped
2	green onions, trimmed and finely chopped
1	clove garlic, minced
2	tbsp. (30 mL) fresh flat-leaf parsley, chopped
1/4	cup (60 mL) extra virgin olive oil
2	tbsp. (30 mL) red wine vinegar
1/2	tsp. (2 mL) salt
1/2	tsp. (2 mL) freshly ground black pepper

1 In a large mixing bowl, combine kohlrabi, carrots, red bell pepper, green onions, garlic and parsley. Toss lightly. In a small mixing bowl, whisk together olive oil, red wine vinegar, salt and pepper. Adjust seasonings to taste. Cover and refrigerate for 2 hours before serving.

garlic butter & lemon kohlrabi

SERVES 4

The thinner you slice the kohlrabi, the quicker it will cook. Vary by combining half the amount of kohlrabi with very thinly sliced pieces of carrot and parsnip.

4	medium-sized kohlrabi bulbs, peeled and thinly sliced
2	tbsp. (30 mL) butter
2	cloves garlic, minced
	Juice of 1 large lemon
	Salt and freshly ground black pepper, to taste

1 Bring a large saucepan of water to a boil. Add kohlrabi and lightly boil for about 15 minutes, until tender. Do not overcook.

2 When kohlrabi is almost ready, melt butter in a skillet over low heat. Reduce heat to lowest point and add garlic. Let garlic sit in the butter for a minute or two (do not brown). Thoroughly drain kohlrabi (pat dry with a clean tea towel) and add to skillet along with lemon juice. Toss together until kohlrabi is coated with butter mixture. Season to taste and serve immediately.

winter

It seems there's an implicit agreement among vegetable gardeners to grow more than they can possibly use. Non-gardeners are of course grateful for the baskets of green beans and tomatoes—and even the never-ending supplies of zucchini—left on the doorstep, but it seems a shame that the gardener doesn't enjoy all the fruits of his or her labours. Thank goodness for vegetables that can be stored well into the winter and still retain their freshness, flavour and nutritional value. A cold cellar or an extra fridge may be necessary to keep the crop, but either would be a good investment in bringing back the tastes and memories of summer. Beets, carrots, potatoes, pumpkins, rutabaga and winter squash are among the vegetables that hold well in cool, dark conditions; just be sure not to keep root crops with apples, pears or other fruits that give off ethylene gas. Even in the fridge it can cause them to deteriorate. And try to harvest vegetables on a dry, cool day. Those picked in heat may not last long in storage.

A familiar red root with year-round appeal

beets

recipes

sautéed beets
with feta cheese

roasted beet soup

Beets have been used since ancient times for medicinal purposes, especially for liver disorders, but the healthful attributes of this classic vegetable are newly appreciated for its anti-cancer properties and the cholesterol-lowering capacity of the roots.

The familiar table beet is one of four types belonging to the species *Beta vulgaris*. The others are sugar beets, widely grown as a source of sugar; mangels, used as a winter feed for livestock; and chard, which is grown for its edible leaves.

Beets can be eaten all year: fresh, tender, sweet roots and greens in spring, summer and fall; or canned, pickled or frozen for enjoyment throughout the winter—special varieties have been bred for storage purposes.

Most people think of beets as round and red, but they can also be golden or white, or have attractive red-and-white striped interiors. Some are cylindrical in shape; some are storage varieties that grow into the form of a misshapen volleyball.

BY HEATHER APPLE

GARDENER'S TIPS
▪ The beet's roots, the part most of us eat, are a good source of vitamin C and potassium. The leaves contain oxalic acid, which inhibits the body's ability to absorb calcium, but they're also rich in calcium, iron and vitamins A and C.
▪ If you're growing beets for greens, there's no need to thin plants.
▪ Earwigs like to munch on beet leaves, but they seem to prefer wilted ones. At night, leave a pile of trimmings on the ground beside your rows to distract them from growing plants.

planting

To grow into plump, succulent, tender roots, beets need full sun and well-drained soil rich in organic matter, with a pH of 6.5 to 7.5. Cover the planting area with five to 10 centimetres of compost or well-aged manure, digging it in to a depth of 15 to 20 centimetres and removing any stones or obstacles that might cause misshapen roots. As a rule, don't plant beets or potatoes in the same place in the garden for three years.

Beets require nitrogen, but fresh manure or high-nitrogen fertilizer could result in hairy roots or rough, pointed side shoots and lush leaves at the expense of roots. Good compost should supply the potassium and phosphorus beets need, but if your soil is seriously deficient in these elements, add wood ashes or kelp meal for potassium and finely ground rock phosphate for phosphorus. Beets are susceptible to boron deficiency; add lots of compost or other organic matter to the soil.

Plant seeds two to three weeks before the last expected frost date. Dig a trench two centimetres deep and sow seeds 2.5 centimetres apart. For greens, sow one centimetre apart and cover with one centimetre of soil; press down gently and water.

With early spring plantings, use a floating row cover to increase the temper-ature. Keep the soil moist but not soggy during germination, in about two weeks at soil temperatures of 10°C, or one week at 20°C. For a continuous supply of tender young beets, plant at three-week intervals to the middle or end of July.

growing

Because each beet "seed" is actually a dried fruit containing numerous seeds, several seedlings will come up where each seed is planted. When seedlings are 2.5 centimetres tall, thin to the most vigorous. Pinch or cut off competing seedlings. When plants are five to seven centimetres tall, thin to five centimetres apart, saving the thinnings for salads. When the roots begin to touch each other (gently scrape a bit of soil away at the bases of stems to check), harvest all the beets or every other beet, leaving space for the remaining roots to grow. If you're growing beets just for the greens, there's no need to thin.

Insufficient moisture makes beets tough and stringy. Periods of drought followed by heavy watering may cause roots to split. Check soil moisture regularly; when the top two to five centimetres is dry, water deeply. Mulch to keep soil consistently moist, control weeds and prevent the roots from becoming rough due to exposure to the air. In a dry summer, check soil regularly under the mulch; if it starts to dry out, water deeply until soil is moist 15 centimetres down.

Boost growth by watering with compost tea when you thin or if plants are stunted, growth is slow or leaves are pale. Weeds compete with beets' shallow roots; carefully pull them out by hand.

harvesting and storage

For greens only, pull up the entire plant when the leaves are 10 to 15 centimetres tall. Otherwise, harvest roots at any stage, even when they're tiny. Most varieties are at their sweetest and most tender when the roots are small—about four centimetres in diameter or less—but can be left to grow one to two weeks beyond this size to produce larger roots of still excellent quality.

Beets survive light frosts, but heavy freezing seriously affects the roots' quality and storage potential. For winter storage, harvest late fall beets after a short period of dry weather. Gently brush soil off the roots but don't wash. Cut off the tops, leaving a five-centimetre stem. Use greens immediately or wash, blanch and freeze. Allow the roots to dry completely in the sun for several hours, turning once. Use damaged roots immediately. Fully grown storage varieties keep five to six months at 0°C to 2°C and 95 per cent humidity. If you don't have a root cellar, enclose beets in double plastic bags punched with air holes and place in a cold but not freezing place.

If beets have been planted in well-drained soil, you can store them where they're growing, removing weeds and vegetation that might attract rodents. Where winters are cold enough to freeze the ground, bury beets under 30 to 60 centimetres of mulch, depending on the harshness of the winter, laying it down while the ground is still moist and before it freezes. Extend the mulch 30 to 60 centimetres in all directions around the beets and cover with a plastic sheet. Plastic garbage bags filled with leaves

Beets grow in more than just plain red. Far left: 'Burpee's Golden', with orange skin and golden yellow flesh, and a group including 'Albina Vereduna', 'Burpee's Golden', 'Cylindra' and 'Chiogga'.

make a convenient mulch; throughout the winter, you can lift the mulch and harvest fresh beets. Check regularly to make sure rodents don't make nests under the mulch and eat all the beets.

diseases and pests

Heart rot Not a disease but a nutritional deficiency, heart rot (a boron deficiency) results in corky (hard-textured), black tissue inside the root. Add plenty of compost or composted manure to correct this problem.

Scab A bacterial disease that also affects potatoes, scab produces raised, corky brown lesions on the roots. Make sure the soil is consistently moist. Crop rotation should prevent the disease from returning.

Cerscospora leaf spot A fungal disease that causes small, brown lesions with purple halos on the leaves. As the lesions mature, they become grey and brittle and

may fall out, leaving a hole. Do a good fall cleanup and practise a three-year rotation. 'Red Ace' is a cercospora-resistant cultivar.

Leaf miners The larvae of small flies. The larvae burrow in the leaves, producing white or brown tunnels and blotches. Squash larvae inside the leaf and check the undersides of leaves for small, white egg clusters. Cut and destroy infested leaves. Cover seed bed with a floating row cover after planting to prevent flies from laying eggs.

Leaf hoppers A tiny, wedge-shaped insect that flies or hops away quickly when disturbed and sucks out the plant juices, weakening the plant. It also spreads viral diseases. Keep garden well weeded. For serious infestations, dust plants with diatomaceous earth or spray with insecticidal soap.

Webworms Small green, yellow or black larvae with stripes or spots that fold themselves into leaves after feeding on the foliage. Hand-pick and destroy.

Mice They love to eat beet roots—a serious problem in rural gardens. Make a fence of 0.5-centimetre mesh hardware cloth, 60 centimetres high with 30 centimetres buried underground. Keep the surrounding area weed-free.

ROUND RED
- 'Red Ace' (50 days). Quick to mature, maintains its sweet tenderness even when roots get larger.
- 'Pronto' (58 days). Dutch heirloom; produces superior, sweet baby beets.

CYLINDRICAL
- 'Cylindra' or 'Formanova' (58 days). Produces a large number of uniform slices; can reach 20 centimetres long.
- 'Forono' (55 days). Sweet-tasting.

FOR STORAGE
- 'Lutz Green Leaf' or 'Lutz Green Top' (80 days). Sow two months before first frost and harvest before a hard frost; large, irregular roots stay sweet and tender; abundant greens.
- 'Winterkeeper', 'Long Season' or 'Green Leaf' (75 to 80 days). Abundant greens and large, sweet and tender roots.

FOR GREENS
- 'Early Wonder' or 'Green Top Bunching' (50 days). Abundant greens and a tasty root.
- 'Early Wonder Tall Top' (45 to 55 days). Tall, vigorous greens; especially good in spring, growing quickly in cool soils.

ODDITIES
- 'Bull's Blood' (60 days). Red-purple leaves, great in salads.
- 'MacGregor's Favorite' (60 to 90 days). Scottish heirloom; narrow, spear-shaped, deep metallic purple leaves.
- 'Burpee's Golden' or 'Golden' (55 to 60 days). Orange skin, golden yellow flesh and sweet flavour; low germination rate, so seed thickly; colour doesn't bleed.
- 'Chioggia' (55 to 60 days). A sweet-flavoured Italian heirloom with red skin and red and white rings resembling a bull's eye inside; doesn't bleed.
- 'Albina Vereduna' (55 to 65 days). A large, pure white beet, tender and sweet.

'Bull's Blood', far right, is often grown for its tasty red-purple leaves, great in salads, as well as for its red flesh, a colourful choice for roasted beet soup.

sautéed beets with feta cheese

SERVES 6

A simple yet spectacular pasta dish, the beets turn the pasta a beautiful shade of purple while the feta and poppy seeds provide subtle and unexpected flavours.

3   tbsp. (45 mL) poppy seeds
6   tbsp. (90 mL) unsalted butter
11/2 lb. (675 g) beets, peeled and finely grated
1   lb. (450 g) spaghettini pasta
1   tbsp. (15 mL) balsamic vinegar
2/3 cup (150 mL) feta cheese, crumbled
     Salt and pepper to taste
1/4 cup (60 mL) chives, finely chopped for garnish

1 In a large, heavy saucepan, toast the poppy seeds over high heat, stirring until they are aromatic and slightly darkened (about 2 minutes). Transfer to a small bowl and set aside.
2 Put on a large pot of water to boil for the pasta.
3 Add 5 tablespoons (75 mL) of butter to the saucepan and cook over medium heat until butter turns golden brown, about 4 to 5 minutes.
4 Add beets to butter; reduce heat and sauté for 3 to 4 minutes.
5 Add pasta and 1 teaspoon (5 mL) salt to boiling water; cook until pasta is tender.

6 Meanwhile, add balsamic vinegar to beets and cook, covered, for 10 minutes. Season with salt and pepper to taste.
7 Drain pasta, keeping 1/2 cup (125 mL) of pasta water aside; add pasta to beets. Turn heat off underneath the saucepan, then add pasta water and remaining 1 tablespoon (15 mL) of butter. Toss together; add poppy seeds and feta cheese. Season again with salt and pepper.
8 Garnish with chives.

roasted beet soup

SERVES 6

A healthy fall soup, it tastes best if made ahead and allowed to sit for a day to blend the flavours and bring out the cumin.

Soup

3   lb. (1.35 kg) or 7 medium-sized fresh beets, washed, tops and bottoms removed, and cut into quarters
2   fresh or dry bay leaves
2   medium-sized sprigs of rosemary
8   sprigs fresh thyme
1   head of garlic, left whole, top trimmed
5   shallots, peeled
3   tbsp. (45 mL) olive oil
1/2 tsp. (2 mL) salt
1/2 tsp. (2 mL) fresh black pepper
1   tbsp. (15 mL) cumin seeds
1   tbsp. (15 mL) yellow mustard seeds
1/4 cup (60 mL) water
2   tbsp. (30 mL) chopped parsley
1   tbsp. (15 mL) orange zest
1   tbsp. (15 mL) lemon zest
5   cups (1.25 L) vegetable or chicken stock
2   tsp. (10 mL) Dijon mustard

Dijon crème fraîche
11/2 tsp. (7 mL) Dijon mustard
1/2 cup (125 mL) crème fraîche (or use sour cream)

Garnish

6   fresh basil leaves, cut into very fine strips or 3 or 4 fresh chives, cut on the diagonal into small pieces
     Black pepper

1 Preheat oven to 450°F (230°C). Put beets, bay leaves, rosemary, five sprigs of thyme, garlic and shallots in a roasting pan. Toss with 2 tablespoons (30 mL) olive oil, salt and 1/4 teaspoon (1 mL) pepper. Cover pan with foil. Roast for about 1 1/4 hours until beets are soft. Keep covered and let cool. Remove beet skins; chop beets into 1/2 in. (1-cm) pieces. Squeeze out garlic from head, then chop garlic and shallots together. Discard herbs.
2 In a large pot over medium-low heat, add 1 tablespoon (15 mL) olive oil. When hot, add cumin and mustard seeds. Cook, stirring continuously, just until the seeds are fragrant and golden.
3 Add garlic and shallots; mix well. Add water and cook gently, continuing to stir. After 2 to 3 minutes, add beets, remaining thyme, parsley, and orange and lemon zests, and continue to cook for 5 minutes, stirring occasionally.
4 Add stock and bring to a boil, then reduce heat to low, cover pot and simmer for 20 to 30 minutes.
5 Remove soup from heat and allow to cool for 10 to 15 minutes. Add Dijon mustard and remaining pepper; remove thyme sprigs. Purée soup in a blender in two batches or in pot with a hand blender.

6 For a smoother texture, strain through a fine mesh sieve, pressing on the solids with the back of a large spoon. Return soup to pot and reheat over low. Season with salt and pepper to taste.

7 For Dijon crème fraîche, mix Dijon mustard with crème fraîche.

8 Ladle soup into bowls and add a dollop of Dijon crème fraîche. Garnish with fresh basil or chives and a bit of fresh black pepper.

For sweet flavour, give them food, water, and a little chill-out time

brussels SPROUTS

recipes

brussels sprouts &
red pepper stir-fry

creamed brussels
sprouts with lemon
and parsley

brussels sprout leaves
with ligurian walnut
sauce

One autumn, while eating rutabaga and Brussels sprouts in a motel restaurant, I noticed the woman at the next table looking at her Brussels sprouts with loathing. Then she speared them with her fork and deposited them disdainfully on her side plate.

Brussels sprouts are one of those vegetables people either love or hate. I love them, but I can understand why some don't—they can be unpleasantly bitter, and cooking methods that traditionally boiled them to mush haven't done anything for their reputation. But when they're grown in fertile, well-watered soil, sweetened by frost and freshly picked, cooked until just tender and served with melted butter, they're delicious.

Brussels spouts (*Brassica oleracea* var. *gemmifera*) grow on plants that resemble tiny palm trees with miniature cabbages along the trunk. First recorded in Belgium about 1750, they reached England and France around 1800. The popular sprouts are often seen in English vegetable gardens in winter, where they thrive in the cool, wet weather. They also grow all winter on the coast of British Columbia. Elsewhere in Canada, their cold-hardiness allows gardeners to reap a flavourful harvest extending into late fall and early winter. BY HEATHER APPLE

GARDENER'S TIPS
■ Fresh from the garden, Brussels sprouts are high in vitamin C. But as with other vegetables, the vitamin value decreases quickly once they're picked— a good reason to grow your own.
■ Sprouts are richer in protein than most vegetables and contain significant amounts of vitamin A, thiamin, potassium, iron and calcium.
■ The secret to growing mild, sweet sprouts is timing: plant them so you'll be reaping the harvest after the first frost.

Slow-poke Brussels sprouts require patience—some can take 100 to 200 days to mature. If planted too early, they mature in hot weather and become bitter. Too late, and cold weather cuts short the harvest. Below: the heirloom 'Red Rubine'.

planting and growing

Seed catalogues list the maturity date—the number of days it takes a seedlng planted in the garden to produce its first sprouts—for each variety. If you're starting sprouts from seeds (indoors or in the garden), add four weeks. For example, if a variety takes 90 days to mature, total growing time from seed to harvest is 118 days (90 + 28). To determine when to start seeds, take the date of your first expected fall frost and count back the number of growing days. If you buy seedlings, use the maturity date (90 days), counting back to calculate when to plant the seedlings in your garden.

To start seeds indoors, plant them one centimetre deep in a light potting mix, three seeds per five-centimetre pot. Keep moist during germination. Once seedlings appear, put them under grow lights or in a sunny south-facing window. Eventually thin to one seedling per pot. Harden off seedlings outdoors by gradually exposing them to direct sunlight and cooler temperatures. Once hardened off, seedlings can withstand light frosts.

Choose a sunny site and work plenty of compost or well-rotted manure into the soil: Brussels sprouts are heavy feeders. Plant 60 centimetres apart. Fill good-sized holes with compost, water seedlings well, and keep moist but not soggy. Cover direct-sown seeds with row covers or sprinkle seedlings regularly with rotenone or diatomaceous earth to protect them from flea beetles. Plant 6 millimetres deep, four to five seeds per 2.5 centimetres. Thin seedlings to 60 centimetres. For a winter crop in coastal British Columbia, plant a slow-maturing variety indoors in early July and transplant in the garden by mid-August.

Plants that are well fed and watered produce the best sprouts. Mulch deeply. Once a month, side dress plants with compost, well-rotted manure or organic fertilizer. Plants are shallow-rooted, so don't dig deeply when feeding or weeding. Stop feeding in autumn; fertilizer stimulates new growth that isn't cold-hardy. Mature plants are top-heavy, easily blown over by a strong wind. Stake plants or support with soil mounded up around the base.

diseases and pests

Practise a three- or four-year crop rotation, as for all cabbage-family members. Clean up dead plant material in fall and eliminate weeds, which may harbour pests and diseases.

Aphids Green or grey insects infest leaves, especially succulent new growth, feeding on plant juices and excreting a sticky honeydew. Hose off. Use insecticidal soap or pyrethrum as a last resort.

Flea beetles Shiny black beetles chew tiny holes in the leaves, quickly destroying seedlings. Protect with row covers. For serious infestations, use rotenone or diatomaceous earth.

Cabbage loopers Brown moths lay white eggs on leaves, which hatch into green caterpillars that chew holes in the leaves. Squash eggs or spray plants with Bt (*Bacillus thuringiensis*).

White cabbage butterfly White with black wing spots, the adult lays cream-coloured eggs under leaves: they hatch into green caterpillars that chew holes in the leaves. Squash eggs or spray plants with Bt.

Diamondback moth The grey moth lays yellow eggs on upper surfaces of leaves; the green caterpillars that eat holes in the leaves. Squash eggs or spray plants with Bt.

Cutworms Plump worms live in the soil and feed on the base of the plant, cutting it off at soil level. When planting seedlings, encircle the plants with a cardboard collar (a toilet-paper roll cut in half) that extends 2.5 centimetres into the soil and about five centimetres above.

Cabbage root maggot Grey maggots eat the roots and stems, causing plants to wilt. Protect seedlings with a row cover, or place a 30-centimetre square of tar paper or black plastic directly over the soil, covering the roots, to prevent the adult from laying its eggs in the soil. Cut a slit from one edge to the middle of the square and slip it around the plant.

Black rot A bacterial disease causing yellow, V-shaped lesions on leaves, and black veins. Leaves wilt as the rot progresses. Remove and destroy infected plants. Avoid working among wet plants, which spreads the disease.

Blackleg A fungal disease causing small, dark lesions that gradually enlarge. Severely infected plants wilt and fall over. Remove and destroy infected plants. Don't work among wet plants.

Clubroot Roots swell and form galls. Top growth is stunted and lower leaves yellow and drop off. Plants wilt during the day and recover at night. Remove and destroy infested plants. Good drainage helps prevent the problem.

Fusarium A warm-weather fungus that causes lower leaves to turn yellow and brown, and then drop off. Remove and destroy infected plants.

harvesting

Brussels sprouts start maturing at the base of the stem. When the bottom sprouts are half-size (just over a centimetre in diameter), break off the lower leaves to allow sprouts to develop. Repeat. If you're growing a long-season variety in a mild-winter area, leave foliage on to protect the sprouts.

Many garden books recommend cutting off the top rosette of leaves to encourage sprout formation. This may not be necessary if your growing season is fairly long. In short-season areas, top plants when bottom sprouts are about a centimetre in diameter; the entire stem

should be ready to harvest in about four weeks. Keep half the leaves on the lower part of the stem so the plant can manufacture food. Topping too early leads to a smaller harvest because plants don't have enough leaves to feed developing sprouts.

Start picking the sprouts at the base of the stem when they're firm, well formed and about the size of a walnut. Left unpicked, leaves loosen and sprouts become over-mature.

When night temperatures fall below -5°C, pull up the plant and hang in a cool cellar, where you can continue to harvest sprouts for several weeks. Or leave the plant in the ground but provide extra protection after the first hard frost and when night temperatures fall below -7°C. Bend the stalk to the ground and cover with a thick mulch, or wrap plant in mulch and cover with a plastic bag.

early or late?

Early varieties—the best choice for short seasons—have closely spaced sprouts on stocky plants with thick stems. In some, spacing is so close the sprouts are flat and difficult to pick.

Late varieties are taller, with more distance between the sprouts, and sprouts are less susceptible to rotting in fall and winter rain. The longer days and shorter nights of fall trigger plants to sprout. If sown too late, plants will be short and produce fewer sprouts. Late varieties suit milder, long-season areas such as coastal British Columbia, although those listed also grow well in most of Canada except northern Ontario, the northern Prairies and mountain areas.

Early Varieties

'Jade Cross E' (97 days). Taller than 'Jade Cross', with dark green oval sprouts. Very cold-hardy.
'Prince Marvel' (90 days). Quick-growing, exceptionally hard; high-quality sprouts.
'Oliver' (95 days). Vigorous, easy-to-grow, with well-spaced sprouts.

Late Varieties

'Red Rubine' (100 days). An heirloom that yields beautiful, rich-flavoured deep red sprouts that retain their colour after cooking.
'Content' (105 days). High-yielding, uniform sprouts where rainfall isn't too heavy.

Disease-resistant.

'Valiant' (110 days). High yield of large, rich-flavoured sprouts on a tall, vigorous stalk. Sprouts frost-tolerant, rot resistant.
'Bubbles' (110 days). Round, dark green, well-spaced sprouts. Some tolerance to drought.
'Lunet' (115 days). High yield of medium-large, firm sprouts.
'JBS 596' (130 days). Tall, cold-tolerant plants produce a high yield.
'Vincent' (200 days). Sturdy, late-maturing plants with well-spaced sprouts protected by generous leaf cover.

Although started plants are easier, the choice of varieties is usually limited in garden centres, and often they're available so early they mature in the heat of summer. Those are two good reasons to grow your own Brussels sprouts from seed.

brussels sprouts & red pepper stir-fry

SERVES 4 TO 6

Especially good served over steamed brown rice. Substitute lightly toasted cashews or slivered almonds for the sesame seeds.

2   tsp. (10 mL) olive oil
1   lb. (450 g) small Brussels sprouts, trimmed and halved
1   small red onion, sliced
2   cloves garlic, minced
1   red bell pepper, seeded and sliced
2   tbsp. (30 mL) light soy sauce
    Freshly ground black pepper
2   tbsp. (30 mL) sesame seeds, toasted
    Cooked rice or pasta

1 In a skillet, warm oil over medium heat. Add Brussels sprouts and stir-fry about 2 minutes. Add sliced onion, garlic and red pepper, and continue to stir-fry another 2 minutes.
2 Just before cooking time is completed, add soy sauce, black pepper to taste and sesame seeds. Toss together and serve immediately over rice or pasta.

creamed brussels sprouts with lemon and parsley

SERVES 6

This variation of the classic French creamed celery makes a lovely accompaniment to grilled or roasted chicken or guinea fowl.

1 1/2 lb. (675 g) Brussels sprouts, trimmed
2   tbsp. (30 mL) butter
3   tbsp. (45 mL) all-purpose flour
1   cup (250 mL) milk
    Salt
1/2   tsp. (2 mL) white pepper
    Finely grated zest of 1 lemon
    Juice of 1 lemon
3   tbsp. (45 mL) chopped fresh parsley

1 Bring a pot of water to boil, add a little salt, and boil whole Brussels sprouts until tender, about 12 minutes. Drain and keep warm.
2 In a heavy-bottom saucepan, melt butter over moderate heat. Whisk in flour and cook 2 or 3 minutes. Add milk gradually and stir mixture together until smooth and thickened. Salt to taste. Whisk in white pepper, lemon zest and juice; add Brussels sprouts. Garnish with chopped parsley.

brussels sprout leaves with ligurian walnut sauce

SERVES 4 TO 6

In Italy, this nutty sauce is used to complement stuffed pastas such as tortellini or agnolotti. If you have the time, start with walnuts in the shell; they're fresher than packaged ones. A pound allows for extra in case a few nuts are shrivelled or stale. Leave the Brussels sprouts whole, if you prefer.

1 1/2 cups (375 mL) fresh walnuts, shelled, blanched in boiling water and rubbed clean of their skins

1 thick slice of homestyle white bread, crusts removed

1/4 cup (50 mL) milk

2 cloves garlic, minced

3 tbsp. (45 mL) extra virgin olive oil
Salt and freshly ground black pepper

1 tbsp. (15 mL) chopped fresh marjoram

3 tbsp. (45 mL) butter

1/3 cup (75 mL) mascarpone cheese

1/2 cup (125 mL) grated Parmigiano-Reggiano cheese

1 lb. (450 g) Brussels sprouts, trimmed, steamed 3 minutes and chopped

1 Place bread in a small bowl and pour the milk over it. Let soak 5 minutes.

2 In a skillet over medium heat, toast blanched walnuts for a few minutes, shaking the pan frequently so they don't burn.

3 Pour the bread and milk into a sieve, squeezing the bread dry with your hands.

4 Chop the toasted walnuts in a food processor or blender, using an on-off motion, until finely powdered. Transfer nuts to a mixing bowl and add the bread, blending it into the chopped nuts with a fork. Add garlic, olive oil, salt and pepper to taste, marjoram and a few tablespoons of hot water as needed for a creamy consistency. Blend well. In the same skillet, melt butter over medium heat. Reduce heat to low, add mascarpone cheese and stir for about 2 or 3 minutes, or until smooth and creamy. Add the nut mixture to the mascarpone mixture and warm through gently for 1 minute. Add grated Parmigiano-Reggiano and steamed Brussels sprouts. Toss together and serve immediately.

A traditional Christmas berry with both domestic and commercial appeal

cranberries

recipes

cranberry
upside-down cake

spiked cranberry orange
marmalade

Cranberries have a long history in North America. The Pequot Indians in the Cape Cod area called them *ibimi* (bitter berry); to the Algonquin, they were *atoqua* (good fruit) and were used fresh, cooked and dried. They were known originally as craneberry by early European settlers, who thought the flowers resembled a crane's head, but the word eventually metamorphosed to cranberry. Cranberries (*Vaccinium macrocarpon*) are native to northeastern North America but are grown across the continent. They're hardy to Zone 3 with some winter protection. British Columbia is the largest Canadian producer, growing more than 25,000 tonnes on 1,400 hectares in 1997. But the world leader is the United States, which produced nearly 255,000 tonnes the same year.

BY JODI DELONG

GARDENER'S TIPS
■ Cranberries contain potassium and vitamins A and C, but their high levels of flavanoids are valuable because they reduce cardiovascular disease and inhibit the growth of some cancers.
■ Native North Americans recognized the medicinal value of cranberries and used them to treat urinary infections centuries ago.

Cranberry plants are happy in ordinary garden conditions as long as generous amounts of sphagnum peat are added to the soil to keep it moist. They make a lovely ground cover, with glossy dark green foliage that grows up to 15 centimetres high and turns reddish bronze in fall. The species *V. macrocarpon* can be grown from seed.

home-grown cranberries

- In his former career as a landscaper, Blake Johnston frequently incorporated plantings of cranberries in his designs. Their use as a ground cover has been overlooked, he says.
- The key to success in growing cranberries, whether for food or ornamental purposes, is to create the conditions they prefer: a moist but well-drained substrate using sand and organic matter is essential, with a soil pH of between 4.0 and 5.5. The biggest difficulty for the backyard grower is finding cuttings to plant; most nurseries don't stock them, and cranberry cultivars don't propagate from seed. Cuttings can be divided into smaller segments, pressed down into a prepared bed and kept moist with regular watering.
- Pest control is not usually an issue for home gardeners, other than removing weeds. If your plants receive adequate moisture and minimal nutrition, they should be able to resist the occasional predatory insect without substantial losses.
- The most dangerous time for plants to be exposed to frost is at bloom and just before harvest. To protect against frost, mulch plants with evergreen boughs or burlap.

commercial growing

Commercial cultivation of cranberries in Canada began in 1870, when William McNeil put in a few plants at the edge of a bog on his farm in the Annapolis Valley, Nova Scotia. Today there are almost 65 hectares of cranberries in the province.

Carrying on the tradition is Blake Johnston in Aylesford, Nova Scotia. For Blake, it's a family affair. His father, Orville Johnston, began growing cranberries in 1952, planting his first acres in Bala, Ontario. Blake worked in construction and landscaping while maintaining his involvement in the Bala operation until 1997, when he sold his share to his brother. Blake moved to the marsh in the Annapolis Valley with his wife, Kate, and their children, Jessie, Amelia and Walker. Today, Johnston's Cranberry Marsh in Aylesford is the largest producer of cranberries in Nova Scotia, with nine hectares in production and 11 recently planted hectares.

It costs $75,000 per hectare, on average, to develop a cranberry operation. After selecting an appropriate site—marshland, as level as possible to make planting, flooding and harvesting the field easier—a ditch is installed around the perimeter to lower the water table and provide drainage; a system of reservoirs, dams and floodgates is needed to manage water levels. Then the planting bed is built up: a layer of clay to maintain the water table; an organic layer such as peat moss; and finally a layer of sand, which not only allows the plants, propagated by cuttings, to root easily, it also drains quickly when the beds are flooded. Plants spread by runners, forming a thick mat 15 centimetres high that helps keep weeds down. After planting, an irrigation system is installed.

Right: the harvest from Johnston's Cranberry Marsh in the Annapolis Valley is inspected visually before it's packed. On opening page: Amelia (foreground) and Jessie Johnston. Cranberry growing is a long-standing tradition in the Johnston clan.

It can take three to five years for plants to produce a viable crop. Some farmers plant small areas to complement other aspects of their operation, but Blake relies solely on cranberries for the farm's income. He has seen prices rise and fall as supply outstripped demand, or vice versa, but he's philosophical if there's a disappointing harvest or prices aren't up to par. "There's always next year," he says. He wryly observes that Kate, a stockbroker, has been supporting his "cranberry habit" for nearly 20 years.

Different cultivars are planted according to their productivity, keeping quality and season length. Blake plants 'Stevens', which he calls cranberries for dummies, because the cultivar is so undemanding and productive, as well as 'Ben Lear'. Planting is usually done in May, and it takes almost five tonnes of cuttings to plant a hectare of marsh.

A common misconception about cranberries is that they grow in water. At harvest time, beds are flooded for six to 48 hours to allow the plants to untangle and the berries to float to the top for easier gathering. In winter, flooding forms a protective barrier of ice that keeps the plants from drying out. In spring, a bed may be flooded to protect growing plants from drying winds and to keep buds from opening too early. Some producers also flood in late fall or early spring to kill off fungus or pests. Frost is always a danger in low-lying marsh areas, where cold air can settle even in July and August. Blake uses a sprinkler system to protect his plants.

During the growing months, April to October, constant vigilance is needed to keep insects at bay. As Blake puts it, "If you have a monoculture, you're going to have pests." To keep close tabs on pest populations, he sweeps a special insect net over the vines, then checks the net to see what pests or beneficial insects are present, and in what numbers. Using target-specific pesticides (*Bacillus thurengiensis*, for example), he can keep pests such as black-headed fireworm down to acceptable levels while not harming beneficials such as spiders. Blake uses an Integrated Pest Management program (commonly called IPM), using a combination of chemical, cultural and biological controls to keep losses from pest damage to an acceptable minimum.

Once harvested, the bad berries are separated from the good by machine, then discarded. Visual inspection and packing follow. A good yield is 22,000 kilograms per hectare. Blake estimates that 98 per cent of his crop is marketed as fresh fruit in the Maritimes, Quebec and Ontario, and the Eastern Seaboard. Some of it goes into Mrs. J's Preserves, a line developed and still managed by Blake's mother, June, and sold in the farm's gift shop.

For 17 years, Johnston's Cranberry Marsh in Ontario has been a major part of the Bala Cranberry Festival. In October, 2000, Blake and Kate carried on the tradition in Aylesford, and nearly 1,000 people showed up. The Bala Festival has attracted close to 25,000 people, Blake says. With that kind of interest, the Johnstons are hoping the future for the Aylesford marsh will be just as rosy.

As chilled juice for kids or in summer drinks, or cooked into cranberry sauce for the Christmas turkey... these are the traditional ways to serve cranberries, but they have much more potential in the kitchen.

cranberry upside-down cake

SERVES 6 TO 8

A festive-looking cake that's a refreshing ending to any holiday dinner, and it is quite simple to make.

For topping

6	tbsp. (90 mL) unsalted butter
3	cups (750 mL) fresh cranberries, washed
9	tbsp. (135 mL) maple syrup
1/2	cup (75 mL) brown sugar
1	cinnamon stick
1	tbsp. (15mL) lemon zest

For cake

1 1/4	cups (310 mL) all-purpose flour
2 1/2	tsp. (12 mL) baking powder
1/2	tsp. (2 mL) cinnamon
1/4	tsp. (1 mL) salt
1/4	tsp. (1mL) nutmeg
3/4	cup (175 mL) yellow cornmeal, preferably coarse
1/3	cup (75 mL) granulated sugar
6	tbsp. (90 mL) melted unsalted butter
3/4	cup (175 mL) buttermilk
1/4	cup orange juice, preferably freshly squeezed
1/2	tsp. (2 mL) vanilla extract
1	large egg, beaten
1	tbsp. (15 mL) lemon zest

1 Preheat oven to 350°C (180°F). Line a baking sheet with aluminum foil and set it aside. Butter and flour an 8-inch, non-stick cake pan, set aside.

2 In a large, heavy-based skillet, melt butter for topping over medium heat until it sizzles. Add cranberries and cook gently until shiny, about 2 to 3 minutes. Add remaining ingredients for topping and cook, stirring frequently, until cranberries are softened but still retain their shape, about 5 minutes. Remove cranberries with a slotted spoon and transfer to the prepared baking sheet. Set syrup mixture aside. When cranberries are slightly cooled, spread evenly over bottom of cake pan.
3 Return skillet to medium heat and bring mixture to a boil. Reduce heat and continue to simmer for 10 minutes. Do not overcook syrup or it will burn. Immediately, pour over cranberries and let cool.
4 Meanwhile, sift flour, baking powder, cinnamon, salt and nutmeg together in a medium-sized bowl. Add cornmeal and sugar; mix well with a fork. In a smaller bowl, add melted butter, buttermilk orange juice, vanilla, egg and lemon zest. Make a well in dry ingredients and pour in wet ingredients. Gently fold together until batter is just blended. Carefully spread evenly over cranberries.
5 Place cake on baking sheet, lined with new aluminum foil, and place in oven. (The cake will temporarily rise higher than the pan while it is baking.) Bake for 40 to 45 minutes until golden brown or until toothpick comes out clean.

6 Place on cooling rack for 15 to 20 minutes. Gently slide a plastic knife or spatula around the edges of pan to loosen cake. Invert cake pan on a flat plate and let it rest upside down for 3 to 5 minutes. Carefully remove pan. Serve slightly warm or at room temperature. Enjoy with a dollop of sweetened whipped cream or ice cream.

spiked cranberry orange marmalade

MAKES 3 CUPS (750 MILLILITRES)

A nice change from traditional cranberry sauce, this spread has a subtle savoury flavour. Try it with turkey or on toast.

2	large thick-skinned navel oranges
1	fresh or 2 dried bay leaves
1	medium-sized cinnamon stick
6	green cardamom pods
1	sprig rosemary
1	cup (250 mL) orange juice, preferably fresh squeezed
1/2	cup (125 mL) dry red wine
1	cup (250 mL) plus 2 tbsp. (30mL) granulated sugar
1	package (12 oz./340 g) fresh cranberries, washed
1 1/2	tsp. (7 mL) bourbon
1/4	tsp. (1 mL) ground black pepper
	6 x 6-in.-square (15 x 15-cm) piece of cheesecloth
	4 to 5 in. (10 to 13 cm) length of kitchen string

1 Using a sharp paring knife or vegetable peeler, carefully peel oranges and cut the orange part only into strips approximately 1 1/4 inches (3 centimetres) in length. Remove all white pith left on peelings and on the orange flesh. Cut strips of peeling lengthwise into very fine julienne. Soak in cold water for about 30 minutes, or overnight. Strain and discard water.
2 Working over a bowl, cut between membranes of oranges to release individual segments. Cut segments into 1/2-inch (1-centimetre) pieces.
3 Place bay leaf, cinnamon stick, cardamom pods and rosemary on cheesecloth. Bring corners together to make a bundle. Tie with kitchen string.
4 Bring orange juice, red wine and sugar to a boil in a heavy, medium-sized saucepan. Reduce heat and stir until sugar is dissolved. Add spice bundle. Simmer for 15 minutes, stirring occasionally. Add cranberries, half the orange peel and half the orange segments. Simmer for 15 to 20 minutes or until slightly thickened, continuing to stir occasionally. Add remaining orange peel and segments. Continue simmering and stirring for 15 minutes.
5 Remove from heat. Add bourbon and black pepper. Transfer to an airtight container and cool completely before refrigerating (about 2 hours). When cool, remove spice bundle from marmalade. Keep refrigerated.

Sweet, succulent and good for you, onions have it all

onions

recipes

cipolline in agrodolce
(sweet & sour onions)

red onion confit

french onion tart

Onions are one of our oldest cultivated crops: the labourers who built Egypt's pyramids ate them to increase their strength and stamina, and the ancient Greeks and Romans always consumed the pungent vegetable before going into battle.

The common onion (*Allium cepa*) is part of the Allium genus, which includes shallots, chives, leeks and garlic as well as many ornamental varieties, and all alliums are members of the *Liliaceae* family, which includes lilies (naturally), hostas and tulips.

Low in calories and high in health-promoting chemicals that help fight disease, onions are also a rich source of organic sulfur compounds. These substances are released when onions are cut and they combine with the moisture in your eyes to form mild sulfuric acid, which stings and causes tears.

And while we enjoy the mighty onion's health benefits, the flavourful vegetable enhances and enriches our cuisine. The familiar yellow cooking and Spanish onions are called bulb onions, and can be grown from seeds or sets (small bulbs harvested the previous summer and stored over winter). While sets are easy to plant and give a quick start, they yield onions more prone to disease and bolting to seed, and don't store well. Seeds take more work, but offer a wider choice of varieties, including types with excellent storage qualities. BY HEATHER APPLE

GARDENER'S TIPS
- Eating onions regularly can lower blood pressure, decrease blood lipid levels and lower blood sugar in diabetics. Half a raw onion a day raises good HDL blood cholesterol by about 30 per cent.
- When harvesting, pick onions that have flowered first. Although flowering plants are pretty to look at, the bulbs don't keep as well.
- Shallots are a culinary treat, expensive to buy in stores. But they're a cinch to grow in the garden.

other onions

Gardeners aren't limited to the standard bulb and storage onions. Here are five varieties to find space for in the vegetable plot.

■ Scallion is a fancy name for green bunching onions. You get scallions by harvesting nearly any onion early, but some are grown specifically for their delicately flavoured white stems and juicy green tops. 'White Lisbon', 'Long White Summer Bunching' and 'Southport White' ('Green Bunching Strain') form mild scallions. 'Red Beard' has a white bulb and rhubarb-red stalk.

Sow seeds six millimetres deep and one centimetre apart, in closely spaced rows. Don't thin seedlings—start harvesting when plants are nine millimetres in diameter. For long white stems, hill up the plants with loose soil as they grow. Make successive sowings for fresh scallions all summer.

■ Shallots have a mild flavour, between regular onions and garlic. Plant cloves 10 to 15 centimetres apart with the tip just below the soil surface. Sprouts appear in one or two weeks. Harvest when the tops start to wither; each clove will have formed a bunch of six to 10 shallots near the soil's surface.

■ Multiplier onions are heirlooms that produce delicious cooking onions. Plant sets in the fall so they have time to grow roots before the ground freezes (spring planting is possible, but not as productive). Space 20 centimetres apart, tips just below soil level. Mulch deeply Zone 5 and colder. Remove the mulch in the spring and fertilize.

Plant a mixture of large and small multiplier onions each year to have onions and sets for planting next year. Each fall-planted small onion grows into a large bulb by the following midsummer. Harvest some for eating and store the rest in a cool, dry place to plant in the fall. Large onions planted in the fall each produce a spring harvest of five to 20 scallions.

■ Welsh onions are hardy, perennial scallions that originated in Siberia, not Wales. Sow seeds in spring, two per 2.5 centimetres. 'Kincho' is hardy in southern Ontario and milder parts of British Columbia; 'Hardy White Bunching' survives in colder areas. When green onions are large enough to harvest, thin to 10 centimetres. Leave the rest in the ground the first season; mulch heavily in cold regions. The following spring, each plant forms a clump of green onions. Harvest some and divide the rest; plant divisions 10 centimetres apart. Toward the end of summer each plant again forms a cluster of green onions; harvest some and leave the rest to overwinter. Hilling up the soil around the plants produces longer white stems. Break off flower stalks. By thinning clumps and refreshing the soil with compost, you'll have Welsh onions indefinitely.

■ Bizarre-looking perennial Egyptian onions form clusters of small onions on top of flower stalks, not underground. The little onions are stronger and richer in flavour than other onions, and can also be pickled. Plant bulbs any time, 10 centimetres apart, tip just below soil level. Mulch for winter in northern areas and uncover in spring. Green shoots can be harvested as scallions. Summer's flower stalk is topped with clusters of bulblets. Eventually the stalk collapses and bulblets fall to the ground and take root, enlarging the patch and giving the plant the nickname "walking onion." Maintain permanent beds by thinning plants and refreshing soil with compost.

If your aim is green onions, or scallions, as they're also called, plant onion sets deep—as deep as 10 centimetres. They'll stretch toward the light as they grow, leaving a long white stalk to bleach white and sweet underground. Alternatively, you could mound earth up around the stalks as plants grow, bleaching the stems that don't receive light.

growing from seed

Spanish-type onions take the longest to mature. Start seeds indoors at the end of February; later sowing results in small, pungent bulbs. Onions grown for storage can be seeded directly in the garden as soon as the soil is workable, although in most parts of Canada (except for coastal British Columbia) a better crop results from starting seed indoors in early April.

Sow seeds six millimetres deep and six millimetres apart, in closely spaced rows. Expose the flat to indirect light and maintain a temperature of 18°C to 21°C. When seeds germinate, place under fluorescent lights or in a sunny window, and grow at a cool temperature. When seedlings are 2.5 centimetres tall, thin to two per 2.5 centimetres. In a soil-free mix, feed weekly with compost tea or a half-strength fish emulsion; in a mix without soil, feed every 10 to 14 days. Keep plants well watered and trim tops to 10 centimetres. When the danger of frost has passed, harden off seedlings.

Plant in fertile, well-drained soil in full sun. Dig in compost or well-rotted manure; heavy clay soils need organic matter and coarse sand. In poorly drained sites, use raised beds. To plant, dig holes or trench five centimetres deep. Using a knife, remove a row of seedlings from the flat and gently separate plants. Set seedlings 10 to 15 centimetres apart (depending on mature size). Keep seedlings watered, but not soggy.

growing from sets

Buy firm, unsprouted sets. Choose small sets; larger ones may already have an embryonic flower stalk inside, which will result in the plant going to seed. Plant them outdoors as soon as the soil is workable in the spring, with tips just below the surface, and spaced 10 to 15 centimetres apart. Firm down the area with the back of a hoe so the sets are in contact with the soil.

During the growing season, keep seed- and set-grown onions well watered. Water-stressed plants produce small, pungent bulbs. Once a month, side dress with compost or organic fertilizer, scratching it just into the soil surface to avoid damaging the onions' shallow roots. Keep the bed carefully weeded; onion seedlings grow slowly and weeds compete for water and nutrients. If you let weeds get too big before yanking them out, you may damage the onion roots and set the plants back.

pests and diseases

Onions are susceptible to a number of fungal diseases and pests. To minimize diseases, plant in well-drained soil, practise three- or four-year crop rotation, destroy infested plants and clean up plant debris in the fall. Water in the morning and grow onions from seed or buy certified disease-free sets. Two pests to watch for are onion maggots and thrips.

Onion maggots They overwinter in the soil as pupae. Adult flies emerge in spring and lay eggs at the base of young plants. The white maggots, about nine millimetres long, burrow into the underground stems, causing them to wilt and turn yellow. Later generations burrow into the bulbs of larger onions and cause them to rot. Dust the soil around onions with diatomaceous earth,

destroy infested plants and clean up garden debris in the fall.

Onion thrips These pests pierce the leaves and suck out plant juices, causing silver streaks that develop into white patches. Serious infestations cause stunted, bleached leaves that die back. Plants ripen prematurely, produce small bulbs and may die. Damage is worst in hot, dry weather. To control, spray the onions with insecticidal soap, don't plant near fields of alfalfa, grain or other commercial crops, and remove nearby weeds and debris to prevent thrips from overwintering.

harvesting and curing

Onions that have been properly harvested and cured keep longer. Toward the end of summer, when about half the onion tops are falling over and the bulbs have a papery skin, gently knock over the rest of the tops by hand or with a hoe, bending but not breaking them. Pull out those with flower stalks and eat first because they won't store well. Leave the remaining onions in the ground for about a week; don't water them. Then dig them up and gently brush off the soil, but don't wash them. Spread them out to dry for a couple of weeks in a warm, airy place, out of rain and direct sun. Leave the tops on and braid for storage, or cut off the tops, leaving a short stub. Store in a cool, dry place (2°C to 10°C) in mesh bags or old pantyhose or on a wire-mesh shelf. Check regularly and remove sprouting or rotting onions.

varieties

Onions form bulbs in response to the number of daylight hours. Varieties are described as short-day (12- to 14-hour days) and long-day (14- to 16-hour days). Grow long-day onions; short-day varieties produce small bulbs in Canada.

Unfortunately, we can't grow mild, sweet Spanish onions such as the famous 'Vidalia', so plentiful in the southern U.S., in our northern latitudes. The closest we can manage is 'Walla Walla', a mild, sweet, jumbo Spanish onion best suited to coastal British Columbia. In the rest of Canada it forms smaller, more pungent bulbs. Outside of B.C., try 'Kelsae Sweet Giant', with huge, mild, sweet bulbs, and 'Riverside Sweet Spanish', which yields mild bulbs that store well until early winter.

Not all varieties of cooking onions store well. 'Copra', a dark yellow-skinned variety, is best. 'First Edition' and 'Redskin' also store well; 'New York Early' isn't as suitable but it's more tender and flavourful.

Onions are more than the cook's greatest flavour ally, they're delicious on their own. Try them roasted whole with a bit of port and rosemary in the same pan as prime rib of beef.

cipolline in agrodolce (sweet & sour onions)

SERVES 8 TO 10

Agrodolce is a cooking method Italians use with cipolline, which are small, flat, dense and exceedingly sweet little onions. While you can use small new cooking onions or pearl onions successfully, cipolline, sold at specialty produce markets and some supermarkets, yield the best results. Add the red wine if the balsamic vinegar is of average quality. Omit the wine if you use a good quality aceto balsamico, aged eight years or more.

2   lb. (1 kg) cipolline (or small new onions or pearl onions)
2   tbsp. (30 mL) butter
2   tbsp. (30 mL) extra virgin olive oil
1/4 cup (50 mL) balsamic vinegar
1   tbsp. (15 mL) granulated sugar
3   tbsp. (45 mL) robust red wine (optional)
1/4 cup (50 mL) chopped fresh mint
     Salt and freshly ground black pepper to taste

1 Blanch unpeeled onions in boiling water 3 minutes—no longer or they'll be too soft. Plunge into cold water and peel; keep the stem end intact.

2 In a skillet large enough to hold all the onions, melt the butter over medium heat and add olive oil. Add onions and cook gently, turning them occasionally, 5 or 6 minutes, or until they start to brown on all sides. Add vinegar and sugar, and wine, if using. Increase heat and cook, stirring, until onions start to caramelize, about 3 minutes. Shake the pan from time to time as they cook.

3 When mixture is thick and syrup-like, add chopped mint; season with salt and pepper. Turn out on a serving dish, let cool and serve at room temperature.

red onion confit

MAKES 1 JAR

A luxurious, brilliantly coloured relish that's magnificent spread over warm crusty bread and paired with a wedge of cheese. Or use it in omelettes or with grilled sausages.

2   tbsp. (30 mL) butter
2   tbsp. (30 mL) extra virgin olive oil
1/2 cup (125 mL) granulated sugar
1 1/2 lb. (680 g) red onions, thinly sliced
3/4 cup (175 mL) dry red wine
1/3 cup + 1 tbsp. (90 mL) red wine vinegar

1 In a large saucepan, melt the butter in the oil over low heat. Add sugar and stir to dissolve completely.

2 Add onions all at once; stir to cover with butter and sugar mixture. Cover loosely and cook about 30 minutes, stirring occasionally. Stir in wine and vinegar and increase heat to bring to a boil. Reduce heat and simmer gently, uncovered, for another 30 minutes.

3 Increase heat once more and cook, stirring, 5 to 8 minutes, or until mixture becomes thick and jam-like. Remove from heat and allow to cool. Pack into a sterilized jar and store in the refrigerator for up to a month.

french onion tart

SERVES 6

Any type of onion may be used, just be sure to allow enough cooking time for the onions to caramelize and darken.

4   tbsp. (50 mL) butter
1   lb. (500 g) onions, very thinly sliced
1/2 tsp. (2 mL) salt
1/4 tsp. (1 mL) freshly ground black pepper
3   eggs
1/2 cup (125 mL) milk
1/2 cup (125 mL) light cream
1/4 tsp. (1 mL) freshly grated nutmeg
1   10-in. (25-cm) baked pastry crust

1 In a large skillet, melt butter over medium heat. Add onions, salt and pepper; stir to combine. Cover and cook, stirring occasionally, until onions begin to caramelize, about 30 minutes. Remove from heat and set aside. Preheat oven to 350°F (180°C).

2 In a mixing bowl, combine the eggs with the milk, cream and nutmeg. Whisk together until well blended.

3 Spread cooled onions over the surface of the baked pastry shell. Pour the egg mixture over the onions. Bake in preheated oven until filling is set, about 30 minutes. Serve warm.

White, purple, red, gold, blue—there's a potato for every palate

potatoes

recipes

spinach & potato dumplings

savoy cabbage with potatoes

potato-tomato gratin

Russian peasants called them "the Devil's apples." Europeans blamed them for ills ranging from warts and rickets to consumption and leprosy. An early American farmer's manual recommended growing them conveniently close to those most suited to feed on them—hogs.

Also woven into the potato's history is the great tragedy of the Irish potato famine. After they were brought to Ireland from South America by Sir Walter Raleigh about 1590, potatoes became the main source of food for Irish peasants. When blight destroyed the crop in 1846, the consequences were disastrous. Over a five-year period, more than a million people died, and another million immigrated to England and North America.

Despite its checkered past, the potato is a popular vegetable today. Enjoyed baked, boiled, chipped, fried and mashed, the humble spud is the fourth most important food crop in the world, after wheat, rice and maize. Yet it's still misunderstood and unjustly accused of being fattening.

Freshly dug new potatoes are one of the garden's most delicious gifts. Even gardeners with limited space can enjoy this treat, and with so many new varieties and different colours available, you can choose a potato that best serves your needs. BY HEATHER APPLE

GARDENER'S TIPS
- Potatoes have an unfair reputation for being fattening. In fact, one medium-sized potato without butter or sour cream is no higher in calories than a large apple.
- One potato supplies one-third the daily requirement of vitamin C, significant amounts of riboflavin, thiamin and niacin, and a whopping 650 milligrams of potassium.

Some gardeners swear by marigolds in the potato patch to repel the Colorado potato beetle. Or try bran sprinkled on the leaves—it's said that after bugs eat it they swell up and explode. Cedar boughs boiled into a weak tea and sprayed on plants is also reported to work. Opposite: 'All Blue', 'Yukon Gold' and 'Banana'.

growing

To prepare large potatoes for planting, cut them into pieces with two eyes or recessed dormant buds. Let pieces dry two days to help seal the cut surface and reduce the chance of rotting. Small, egg-sized potatoes can be planted whole. Some mail-order seed potatoes are shipped as marble-sized plugs cut from whole tubers, and these should be planted whole.

If your soil is wet and cold in the spring, plant potatoes whole to reduce the risk of rotting. Tubers can be sprouted before planting, known as "chitting," for early maturing. Two or three weeks before you plan to plant, spread potatoes in a single layer on a tray in a bright location. Spritz with water if they start to shrivel. Eventually they turn green, and stubby shoots appear.

Tubers stored over the winter in a dark

place may send out long, weak shoots well before planting time. In that case, start chitting up to six weeks before planting. Cut shoots back to 2.5 to five centimetres first.

Potatoes need sun and well-drained, loose, humus-rich, slightly acidic soil. Add lots of compost or well-aged manure to sandy or clay soils. Practise a three-year rotation plan: don't plant tomatoes, peppers or eggplants in the same location for three years.

Seed potatoes may rot in cold, wet soils. Dig 15-centimetre-deep furrows in rows 75 to 90 centimetres apart—wide enough to allow tilling, hilling and mulching. In raised beds, rows can be 30 to 45 centimetres apart. Set potatoes 25 to 30 centimetres apart with the eye on top. The first green shoots appear in about two weeks. Two weeks after, use a broad hoe to pull soil gently up around the plant's stems. The new crop of potatoes forms above, not below, the seed potato, and hilling prevents tubers from becoming exposed to the sun and turning green, producing the toxic alkaloid solanine. Hill up plants again in another two or three weeks, adding compost to the soil and banking it high, but leaving 25 to 30 centimetres of stem and leaves uncovered.

Water regularly and deeply at the base of the plant. Use overhead watering early in

the day so foliage dries by nightfall. In hot, dry areas, mulch to keep soil cool and moist. Tuber development decreases at prolonged high temperatures (above 32°C).

harvesting and storing

Tubers begin forming before the plants bloom and continue until vines die. Harvest small new potatoes after the plants begin to flower—usually 10 weeks after planting. Dig around with your hands and gently remove egg-sized tubers, disturbing the roots as little as possible and replacing soil carefully to allow smaller tubers to continue maturing. As the season progresses, dig up whole plants and harvest everything from tiny new potatoes to full-sized tubers. Dig a garden fork into the soil about 30 centimetres away from the plant, wiggle it gently to loosen the potatoes, then lift up the fork. Lift out any potatoes you can find and then feel around in the soil for others.

Never eat green tubers. You can, however, cut away the poisonous green areas and safely eat the rest of the tuber. Leaves and small green fruits that form later on the plants are also poisonous.

For a storage crop, grow varieties that are good keepers. After tops die, leave tubers in the ground a couple of weeks to toughen skins—up to six weeks, if necessary. Harvest on a cool day when the soil's not wet, and leave potatoes on the ground for only an hour or two if they're damp. Before long-term storage, cure tubers one to two weeks: spread out in a totally dark place with a fairly high humidity and about 13°C to 18°C. Turn halfway through the curing period. Store in a cold, dark place, 2°C to 4°C, with high humidity. At 2°C and below, some of the starch converts to sugar, resulting in an unpleasant sweet taste. Don't store with apples, which give off ethylene gas that stimulates sprouting.

diseases and pests

Colorado potato beetle Adults and larvae feed on leaves and can defoliate plants. Squash adults. Check under leaves for orange egg masses and squash those, too. Shake foliage over a pail of soapy water or use rotenone.

Aphids Control aphids by washing off with a stream of water or spraying with insecticidal soap.

Hollow heart Caused by feast-and-famine fertilizing or watering. Provide plants with a steady supply of food and water evenly.

Scab Irregular brown lesions on the surface, but peeled tubers can be eaten. Severe in light, dry soils. Maintain adequate soil moisture. Add organic matter.

Black scurf Forms on skin. Causes swollen stems and cankers, leaf rolling, wilting and purpling, and plant death. Plant in well-drained soil.

Bacterial ring rot Foliage wilts, gradually affecting the whole stem. Tubers turn brown and decay near stem end, which may ooze a cheesy substance. No cure. When cutting tubers for seed, disinfect knife with bleach or alcohol.

Early blight Small brown lesions on foliage can reduce yield. Symptoms appear on tubers during storage. Don't harvest tubers when soil is wet.

Late blight (seen at far left) Cause of Irish potato famine. Dark green, water-soaked areas at leaf tips spread inward and become dark brown and brittle. Spreads rapidly. Cut off stalks just above the ground so spores don't enter the soil and infect tubers. Wait two weeks to harvest tubers.

Viruses Cause rolling, discoloured, mottled and deformed leaves, and stunted plants.

varieties

The performance, taste and colour of potato cultivars varies with soil and climate.

- European fingerlings are long thin varieties with waxy yellow flesh that's firm but tender: 'Banana', 'German Fingerling' and 'Slovenian Crescent'.
- 'Red Dutch' is a red russet-skinned, yellow-fleshed variety.
- Unusual blue-skinned, blue-fleshed varieties: 'All Blue', an excellent baker, retains its colour after cooking; 'Congo' is an old Swedish variety with dark purple flesh; and 'Blue-Noser' is a Canadian heirloom from Tancook Island, Nova Scotia. Traditionally boiled with salt fish, 'Blue-Noser' has lavender skin with a dark blue nose, and white flesh with blue markings.
- For storage: russet-skinned 'Nooksack'; Canadian-bred 'Yukon Gold', a delicious all-round potato.
- 'Kennebec' is a high-yielding white-fleshed variety.
- 'Sebago' is an all-purpose potato adaptable to clay soil that produces many white tubers. It's resistant to early and late blight and moderately resistant to scab.
- For beautiful new potatoes, try 'Warba'; it has golden skin and pink splashed around its deep eyes.
- 'Acadia Russet' produces long tubers with a light, netted skin; it's excellent boiled or baked.

a barrel of spuds

- Even in a small garden, it's worth growing a few plants for new potatoes. Early varieties such as 'Yukon Gold' (yellow-fleshed), 'Norland' (red-skinned) and 'Warba' (white-fleshed) yield plenty of superior-tasting spuds. Once the potatoes are harvested, remove the vines, work compost into the soil and plant peas, lettuce, spinach, turnips or Chinese greens for a late-summer crop.
- No garden space at all? Plant potatoes in a large container such as a half-barrel or garbage pail. Fill the container to within 25 centimetres of the top with a mixture of good soil and compost. Place one tuber on the soil and cover with 10 centimetres of soil/compost mixture. As the plant grows, add more soil/compost mix to hill it up.
- Keep container soil evenly moist but not soggy. Soil that heats up quickly on a sunny day could adversely affect tuber production; wrap burlap around the container, or shade it by clustering other potted plants around its base.

spinach & potato dumplings

SERVES 6 TO 8

Don't be intimidated by the lengthy list of ingredients in this recipe, indigenous to Caserta, Italy. It's not difficult to make, and it's outstanding as a first course. The less you handle gnocchi, the less flour is absorbed and the lighter they'll be.

For the tomato sauce

4	tbsp. (60 mL) olive oil
1	large onion, peeled and chopped
4	cups (1 L) ground or puréed tomatoes
2	cups (500 mL) canned Italian plum tomatoes, drained and chopped roughly
	Sea salt and freshly ground black pepper
1	tsp. (5 mL) granulated sugar

For the meatballs

10 oz. (315 g) lean ground beef
3	cloves garlic, peeled and minced or put through a garlic press
4	tbsp. (60 mL) chopped flat-leaf parsley
	Sea salt and freshly ground black pepper
2	tbsp. (25 mL) olive oil

For the gnocchi

1 1/2	lb. (750 g) boiling potatoes, scrubbed clean and halved
1 1/2	lb. (750 g) fresh spinach, washed and stems trimmed
1 1/2-2	cups (375-500 mL) unbleached all-purpose flour
2	eggs
1	tsp. (15 mL) salt
1 1/2	cups (375 mL) ricotta cheese
1	lb. (450 g) mozzarella cheese, shredded

1 To make the tomato sauce: In a large skillet or saucepan, warm olive oil and sauté onion until softened, about 5 minutes. Add puréed and chopped tomatoes, salt, pepper and sugar, and cook until thickened, about 20 minutes. Distribute sauce evenly over the bottom of a large, shallow glass or terra-cotta baking dish and set aside. Wipe the skillet clean.

2 In a large mixing bowl, combine ground beef with garlic, parsley, and salt and pepper to taste. Shape into tiny meatballs no bigger than a hazelnut. Warm olive oil in skillet and brown meatballs, a batch at a time, shaking the pan to brown all sides. Using a slotted spoon, transfer the meatballs to a bowl or plate lined with paper towelling.

3 Cook potatoes in a large saucepan in lightly salted water just to cover. In another saucepan, cook spinach in just the water that clings to the leaves. Transfer cooked spinach to a fine sieve and press firmly to remove all the water. When cool enough to handle, squeeze spinach as dry as possible with your hands; chop finely and set aside. When potatoes are cooked, drain and return them to the heat. Lower heat and shake pan once or twice to allow excess moisture to evaporate. Remove from heat. When cool enough to handle, remove skins and mash potatoes. Put a large pot of lightly salted water on to boil.

4 In the bowl of a food processor, combine potatoes and spinach and, using the on-off switch, pulse a few times to blend them. (Or blend by hand.) Turn mixture out onto a clean work surface.

5 Gradually work in the flour and eggs, using just enough flour to keep dough from being too sticky. Try not to knead dough longer than a few minutes. When dough is smooth, divide into several equal-sized pieces. With your hands, roll out each piece of dough into a long sausage shape about 3/4 in. (2 cm) in diameter. Cut off 1/2-in. (1-cm) portions and transfer to a tray. Repeat process until all the dough has been shaped. (At this point, gnocchi can be covered with plastic wrap and stored in the refrigerator for several hours.)

6 Preheat oven to 350°F (180°C). Add salt to a large pot of boiling water, and cook gnocchi in batches of about 20 at a time. After a few minutes, they'll bob to the surface; cook for about 2 more minutes, then remove with a slotted spoon or small sieve to a warmed mixing bowl.

7 When all gnocchi are cooked, add ricotta and mozzarella cheese. Add meatballs and toss gently together. Pour mixture over tomato sauce in baking dish and bake about 20 minutes, or until heated through and gnocchi and ricotta are beginning to brown slightly. Serve immediately.

potato-tomato gratin

SERVES 6 TO 8

A combination of potatoes and tomatoes
makes a light dish substantial enough
for a main course. Prepare up to a day
ahead and reheat before serving. Make
it in late summer when fresh plum
tomatoes are plentiful.

4   tbsp. (60 mL) extra virgin olive oil,
     and a little more for the baking dish
4   lb. (2 kg) baking potatoes (about
     6), peeled and cut crosswise into
     1/4-in. (6-mm) slices
2   medium onions, thinly sliced
1   lb. (450 g) ripe, firm plum tomatoes
     (about 6), seeded and diced
3   garlic cloves, finely chopped
1 1/2 tsp. (20 mL) chopped fresh oregano
     Sea salt and freshly ground
     black pepper
1   cup (250 mL) freshly grated
     Pecorino Romano cheese

1 Preheat oven to 400°F (200°C). In a
large mixing bowl, combine 2 tbsp. (30
mL) olive oil with the potatoes, onions,
tomatoes, garlic, oregano, salt, pepper
and 1/2 cup (125 mL) of the Pecorino
Romano cheese. Using your hands,
combine well.
2 Brush a little more olive oil over the
surface of a large, shallow baking dish.
Transfer potato mixture to the baking
dish and drizzle remaining 2 tbsp. (30
mL) olive oil over top. Evenly distribute
remaining Pecorino Romano cheese
over all.
3 Bake on top rack of oven until potatoes are tender, about 1 hour. Allow to
stand for 15 minutes before serving.

savoy cabbage with potatoes

SERVES 4 TO 6

Canadians with Irish origins will love this
Italian version of colcannon. Garlic and
olive oil are used instead of a large quantity
of butter. Wonderful with grilled sausages
or roast pork.

2   lb. (900 g) boiling potatoes,
     peeled and quartered
2   lb. (900 g) Savoy cabbage,
     cored and chopped
1/4 cup (50 mL) olive oil
1   tbsp. (15 mL) butter, softened
4   cloves garlic, minced
3   tbsp. (45 mL) chopped flat-leaf
     parsley
     Salt and freshly ground black
     pepper to taste

1 Bring a large pot of lightly salted
water to boil. Add potatoes and cook
about 15 minutes; they should not be
fully cooked. Add cabbage and cook a
further 15 minutes, until both vegetables are cooked through.
2 Drain vegetables and return to pot.
Shake pot over very low heat to allow
moisture to evaporate. Potatoes and
cabbage should be relatively dry.
Remove pot from heat and cover.
3 Warm olive oil and butter in a skillet
over medium heat. Add garlic and
sauté for a few minutes until softened.
Add chopped parsley, stir to combine
with garlic, then immediately pour mixture over cabbage and potatoes, scraping with a rubber spatula to get all the
oil, garlic and parsley.
4 Roughly mash vegetables with
warmed oil mixture and stir everything
together well. Season to taste with salt
and pepper and serve immediately.

An old-fashioned vegetable both beautiful and delicious

winter SQUASH

recipes

buttercup corn muffins

squash soup with pasta

acorn squash with apple ale & garlic

I've always loved squash. As a child, I got a vicarious thrill seeing my grandmother raise her axe to cleave open a monstrous 'New England Blue Hubbard' squash, grown on her three-hectare market garden farm in Churchill, Ontario. It was always a cold winter day when the leathery, green, warty hide was breached, revealing a glowing, golden interior. Glimpsing the tasty flesh was like a vision of pure summer sunshine kept hidden through the dreary months of late fall and early winter. That was more than 35 years ago and Hubbard squash is still my favourite winter vegetable. Four years ago, I moved to a house with a large yard, where I hoped to cultivate my own 'New England Blue'. I realized they might take over the entire neighbourhood, so I opted for the 'Mini Green Hubbard'. Still, the vines greedily clambered everywhere—even into the neighbour's yard—in search of sun.

Squash can be divided into two groups: thin-skinned, summer squash (*Cucurbita pepo*), such as zucchini and vegetable marrow; and hard-skinned, winter squash (*Cucurbita maxima* and *Cucurbita moschata*). Winter squash need lots of room, plenty of water and full sun, as well as warm earth and a long season. Along with pumpkins and melons, they rate low for garden-space efficiency, but give relatively high yields because of the size of the fruit. BY LESLIE SMITH DOW

GARDENER'S TIPS

■ Yellow squash contains a wealth of vitamins A, B and C, plus iron, calcium, phosphorus and sugars.

■ Summer squash, including the round pattypan or scallop squash, the knobby crookneck and the ubiquitous zucchini lack the flavour of winter squash.

■ Gourds are also squash, and are fun to grow even if they take forever to mature. Start seeds indoors and grow on trellis. Ripen on the vine and cure in a warm, dry spot.

Butternut squash, at left in a butterbowl and on the vine, on opposite page, is a favourite variety. Below, 'Buttercup' on the vine in August, and at at top right with acorn squash.

planting

"You can grow squash just about any-where in the country below the treeline," says Chris Chechak, farm trial co-ordinator for Stokes Seeds in St. Catharines, Ontario. The biggest mistake gardeners make is to plant seeds too early, she says. Soil temperature should be at least 18.5°C, or warm enough to sit on comfortably, and don't judge its warmth by the temperature of the air—soil is usually 5°C to 6°C cooler. "If the ground is cold and wet, the seeds will rot very quickly, even if treated with anti-rotting agents," Chechak says. To warm the soil, cover the planting area with black landscape fabric or plastic.

Dig holes 15 centimetres deep and 60 centimetres in diameter. Space planting holes one to 2.5 metres apart, depending on the type of squash and expected fruit size, and fill with well-rotted manure. Mix a handful of 6-12-12 fertilizer with the excavated soil, place it on top of the manure and hill it up. When the weather is consistently warm and danger of frost is past, plant six to 10 seeds per hill.

For an earlier start, plant seeds indoors in peat pots four to six weeks before you expect the weather to warm up. Thin seedlings to three vigorous shoots when vines are 15 centimetres long. Although they're unsightly, old tires placed around seedlings are perfect for growing squash—they warm the ground and help contain the vines.

growing

Once plants are established, place an organic mulch around plants and under the vines as far as they extend. Fruit resting directly on damp soil may rot. Water weekly, or bury soaker hoses under vines; squash require about six centimetres of water a week. But don't water at night—damp foliage and soil encourage powdery mildew.

To grow plants upright—which doesn't work well with varieties bearing heavy fruit—drape vines on a trellis. Varieties without grasping tendrils must be tied. Support the fruit with slings made of fabric (old pantyhose or J-cloths work well) tied to the trellis; don't use wire or twist ties, which might sever the vines. Be sure the fabric and the trellis, not the vine, take the weight of the squash. Vines can also be trained up wire fencing, a lean-to, tall wooden arches, tripods or teepee-shaped frames.

Be on the lookout for squash vine borers—fat, wrinkled, white caterpillars that tunnel into the squash stem, causing the vine to wilt and die. Slit open the vines, pry out the borer and kill it. If the vine isn't too badly damaged, bury the section you slit; the vine should re-root at that point. Fusarium wilt, bacterial wilt, powdery mildew and downy mildew can also be problems; choose disease-resistant varieties. Rotenone is an effective organic insecticide, but be sure to follow package directions.

Not all squash blossoms grow into fruit—don't be alarmed if some drop off.

Squash vines are space robbers—they greedily clamber everywhere, sometimes even into the neighbour's yard, in search of sun. But growing plants upright doesn't work very well with varieties that produce heavy fruit. Some varieties can be draped over a trellis or fence, with the fruit held in slings of old pantyhose or J-cloths.

(Squash blossoms are edible: early blossoms dipped in batter and deep-fried are delicious.) To keep vine growth in check, pinch off the soft tips once fruit has set. My Grandma came up with her own space-saving solution during the Great Depression: according to family legend, she trained squash vines up the drainpipes and onto the roof to conserve space—the entire backyard was already under cultivation.

harvesting

Harvest squash when the skin is hard (not easily dented by a thumbnail), after the first light frost. Frost improves taste but reduces the storage time of some varieties. Cut the stem 10 to 15 centimetres from the fruit with a sharp knife. Cure in a warm, dry place, about 24°C, for 10 to 15 days, then store in open bins in a cool, dark place at 10°C to 12°C, with plenty of air circulation. Place fruits in single layers, not touching each other. Squash should last two to six months, depending on type.

Seed can be saved for next year, but be warned: squash varieties cross-pollinate, and squash will also cross with pumpkins, so you can never be sure you'll reap what you sow. Plant different squash cultivars as far away from each other as possible.

I've faced squash-growing challenges of a different nature in the past, mainly of the furry kind. A few years ago I planted a packet of 'Golden Hubbard' seeds, but squirrels ate them before they even germinated. Then I planted seeds saved from last year's 'Mini Green Hubbard', and from the sole surviving 'Small Sugar' pumpkin. Nothing came up. Finally, I bought some 'Early Butternut Hybrid' seedlings and a pumpkin of indeterminate variety from my local gardening centre. It wasn't what I'd had in mind, but it was better than being squashless, or eating the store-bought variety. Cracking open my own home-grown squash in the dead of winter has become something of a ritual. It's like being able to save some sun—not just from the previous summer, but from my childhood.

squash varieties

- 'Tay Belle' (10 by 15 centimetres) and 'Tay Belle PM' (12 by 18 centimetres) acorns: 500 grams, 68 days.
- 'Mesa Queen' acorn: 15 centimetres, 680 grams, 71 days.
- 'Hybrid Early Butternut' buttercup: 25 by 10 centimetres, up to two kilograms, 85 to 90 days.
- 'Hybrid Sweet Mama' buttercup: 20 by 12 centimetres, up to two kilograms, 75 days.
- 'Table King' acorn: 10 by 15 centimetres, 600 grams and up, 85 days.
- 'Golden Hubbard': 30 by 25 centimetres, five kilograms, 90 days.
- 'Stripetti', a combination of 'Delicata' and 'Vegetable Spaghetti': 30 by 13 centimetres, 1.8 kilograms, 95 days.
- 'Ambercup' buttercup: 15 by 12 centimetres, up to 1.5 kilograms, 100 days.
- 'Delicata', or sweet potato squash: 20 by nine centimetres, 500 grams to one kilogram, 100 days.
- 'Mini Orange Hubbard': 30 by 20 centimetres, one kilogram, 100 days.
- 'Mini Green Hubbard': 30 by 20 centimetres, one kilogram, 100 days.
- 'New England Blue Hubbard': 75 by 35 centimetres, eight kilograms, 110 days.
- 'Warted Green Hubbard': 32 by 25 centimetres, 4.5 kilograms, 110 to 115 days.

buttercup corn muffins
MAKES UP TO 12 MUFFINS

You could add a little chopped smoked ham or cooked bacon and a fresh chili or two to these muffins and serve them alongside brunch or breakfast dishes. Vary the fresh herbs as you wish. Acorn, Hubbard, butternut or sugar pumpkin (the young, small pumpkins that are more flavourful and less stringy than more mature gourds) may all be substituted for the buttercup squash.

1   cup (250 mL) cornmeal
1   cup (250 mL) all-purpose flour
1 3/4 tsp. (7 mL) baking powder
1   tsp. (5 mL) baking soda
1   tsp. (5 mL) salt
1   tbsp. (15 mL) chopped fresh
    marjoram or oregano
1   tbsp. (15 mL) chopped parsley
1   or 2 green onions, finely chopped
1   cup (250 mL) fresh or frozen
    (thawed, drained) corn
2   large eggs
3/4 cup (175 mL) plain yogurt
3/4 cup (60 mL) olive oil
1   cup (250 mL) mashed, cooked
    buttercup squash

1 Preheat oven to 425°F (220°C). Lightly butter muffin tin and set aside.
2 In a large mixing bowl, combine cornmeal, flour, baking powder, baking soda, salt, marjoram, parsley, green onion and corn. Stir together well, then set aside.

3 In another mixing bowl, beat eggs together lightly, then incorporate yogurt and olive oil. Blend in squash until mixture is smooth. Add squash mixture to the cornmeal mixture and stir until well incorporated, but do not beat heavily.
4 Spoon mixture into muffin cups about 2/3 full. Bake for 25 to 30 minutes, or until nicely browned and a tester emerges cleanly. Let cool for a few minutes in the muffin tin. Serve warm with butter and red pepper jelly.

Squash can be baked into a pie, like pumpkin (in fact, many canned pumpkin pie fillings contain squash to some degree), as well as in the delicious muffins here. Puréed squash with garlic, curry and a touch of cream also makes a good filling for ravioli.

squash soup with pasta

SERVES 6

This creamy soup has few ingredients, but it boasts style and flavour. The Italians, who call it *minestra di zucca e spaghetti*, usually mean butternut squash when they refer to *zucca*, but small sugar pumpkins could be used instead. Make this even more substantial by placing thick slices of toasted Italian bread brushed with extra virgin olive oil in the bottom of each serving bowl, then spooning the soup over.

5	cups (1.25 L) whole milk
1	cup (250 mL) chicken stock
1	lb. (500 g) butternut squash, peeled, seeded and chopped
	Salt and freshly ground black pepper to taste
1	cup (250 mL) broken spaghetti
2	tbsp. (30 mL) butter
3/4	cup (175 mL) grated Parmigiano-Reggiano cheese
	Freshly grated nutmeg to taste

1 In a large saucepan, combine milk and chicken stock. Bring to a boil over medium-high heat. Stir in squash or pumpkin; cook 10 minutes or until tender. With a slotted spoon, transfer squash to a food processor or blender; purée. Return purée to saucepan; stir to blend and season to taste.
2 Bring soup to a boil over medium-high heat. Stir in spaghetti; cook for 10 minutes or until pasta is tender but firm. Remove from heat. Stir in butter. Serve sprinkled with Parmigiano-Reggiano cheese and nutmeg.

acorn squash with apple ale & garlic

SERVES 6 TO 8

As every garlic lover knows, once garlic is cooked—roasted, baked or sautéed—it loses its intensity and becomes nutty and delicious. Paired here with winter squash, it results in a rich-tasting side dish that begs to be served with roast pork, turkey or game. Toss in a peeled, cored and chopped apple or two if you like.

1/2	cup (125 mL) any good-quality apple ale or dry (not sweet) cider
1	head garlic (8 to 10 cloves are needed), separated and peeled
1/3	cup (75 mL) butter
2 1/2	lb. (1.5 kg) acorn squash, peeled, seeded and diced
	Salt and freshly ground black pepper to taste
3	tbsp. (45 mL) chopped fresh parsley
3	tbsp. (45 mL) chopped fresh thyme

1 In a large, heavy skillet, melt 3/4 of the butter. Add the ale and all of the cloves of garlic and cook, covered, stirring now and then, for about 20 minutes. Be careful not to let the garlic burn. When garlic is browned and softened, mash it with the back of a fork.
2 Add remaining butter and diced squash and cook, covered, stirring occasionally, until squash is tender, another 15 minutes or so. (If necessary, add a little more ale.) Season to taste, add fresh herbs and serve.

sources

Good places to buy seed to grow the vegetable garden of your dreams.

Most of the sources listed below sell seeds by mail order; some sell plants as well. Phone or e-mail for catalogue information.

The Abundant Life Seed Foundation
Box 772, Port Townsend, Washington 98368;
360/385-5660;
www.abundantlifeseed.org
Organic heirloom seed.

Alberta Nurseries & Seeds Ltd.
Box 20, Bowden, Alta., T0M 0K0,403/224-3545, fax 403/224-2455

Ken Allan
61 South Bartlett St., Kingston, Ont. K7K 1X3;
allan@kingston.net
Sweet potato seed-roots; peas, tomatoes, tetraploid watermelons.

Aurora Biodynamic Farm
3492 Phillips Rd., Creston, B.C. V0B 1G2; 250/428-4404;
www.kootenay.com/~aurora
Heirloom herbs, vegetables.

Carolina Seed Co.
3580 Main St., Bldg. 10, Hartford, Connecticut 06120; 800/783-7891;
www.carolinaseeds.com
1,100+ seeds.

Circle Dance Seeds
84354 McNabb Line, RR 3, Brussels, Ont. N0G 1H0; 519/887-9793.
Heirloom organic vegetable seeds.

The Cook's Garden
Box 535, Moffits Bridge, Londonderry, Vermont, 05148.

Corn Hill Nursery Ltd.
2700 Rte 890, Corn Hill, N.B. E4Z 1M2; 506/756-3635;
www.cornhillnursery.com
Fruit trees, vines.

The Cottage Gardener
4199 Gilmore Rd., RR 1, Newtonville, Ont. L0A 1J0; 905/786-2388;
www.cottagegardener.com
Heirloom vegetable seeds & plants.

Country Meadows Gardens
1165 Ravenshoe Rd., Queensville, Ont. L0G 1R0.
Certified organic, heirloom vegetables; gourds.

William Dam Seeds
Box 8400, Dundas, Ont. L9H 6M1; 905/628-6641;
www.damseeds.com
900+ vegetables, flowers, herbs.

Howard Dill
RR 1, Windsor, N.S. B0N 2T0; 902/798-2728;
www.howarddill.com
Pumpkin seeds, incl. 'Dill's Atlantic Giant'.

DNA Gardens
Box 544, Elnora, Alta. T0M 0Y0; 403/773-2489;
www.dnagardens.com
Fruit-bearing plants; tissue culture lab.

Dominion Seed House
Box 2500, Georgetown, Ont. L7G 5L6; 800/784-3037;
www.dominion-seed-house.com
Flower, veg. & herb seeds, plants, bulbs.

Early's Farm & Garden Centre
2615 Lorne Ave., Saskatoon, Sask. S7J 0S5; 306/931-1982;
www.earlysgarden.com
Flower & veg. seeds.

Eternal Seed
657 Pritchard Rd., Farrelton, Que. J0X 1T0; 819/827-8881;
edecas@travel-net.com
Heirloom, non-hybrid veg.

Fish Lake Garlic Man
RR 2, Demorestville, Ont. K0K 1W0; 613/476-8030.
Organically grown garlic.

Forget Me Not Heritage Seed
729 Erbsville Rd., Waterloo, Ont. N2J 3Z4; 519/888-0339;
www.forgetmenotseeds.com
Heirloom veg., herb seeds.

Greta's Organic Gardens
399 River Rd., Ottawa, Ont. K1G 3N3; 613/521-8648;
www.seeds-organic.com
Organic and heirloom veg. seeds, 100+ tomatoes.

Grimo Nut Nursery
979 Lakeshore Rd., RR 3, Niagara-on-the-Lake, Ont. L0S 1J0; 905/934-6887;
www.grimonut.com
Hardy, edible-nut trees; seedlings; minor fruits.

Halifax Seed Co. Inc.
5860 Kane St., Box 8026, Stn. A, Halifax, N.S. B3K 5L8; 902/454-7456. Also 664 Rothesay Ave., Box 2021, Saint John, N.B. E2L 3T5; 506/633-2032;
www.halifaxseed.com
Herb, veg. seeds.

Heavenly Herbs & Reiki
478246 3rd Line, RR 2, Shelburne, Ont. L0N 1S6; 519/925-0626.
Culinary & medicinal herbs.

Hole's Greenhouses & Gardens Ltd.
101 Bellerose Dr., St. Albert, Alta. T8N 8N8; 888/884-6537;
www.holesonline.com
Fruit, seeds.

Ed Hume Seeds Inc.
Box 73160, Puyallup, Washington 98373;
fax 253/435-5144;
www.humeseeds.com
Veg., herb seeds for short-season climates.

J.L. Hudson, Seedsman
Box 1058, Redwood City, California, 94064

Johnny's Selected Seeds
184 Foss Hill Rd., Albion, Maine 04910; 207/437-4301;
www.johnnyseeds.com
900+ veg. & herb seeds.

Kettleby Herb Farms
15495 Weston Rd., RR 2, Kettleby, Ont. L0G 1J0. 905/727-8344;
www.kettlebyherbfarms.com
Herbs.

McConnell Nurseries Inc.
Box 248, Strathroy, Ont. N7G 3J2; 800/363-0901, French 800/461-9445;
www.mcconnell.ca
Hardy fruit trees.

McFayden Seed Co. Ltd.
30 9th St., Brandon, Man. R7A 6N4; 800/205-7111;
www.mcfayden.com
Veg. seeds.

Mapple Farm
129 Beech Hill Rd., Weldon, N.B. E4H 4N5; 506/734-3361;
wingate@nbnet.nb.ca
Sweet potato slips, French shallots, Egyptian & potato onions, Jerusalem artichokes, chufa nuts, Indian tomatillo, horseradish; early, storage & distinctive tomatoes.

OSC Seeds
330 Phillip St., Box 7, Waterloo, Ont. N2J 3Z6; 519/886-0557; www.oscseeds.com
Veg., herb seeds.

Park Seed Company
1 Parkton Ave., Greenwood, South Carolina 29647; 800/845-3369; www.parkseed.com
Veg. seeds.

The Pepper Gal
Box 23006, Fort Lauderdale, Florida 33307-3006; 954/537-5540; peppergal@mindspring.com
Peppers, gourds, herbs, tomatoes.

The Redwood City Seed Co.
Box 361, Redwood City, California 94064; www.ecoseeds.com
Ancient veg., hot peppers.

Rhora's Nut Farm & Nursery
32983 Wills Rd., RR 1, Wainsfleet, Ont. L0S 1V0; 905/899-3508; www.nuttrees.com
Hardy edible-nut trees; minor fruits.

Richters Herbs
357 Hwy. 47, Goodwood, Ont. L0C 1A0; 905/640-6677; www.richters.com
Herbs, organic gourmet veg.

Sage Garden Herbs
3410 St. Mary's Rd., Winnipeg, Man. R2N 4E2; 204/257-2715; www.herbs.mb.ca
Hardy lavenders, rare plants.

Salt Spring Seeds
Box 444, Ganges P.O., Salt Spring Island, B.C. V8K 2W1; 250/537-5269; www.saltspringseeds.com
Beans, grains, tomatoes, lettuce, garlic, amaranth, quinoa.

Scents of Time Gardens
11948 207th St., Box 402, Maple Ridge, B.C. V2X 1X7.
Heirloom veg., old-time herbs.

Seeds of Diversity Canada
Box 36, Stn. Q, Toronto, Ont. M4T 2L7; 905/623-0353; www.seeds.ca
Seed exchange for heirloom veg. herbs.

Seeds of Victoria
395 Conway Rd., Victoria, B.C. V9E 2B9; 250/881-1555; www.earthfuture.com/gardenpath
Organic & heirloom veg.

Shepherd's Garden Seeds
30 Irene St., Torrington, Connecticut, 06790.

Siloam Orchards
7300 3rd Concession, RR 1, Uxbridge, Ont. L9P 1R1; 905/852-9418; www.siloamorchards.com
Fruit trees; antique & disease-resistant apple trees.

Stokes Seeds Ltd.
Box 10, Thorold, Ont. L2V 5E9; 800/396-9238; www.stokeseeds.com
Flower, herb & veg. seeds.

Terra Edibles
Box 164, Foxboro, Ont. K0K 2B0; 613/961-0654; www.terraedibles.ca
Organic veg., herbs; rare & heirloom var.

Territorial Seeds
(Canada) Ltd.
Unit 206, 8475 Ontario St., Vancouver, B.C., V5X 3E8.

Thompson & Morgan Inc.
Box 1308, Jackson, New Jersey 08527; 800/274-7333; www.thompson—morgan.com
Traditional, rare & unusual seeds.

Tomato Growers Supply Co.
Box 2237, Fort Myers, Florida, 33902, 941/768-1119, fax 941/768-3476

Upper Canada Seeds
8 Royal Doulton Dr., Don Mills, Ont. M3A 1N4; 416/447-5321; upper-canadaseeds@rogers.com
Heirloom veg., melons, herbs, tomatoes.

Veseys Seeds Ltd.
Box 9000, Charlottetown, P.E.I. C1A 8K6; 800/363-7333; www.veseys.com
Veg. seeds.

West Coast Seeds Ltd.
3925 64th St., RR 1, Delta, B.C. V4K 3N2; 604/952-8820; www.westcoastseeds.com
Specialty veg. incl. Oriental.

Western Biologicals Ltd.
Box 283, Aldergrove, B.C. V4W 2T8; 604/856-3339; western@prismnet.bc.ca
Mushroom spawn; rare & medicinal herbs.

Woodwinds Nursery
Box 21-13, Bluevale, Ont. N0G 1G0; www.woodwindsnursery.com
Rare pears & apples. Heritage, hardy, disease-resistance varieties.

index

index

contributors

The editors and publishers sincerely thank the following people for contributing to this book. Without people who really care about the best way to grow and cook the vegetables and fruits we eat, and to photograph them at their most seductive, *The Cook's Garden* would not have been possible.

growing

Heather Apple: beans, 56; beets, 174; blackberries and raspberries, 62; Brussels sprouts, 180; chicory, 74; cucumbers, 86; Jerusalem artichokes, 154; kohlrabi, 166; okra, 104; onions, 192; peppers, 116; potatoes, 198; radishes, 36; salad greens, 24; spinach, 42; strawberries, 48; tomatillos, 122;
Jennifer Bennett: tomatoes, 128
Jodi DeLong: cranberries, 186
Maribeth Fitts: peaches and pears, 110
Mark Forsythe: rhubarb, 30
Larry Hodgson: asparagus, 12; corn, 80; kiwi, 160; melons, 98
Jim Hole: cherries, 68
Laura Langston garlic, 142; lavender, 92; peas, 18
Marlene Orton: grapes, 148
Bob Osborne: apples, 136
Leslie Smith Dow: winter squash, 204

recipes

John Ash: Fetzer Vineyards Lavender Blueberry Soup, 96
Carol Dudar: beets, 178; cranberries, 190
Laura Langston: peas, 22-23 (Maltese Scampi with Peas from *Tastes of the Pacific Northwest* by Tina Bell and Fred Brack, Doubleday, 1988, and Fresh Pea Soup from *Victory Garden Cookbook* by Marian Morash, Alfred Knopf, 1982).
Kathleen Sloan-McIntosh: apples, 140; asparagus, 16; beans, 60; blackberries and raspberries, 66; Brussels sprouts, 184; cherries, 72; corn, 84; cucumbers, 90; Jerusalem artichokes, 158; kiwi, 164; kohlrabi, 170; Lavender Hill Butter, 96; melons, 103; okra, 108; onions, 197; peaches and pears, 114; peppers, 120; potatoes, 202; radishes, 34; rhubarb, 34; salad greens, 40; strawberries, 52; tomatillos, 126; winter squash, 208
Sooke Harbour House: Lavender Honey Ice Cream, 96
Tracy Syvret: chicory, 78
Lucy Waverman: garlic, 146; grapes, 152; spinach, 46; tomatoes, 132;

photographs

Paul Bailey: lavender, 92-97
David Barr: corn, 83 bottom right
Yvonne Duivenvoorden: beets, 179 top; chicory, 79; cranberries, 190
Wally Eberhart: peppers, 118
Turid Forsyth: peas, 18-21; radishes, 26 bottom left, 27-28; salad greens, 39 both; spinach, 42-45; strawberries, 49, 51; beans, 56-58, 59 top left and bottom right; cucumbers, 86-90; okra, 105-107; tomatilloes, 123; tomatoes, 128, 130 top right, 131, 133; garlic, 144-145; grapes, 150; Jerusalem artichokes, 155-157; kohlrabi, 167; Winter, 172; beets, 174; Brussels sprouts, 181, 183-84; onions, 192-95; potatoes, 199-201; winter squash, 204-07, 209
Gibson & Smith: peppers, 120; kohlrabi, 168, 170
Anne Gordon: rhubarb, 33 top
Michael Grandmaison: cherries, 70 top, second from left
Rachel Heikoop: peaches and pears, 100-115
Linda Hink: rhubarb, 37; kiwi, 162, centre
Bert Klassen: peas, 22; radishes, 29; rhubarb, 35; spinach, 46-47; strawberries, 52-53; beans, 61; cherries, 68-69, 70 bottom left, top left, middle, right, 71-73; cucumbers, 91; lavender, 96; melons, 102; okra, 109; tomatillos, 127; tomatoes, 132; Fall, 134; apples, 136-38, 140-41; garlic, 143, 146-47; grapes, 148-49, 151-52; Jerusalem artichokes, 159; kiwi, 129 top left, 164; Brussels sprouts, 185; onions, 196; potatoes, 203; winter squash, 208
Marilynn McAra: peas, 18; salad greens, 36, 38; beans, 59 top; grapes, 153; kohlrabi, 166
James Noble: salad greens, 41; blackberries and raspberries, 66
Jerry Pavia: blackberries and raspberries, 65 centre
Beth Powning: apples, 139; kiwi, 160-61,165
David Shuken: tomatillos, 122
John Sylvester/firstlight.ca: strawberries, 50 top left
Aleksandra Szywala: kiwis, 162
Debra Their: cranberries, 186-189
Roger Yip: Spring, 10; asparagus, 12-16; radishes, 24-25, 26 bottom left; salad greens, 37-38; Summer, 54; raspberries and blackberries, 62-64, 65 top, 67; chicory, 75-78; corn, 80-82, 83 top, 84-85; melons, 98-101, 103; peppers, 117,119,121; tomatoes, 129, 130 bottom left; beets, 175-177, 179 bottom; Brussels sprouts, 182

editors

Before Liz Primeau joined *Canadian Gardening* magazine as its first editor in 1990, she spent 20 years as an editor and writer at *Weekend, Toronto Life, Chatelaine, City Woman, Ontario Living* and *Vista* magazines. For three years in the late '90s she was also co-host of Canadian Gardening's television show on HGTV. Since the beginning of 2000 she's been freelancing as a writer and editor, and speaks on garden design and care at conferences and garden shows.

Her gardening articles, including a regular column in *Canadian Gardening* magazine, have appeared in several newspapers and magazines. Writing and editing credits also include a series of gardening books produced by Madison Press Books for Penguin Studio and *Canadian Gardening*; 1999's *Gardening for Canadians for Dummies,* for CDG Books Canada Inc., plus a second edition published in January, 2002; and two small children's garden books, *Grow a Salad* and *Grow a Butterfly Garden,* published in 1999 by Somerville House. Her most recent book is *Front Yard Gardens: Growing More Than Grass,* released by Firefly Books in March, 2003.

Liz has been an avid gardener since her early 20s, and her Mississauga garden has been featured on several garden tours.

Aldona Satterthwaite learned about the joys of gardening from her grandmother and the pleasures of cooking from her mother. Her career has taken her from magazines to advertising to museums and back to magazines. Prior to joining *Canadian Gardening* as its editor, she was director of writing services at The Museum of Modern Art, New York. Aldona completed her journalism studies at the Regent Street Polytechnic in London, England, studied landscape architecture at Ryerson University and trained as a master gardener at the Civic Garden Centre, Toronto. She is the author of the guidebook to Royal Botanical Gardens in Burlington.